About the author

Mark Peters is the Value Stream Director for Engineering Ops at BrainGu, which develops custom and specialized DevOps software for leading corporations such as Deloitte, American Express, Nestlé and Coca Cola. He is the North America Chapter Chair for the DevOps Institute. He also holds a variety of technical certifications such as CISSP, PMP and CHSCL.

Confident DevOps

*The essential skills and insights
for DevOps success*

Mark Peters

KoganPage

First published in Great Britain and the United States in 2024 by Kogan Page Limited

2nd Floor, 45 Gee Street	8 W 38th Street, Suite 902
London	New York, NY 10018
EC1V 3RS	USA
United Kingdom	

www.koganpage.com

Kogan Page books are printed on paper from sustainable forests.

ISBNs

Hardback	978 1 3986 1659 2
Paperback	978 1 3986 1657 8
Ebook	978 1 3986 1658 5

British Library Cataloguing-in-Publication Data

A CIP record for this book is available from the British Library.

Library of Congress Control Number

A CIP record for this book is available from the Library of Congress.

Typeset by Integra Software Services, Pondicherry
Print production managed by Jellyfish
Printed and bound by CPI Group (UK) Ltd, Croydon, CR0 4YY

To my wonderful, loving wife and beautiful daughter,
without whom none of my success would be possible

Contents

Foreword x

Acknowledgements xii

Introduction 1

PART ONE
Learning about DevOps 9

01 What is DevOps? 11
   Introduction 12
   History 14
   Defining DevOps 21
   Applying DevOps today 24
   Notes 27

02 Comparing DevOps methods 30
   The software development lifecycle (SDLC) 31
   The DevOps SDLC 41
   The Waterfall SDLC 45
   Extreme Programming and Agile SDLC 52
   SDLC implementation processes (SAFe, GitOps) 59
   Summary 63
   Notes 64

03 Beginning with DevOps 66
   The Three Ways explained 67
   Flow 75
   Feedback 80
   Improvement 84
   Summary 88
   Notes 88

PART TWO
Fundamentals of DevOps 91

04 DevOps architecture 93
The basics of architecture 94
The language of architecture 100
Servers and serverless, monoliths and microservices 108
Architecture people, processes and technology 112
Summary 116
Notes 117

05 Managing observability 119
Basics of observability 120
Observability metrics 124
Advancing metrics 129
Observable people, process and technology 134
Summary 140
Notes 141

06 Routing the pipeline 142
What is a pipeline? 142
Setting up an effective pipeline 145
Technical pipeline solutions 152
Picking pipeline people, process and technology 157
Summary 163
Note 163

07 Testing the process 164
The basics of testing 165
Continuous testing and monitoring 172
Testing for improvement 177
People, processes and technology for testing 181
Summary 185
Notes 186

PART THREE
The DevOps mindset 187

08   The DevOps mindset 189
     Understanding interaction with individuals and teams 190
     Overcoming bias 198
     Preparing the culture 202
     Summary 207
     Notes 208

09   DevOps practices 210
     Finding, hiring and training people 211
     Establishing effective processes 217
     Learning technological solutions 226
     Summary 232
     Notes 232

10   Stability and security 233
     Security and stability professionals 234
     Processing for security and stability 243
     Stable and secure technologies 253
     Summary 257
     Notes 258

PART FOUR
The future of DevOps 261

11   The future of DevOps 263
     Advancing people 264
     Advancing process 266
     Advancing technology 271
     Final thoughts 275
     Notes 277

Index 279

Foreword

DevOps has been literally life-changing for millions, perhaps even billions, of people. At its core, DevOps is human, seeking to resolve conflict to remove friction and optimize organizational flow. It is the key driver in the digital economy when leaders realize that success depends on their ability to treat software engineering as a strategic advantage, not a cost centre. But what is it?

The progenitors of DevOps in 2009 resisted providing the market with strict definitions or manifestos. It's always been a delicate balance between letting DevOps fly free to evolve as we learned more about the practices and caging those practices to apply them usefully in the real world. This has been challenging for those change agents and transformation leads wanting to reap the benefits of DevOps and see it deliver on its promises of high throughputs with simultaneous increases in the quality of outputs. All of this resulting in customer outcomes that make businesses thrive, not just survive.

In his book, Mark Peters shows how DevOps connects to the frameworks that led to it – how it stands on the shoulders of the giants of Lean, Agile, and programme management. Readers will learn how Software Development Lifecycles change when you execute them under different philosophies and why DevOps principles ultimately lead to higher levels of organizational performance. *Confident DevOps* combines the technical know-how of building CI/CD pipelines with the human elements of creating cultures and mindsets that embrace the federated, end-to-end ownership, 'shift left' capabilities that make DevOps work.

DevOps is a complex field, requiring nuanced understanding and careful implementation. It's a journey that demands time, care and effort. Mark Peters, a respected figure in the DevOps community, is known for his generosity in sharing his experience, knowledge and expertise. He's always at the forefront, assisting others in developing their own DevOps skills and understanding that collective growth is the key. His extensive research into the evolution and impact of DevOps on global organizations has provided him with profound insights and understanding. In this book, he shares all of this, empowering you to confidently apply DevOps principles in your own context.

Helen Beal
Head of Ambassador Program
PeopleCert (DevOps Institute, ITIL, Prince2, LanguageCert)

Acknowledgements

No book is possible without the dedicated support of those around you. The hours spent in writing, editing and researching were matched or exceeded by the wonderful team at Kogan Page. Their assistance in assembling graphics, correcting initial drafts and creating the final version in your hands was essential to an on-time completion.

For this book in particular, my thanks go out to Helen Beal, a long-time mentor. Helen and I have worked together for over four years and she tossed this opportunity into my lap. Her schedule was full up at the time, and she suggested to the editors at Kogan Page that if they needed an author they should talk to me. That opportunity turned into the book in your hands, so thanks again Helen.

More thanks go out to all the great individuals I have engaged with over the years to formulate my own ideas for DevOps: Garima Bajpai, Trac Bannon, Patrick Debois, Bryan Finster, Maran Gunsakeran, Suresh GP, Maciej Jarosz, Rafal Los, Larry Maccherone, Leo Murillo, Gautham Pallapa, Steve Perierra, Tracy Ragan, David Webb. Each of these helps contribute and I always appreciate our discussions.

Finally, as mentioned in the dedication, no book is possible without the support of family. I would again thank for wonderful wife for putting up with late nights, reading every word I write, and offering her valuable input. My daughter also contributes, giving her ideas and making sure the language wanders appropriately from my penchant for storytelling to the more detailed technical language. And, of course, the two Great Danes who provide needed refuge when the writing gets to be too much.

Thanks again for purchasing this book, and I hope you enjoy reading it as much as I enjoyed writing it.

Introduction

First, thank you for picking this book to begin or continue your DevOps journey. Whether you are just setting foot on the trail or eying the summit, we will help you reach those goals. Each chapter will help you broaden your technical and conceptual understanding of how DevOps works and how it supports modern enterprises. DevOps offers an alternative to traditional software development through an iterative approach, offering the most customer value in the fastest possible manner. In the past decade, the DevOps industry has snowballed. In 2022, the DevOps market value was US $8 billion, with an expected 20 per cent compounded annual growth rate and a predicted 2033 global market size of over US $70 billion.

One frequently overlooked yet vital element is that DevOps offers a cultural transformation rather than a technical one. Many vendors offer technical-based solutions to allow fast access to continuous integration/continuous delivery tools, in-line security scans and various integrated development (IDE) environments that will put you on the DevOps path. Consulting companies then offer the leadership and training approach, giving guidance in areas such as Agile, project management or the Scaled Agile Framework (SAFe). Each of these provides part of the story but not the whole solution. In truth, culture drives technological choices, then those choices drive cultural changes. This book will give you all the tools to succeed in your own DevOps transformation.

My journey into DevOps

My transformation into a DevOps junkie came later in my career but shortly after my introduction to contractual software development. I use the term junkie intentionally because I now need my daily DevOps fix. I love to be involved in improving code, setting feature criteria to create value and delivering exceptional products to the customer. There is no better success to my day than when a piece of code finishes testing, improves the overall product and reaches the customers quickly. Speed can be relative, but we mean faster than other options and much faster than competitors. Traditional software design challenges appear in the time gap between development and delivery. One of my compatriots had the experience where, five years after leaving a position, he received a call about code comments because the software was finally ready for production. That is not the goal.

I worked for 22 years in the US Air Force before entering the software design field. During this time I ran systems design, deployed multi-level solutions and managed weapon systems within the intelligence field. On my first contracting job, one of the individuals mentioned that I needed to get smarter about DevOps. Over the weekend, dedicated to learning, I studied DevOps and was surprised to realize that the DevOps mindset was one that I had already been using for the past 22 years without realizing there was a name for that approach.

In the USAF, my job was to find information, format the information usefully, deliver it to a pilot (customer), let them complete the task and then garner feedback about how the information had performed. After receiving feedback, I would then experiment to find a way to deliver more effective products for the next task, whether that was hours, days or months away. This concept of flow, feedback and improvement aligned with my personal beliefs in the best way to get stuff done. Once aligned in this manner, I couldn't help but be a junkie.

After all the research, I started reframing the items I worked on from name-only DevOps to actual DevOps practices. I restructured the local organization, aligned teams and emphasized small-value delivery quickly over extended planning. That team succeeded, and so did the next when I integrated security practices with improved visibility. Implementing the improved processes accelerated the programme delivery from once every 30 months to every three months. In addition, aligning security teams with the development teams allowed the closing of over 1,400 vulnerabilities and smashed the benchmarks. Since then, I've been writing and talking about DevOps globally as a DevOps Institute's Ambassador programme member. I always encourage others to improve themselves because, as software continues to transform the world, better, more secure software helps us all have a more stress-free life.

My approach to DevOps

Every person who approaches DevOps finds a unique approach to success. It is like when one prepares to scale a summit such as Mount Everest. Every basecamp starts at the same location and proceeds with the same tools, but the path to the top is always different. This book will help prepare your basecamp for later success. In preparing, I always find images and well-defined words to be extremely useful. My own DevOps basecamp

FIGURE 0.1   DevOps basecamp

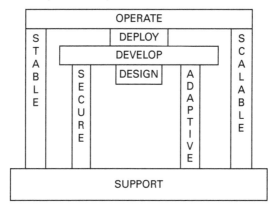

diagram appears here, and then the details will be explained throughout the book, especially in the later sections.

My basecamp succeeds because when I design, implement and deploy, I concentrate on having a foundation with quality layers and sound pillars. From the horizontal view, the most significant, and so the first, layer is support. Support requires documentation, knowledgeable help and a friendly staff, all cultural fixes. Without continually supporting software, everything else falls away. After deciding support requirements, the following layers use customer requirements to design, develop, deploy and operate the code effectively. Each layer's size reflects the relative time spent compared to the other layers. When those times are no longer in alignment, I know the time has come to spend cycles on feedback and improvement.

The vertical parts of the diagram describe the values and commitments needed across those layers to succeed. Any software supporting my DevOps approach should be stable, secure, scalable and adaptive. Each of these terms will be described later but you can return to the summit metaphor. Would you want to proceed on a climb if a tool was poorly made, fell apart often and could not be depended on? Consider the hooks, hammers and lines needed to secure a summit ascent as an image. The hooks should be strong, the hammers should be easy to use and the lines should bear your weight. Additionally, if one hook fails, you should have redundant, adaptive options that limit any fall. You don't want just one option but adaptive options that limit falls and allow continued climbing. It is the same with software. Thanks again for taking this journey, and I am confident we will reach the summit together.

Breakdown of the book

The book contains 11 chapters in four parts. The first part promotes some basic learning about DevOps concepts and principles to ensure a common vocabulary. Each of the chapters in the second part offers a people, process and technology approach to ensure that you can hire the right people, implement the right processes and deploy the right technology for continued success. The third part delves into the all-important DevOps mindset, while the fourth part explores ongoing developments in the DevOps space, uncovering what the future might hold.

Part 1: Learning about DevOps

Chapter 1: What is DevOps? This answers the question for those starting from scratch with DevOps. It details the history of DevOps from programme management to the current day and shows some examples of current usage by successful corporations.

Chapter 2: Comparing DevOps methods. Now that we know how DevOps emerged, a comparison appears between DevOps and other prevalent SDLCs. The distinction is made between traditional Agile formats, Waterfall and Spiral methods, and modified DevOps versions such as SAFE and LeSS.

Chapter 3: Beginning with DevOps. This chapter begins with learning confidence in DevOps cultures through implementing the Three

Ways. Each way appears with examples from the strategic to the operational and the successful to the less than perfect.

Part 2: Fundamentals of DevOps

Chapter 4: DevOps architecture. Much of DevOps depends on automated infrastructure as code and lightweight architectures, so this chapter explains how to model and plan those solutions before starting. It explores the transition from microservice, monolith or on-premise to cloud-native as well as technologies to model those architectures

Chapter 5: Managing observability. Without observability of process and performance, feedback is impossible. This chapter details how to obtain that observability and then measure the results for useful growth.

Chapter 6: Routing the pipelines. Many DevOps organizations base success on implementing CI/CD pipelines. However, pipelines can range from extremely simple to extremely complex. Here, the discussion focuses on creating initial pipelines, establishing processes and software, and creating a stable foundation.

Chapter 7: Testing the process. One of the core maxims for DevOps is to fail often and learn quickly. The best way to measure failures appears through thorough testing. Testing can occur at many levels with characteristic elements and at different times. Bringing security into DevOps requires testing and this chapter explains how to build and implement successful tests.

Part 3: The DevOps mindset

Chapter 8: The DevOps mindset. Cultural transformations affect people, who perform differently than software constructions. Code is simply a set of instructions so the gaps between those instructions are filled by culture. Learn how to understand human transactions, improve emotional intelligence and deploy successfully.

Chapter 9: DevOps practices. Developers are often considered the temperamental artists behind DevOps success. Successful development requires understanding how to hire the right people for various requirements, setting up an effective process for those individuals to be successful and providing them with the right technical tools.

Chapter 10: Stability and security. Many have emphasized the need for a DevSecOps mindset to incorporate security concerns into development. This chapter touches on those security processes and explains how, with a DevOps approach and experienced practitioners, security is already included if the right people, processes and technology are in place.

Part 4: The future of DevOps

Chapter 11: The future of DevOps. DevOps changes rapidly and each new instance of a thing now calls for a new term like AIOps, MLOps or FinOps. The chapter assesses some of the underlying functions associated with these tasks and how they can be integrated into one's current DevOps culture as the ultimate measure of confidence.

Each of these chapters has its nuggets and gems to further your journey. They may be read in order, or you can skip around to find the most valuable pieces. In any case, learning and internalizing these ideas will develop your skills, understanding and potential as a confident DevOps professional.

PART ONE

Learning about DevOps

Beginning your journey to learn DevOps and be a confident practitioner first means learning the basics and terminology. This section aims at those new to this journey or those wishing for a refresher. Sometimes, organizations launch right into the technical transformation aspects without considering the cultural roots, and this element helps create the necessary firm foundation for DevOps transformations.

The first chapter starts with the fundamentals, introducing you to DevOps history and applications. The discussion then compares DevOps and other methods using the SWOT (Strengths, Weaknesses, Opportunities and Threats) model. Using a structured model from other business practices allows linear comparison and expands the reader's understanding of why DevOps is an excellent choice. The final chapter in this section starts the DevOps journey, delving into the Three Ways and how to begin each to ensure transformation success.

CHAPTER ONE

What is DevOps?

If you are a working professional, this conversation will likely be very familiar. The group is gathered around a table or assembled at their video monitors, awaiting the weekly status meeting. The boss, CEO or senior board member walks into the meeting excited about a recent podcast, conference or news article advertising the newest management success story.

Boss: 'I'm so excited, I just heard about this DevOps process on the podcast on my way to work. It increases value exponentially in a short time. Everyone is using it, and we are going to switch now!'

Staff: 'What do you mean by DevOps? How does it apply, and what do we have to do to make it work?'

Boss: 'We will just implement it. It is so easy; all we have to do is have developers talk to operations and all our problems will be solved. We will be able to deliver software in a fraction of the time it takes now, and our customers will love it.'

Staff: 'You got it, boss. We will make that happen, and we can all look forward to rolling in money.'

Then the staff wander away slightly befuddled, change the name of all the current teams to DevOps, search randomly through internet references and try to make the change happen. DevOps is not a simple answer, a checklist or a magical fix; instead, it is a cultural transformation incorporating human and technological elements. This book will provide the confidence to answer questions effectively, implement DevOps practices through cultural change and master the technology that makes DevOps so powerful. This section will cover some of the DevOps basic understanding to launch a transformation.

The history section provides elements of DevOps growth from the original programme management theories. Once grounded with that history, several instances will support how DevOps appears across multiple industry fields today. While the book can be read from start to finish, those looking for a particular solution can certainly skip ahead.

Introduction

The term DevOps is relatively new in terms of technology, emerging within the past 15 years, but the embedded concepts have existed for quite some time. DevOps stands for Development and Operations and embodies the concept that software developers should also be responsible for operating it. This concept emerges from the idea that builders know better than anyone else how to deliver on what they have promised. Linking individuals who know how to create the most effective solutions emerges from a history of Just-in-Time and Lean manufacturing. These things focus on minimizing waste while maximizing productivity, and DevOps accomplishes the same functions for software. At its heart, DevOps focuses on three concepts: flow, feedback and improvement.

FIGURE 1.1   DevOps venn diagram

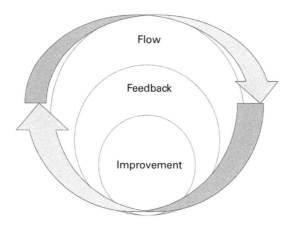

Rather than differentiating between the cycles as separate stages, each item depends on the others throughout the process in a Venn diagram construction. Flow means accomplishing work as fast as possible through prioritizing the smallest possible increments to deliver value. Feedback entails always creating observability, being aware of what creates value and being willing to undertake blame-free discussions of blockers and issues with the flow. Improvement drives the DevOps essence and may be referred to as continuous experimentation. Being able to improve highlights the need for continuous learning, that constantly staying on the cutting edge enables one to best implement improvements through experimentation. Each step provides a needed element for the next progression. The ability to take time and work cycles to experiment allows for continuous improvement as not all changes may be immediately apparent in their success or failure.

DevOps is not the creation of any one individual. The theories and processes emerge from many people who have seen similar work challenges and realized how to experiment to reach continuous improvements. As Isaac Newton wrote in his letter to Robert Hooke in 1675, 'If I have seen further, it is by standing on the shoulders of giants'.[1] One of the unusual items about DevOps compared to other fields is that one not only stands on the shoulders of giants but is also mutually supported by the community. Everyone in the DevOps culture contributes, and each contributes to cooperative success. However, we must also recognize some outstanding contributions leading to the current DevOps patterns.

History

Programme management

It would not be entirely fair to look at DevOps without putting the initial history within the context of programme management. DevOps has proven to be more than just another form of programme or project management but a cultural influence.[2] The specific implications will appear throughout this work but for now the assumption will be that DevOps has some roots in the programme management theories.

Ever since humans have tried to succeed in business, someone has been trying to figure out a better way, an opportunity to do it faster, cheaper, and still maintain value. Scholars generally see programme management theory development as four separate historical distinctions: prior to 1958, from 1958 to 1979, 1980 to 1994 and from 1995 to the present.[3] Each era has different goals and strategies based on the historical perspective. The first era appears as a transition during the industrial age, led by Henry Ford, interchangeable parts and the assembly line. The next era sees the growth of the military-industrial complex and the need to migrate project strategies from the government to the commercial world. The third era begins to take advantage of software interactions and move from manual to electronic outcomes, allowing the implementation of lighter-weight methodologies. Finally, the modern era is the growth of software development, the era we are interested in, in the need to manage continuous development and deployment versus a simplified product end state.

Era 1 (prior to 1958) is characterized by tools such as the Gantt Chart, Critical Path Method, Precedence Diagramming Method and the Project Evaluation Review Technique. All of these are very manually intensive ways to depict programme success, emphasizing observability of all possible events rather than a DevOps flow. Many still use the Gantt chart within DevOps but my professional opinion is that it overcomplicates and focuses too much on end-dates rather than continuously delivering products.

This stage focused heavily on gathering data about project events and streamlining what was necessary through critical paths without the later Lean focus on eliminating waste. Defining projects in this era were the Manhattan Project (1942–1945), the project plan for the Pacific Railroad (1857) and the Hoover Dam (1931–1936).[4]

The second era begins the transition from large government projects to the commercial and corporate model. Appearing in this era were tools like the Work Breakdown Structure (WBS), conflict management and some initial iterative project planning. The WBS creates a more complicated version of the Gantt chart, detailing who is responsible for every step, outlining costs for those items and even further locking down delivery dates. Conflict management focuses more specifically on humans, a critical area for DevOps. Finally, the start of iterative planning, like the Lean solutions in the next section, shows some of the basis for DevOps in realizing that growth can occur over time rather than being a planned event. Representative projects are the Polaris project to build submarine-launched nuclear missiles (1956–1961), the Apollo project to reach the moon (1958–1969) and ARPANET, the precursor to the internet (1962–1979).

Moving into the next era begins some transitions into the modern age. Here, the lightweight methodologies are not yet Agile but are beginning to understand the need. The earlier reliance on charts and diagrams incorporates risk management to understand the probability and impact of various actions. This allowed people to observe where an item occurs along the path and the internal and external events that could affect success. In this era, the certificate transition begins when one could achieve certificates, like the Programme Management Professional from the Programme Management Institute, that could validate credentials short of a degree. This carries forward in many other modern institutions with DevOps, Amazon Web Services and many other certificate options. Examples of projects in this era include the England-France tunnel project (1989–1991), the Space Shuttle Challenger (1983–1986) and the Calgary Olympic Winter Games (1988).

From 1995 to the present, the modern project management era starts with linking the Agile and DevOps mindset to overall management theories. Agile methodologies first appear and begin implementation through Extreme Programming, Pair Programming and eventually Agile. As the era reaches the present, within the past ten years we see transitions to remote work from in-person attendance. This era sees Critical Chain Project Management as expanding the Critical Path method to allow the inclusion of resources and risk into delivery timelines. Finally, the era has seen the introduction of university degrees in project management. Projects exemplifying this era include the Y2K solutions to update computer architectures, the Panama Canal Expansion and the Large Hadron Collider.

Programme management processes are far from DevOps solutions, only starting to contribute in the most recent timeframes. Many who realize DevOps success have previously worked in programme management for physical projects and try to adapt those tools to software development. The next step in learning DevOps history moves from basic programme management to learning Lean contributions.

Lean

DevOps roots begin with Lean and Just-in-Time manufacturing processes generally attributed to Toyota during the 1980s and early 1990s. The earliest roots attribute initial thoughts to Henry Ford with the Model T line in 1913 when he linked interchangeable parts to a production line.[5] This enabled a continuous operations flow but did not accelerate the linkages between development and operations. Toyota incorporated these concepts to provide the best quality, lowest cost and shortest production times by eliminating waste within the system.[6]

Toyota faced numerous shortages in the post-WW2 era, and any hiccup in their process caused an unacceptable slowdown, resulting in value loss. Implementing an idea called Kaizen dedicated Toyota to seeking rapid improvement wherever possible. This concept relies on the two pillars of Just-in-Time and Jidoka. Just-in-Time uses continuous flow, takt time and a pull system. Continuous flow means delivering value never stops; the production line must always continue flowing. Takt time emerges from the German word, *takt*, for a beat or pulse in music to measure production output against customer demand.

Just as in software, the heartbeat of development and production must drive overall business value. The pull system is the last component to ensure that everything produced has value. Pulling means that the next item on the chain appears only with

FIGURE 1.2   Takt time equation

Formula

$$T = \frac{T_a}{D}$$

T = product assembly time required to meed demand
T_a = net time available to work
D = customer demand

valuable customer requests instead of emerging as a bright idea from the operations or development side. In DevOps, one ensures this through value stream measurements and flow.

Jidoka incorporates notification of abnormalities and distinguishing between human and machine work. Toyota emphasized the notification by implementing an 'Andon' cord. When a person pulled the Andon cord, all line work stopped until the identified issue could be addressed and fixed with a value-adding solution. While this caused slowdowns, it ensured that the overall process of delivering value never stopped. The Andon cord process allowed identifying stoppages caused by a person and stoppages caused by the machine. One sees the incorporation of this process into DevOps through the push to automate as much as possible. One quick expression of automation within DevOps is that any process needing manual repetition should become an automation candidate. This concept appears more fully later when we discuss implementing DevOps pipelines, including testing.

These two concepts, Just-in-Time and Jidoka, enabled Kaizen to take effect. Once implemented, Toyota's contribution to these processes drove their revenues and dramatically increased their ability to contribute value.

The Toyota car company dedicated itself to producing good cars and improving every manufacturing aspect tied to production and value delivery. While this mindset was easily implemented in physical manufacturing, bringing these concepts over to the software development side took longer. One first sees the push to incorporate these ideas during the 1990s, and then post-2000 with the introduction of Agile processes.

Agile

Agile history began in 2001 when several experienced software developers realized that the methods used by developers to reach

FIGURE 1.3   Toyota revenue 1937–2003

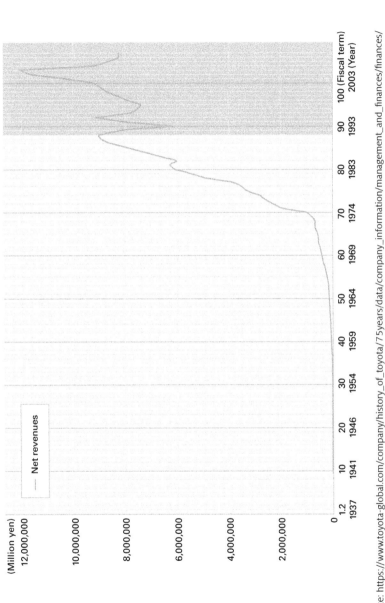

Source: https://www.toyota-global.com/company/history_of_toyota/75years/data/company_information/management_and_finances/finances/income/1937.html

the user were drastically different than the traditional Waterfall methodologies. The group included Kent Beck, Martin Fowler, Ron Jeffries, Ken Schwaber and Jeff Sutherland.[7] As a group, there was a large-scale dissatisfaction with some of the lightweight models such as Extreme Programming, Scrum, Dynamic System Development, Crystal, Feature-Driven Development, Pragmatic Programming and others. While each of these made steps to a more compact process, the traditional reliance on programme management remained. The true genius appears next in the development of the Agile Manifesto, statements to drive human roles in software development rather than management by pre-determined standards:[8]

· Individuals and interactions over processes and tools.
· Working software over comprehensive documentation.
· Customer collaboration over contract negotiation.
· Responding to change over following a plan.

These four statements depend on the caveat that while value appears in the items on the right, the items on the left have a higher value. These basic four statements were later followed by 12 principles, extensively discussed in Chapter 2. In each of these, the emphasis is on delivering a working item over the administrative hurdles common to project management such as scheduled design reviews, precise Gantt charts and mapping every possible project need four to five years in advance. These elements of rapid value persist through the next section's DevOps as almost a statement of core beliefs to further cultural transformation. From a traditional mindset, these elements are the organizational vision describing the long-term vision. DevOps moves forward from these visionary statements to build a cultural process and artifacts to support use over a wide variety of applications.

Defining DevOps

The term DevOps is generally attributed to an individual named Patrick Debois in trying to combine all possible information technology (IT) perspectives within the business.[9] A business may be defined as multiple streams with some specializing in one aspect and some specializing in another. In 2007, when he began formulating DevOps basics, Debois was in charge of testing for a data centre migration. Here he recognized the difficulty in merging the software development on one side of the corporation from those implementations into operations from the other side.

IT development is generally responsible for creating new software, hardware, firmware or configurations that address customer problems and business needs to create value. However, the operations of those functions can become segmented, with the IT operations elements responsible for monitoring and maintaining business technology by handling issues submitted by other departments and resolving their business problems. When testing, Debois began to realize that the new items submitted by development did not always fit operations processes and sometimes the operations fixes did not always travel back to development. This resulted in manual fixes for items that could be automated and delayed the delivery of value to the customer. The thought process and culture to bridge this gap did not exist. This gap likely caused frustration for many in the software development industry, but to Debois's credit he advanced the possibilities for solutions to a like-minded group and today we have DevOps.

The idea was pushed forward in 2008 when a gentleman, Andrew Shafer, arranged a working session at an Agile conference in Toronto, Canada, called Agile Infrastructure. Unfortunately, Shafer received negative feedback and did not attend his own session. Reportedly, Debois found him later at the conference for a hallway discussion, and they formed an online group to discuss ideas further. In a proper DevOps pattern, one can see flow, feedback and improvement in the process. As before, the idea was to bridge the business gap between development and operations.

The next major push occurred in 2009 when Paul Hammond and John Allspaw presented a lecture entitled '10+ Deploys a Day: Dev and Ops Cooperation at Flickr'.[10] Even over 15 years later, watching the video helps us see how many of today's DevOps concepts appear in this presentation. This helped identify what started as a conflict between the two groups who frequently blamed the other for the delay instead of working on the issue. It highlighted the stereotypes between the two groups that Dev is supposed to constantly deliver new things while Ops keeps the site stable and fast. However, the bridge begins to emerge in that the groups have the same goal of advancing the overall business. The presentation explained some initial concepts embedded in DevOps today, such as automated infrastructure, shared version control, one-step build and deploy, and common metrics. Most importantly, the presentation highlighted the need for shared trust between the groups rather than an adversarial approach.

Debois ran with this idea and gathered system administrators and developers to sit together during a DevOpsDays conference in October 2009.[11] Emphasizing the nature of the community, the group focused on the problems they encountered and ways to bridge those gaps. The concept of DevOpsDays has exploded since that initial conference and instances can be found globally in most cities today through devopsdays.org. On average, there are over 50 conferences yearly, and this emphasizes again the feedback and improvement aspects of DevOps that practitioners regularly seek help from others across multiple industries.

Over the next two years, the movement's following grew quickly and many smaller tech enterprises began incorporating some of the ideas into their daily work and experiencing success. DevOps incorporated several ideals, with the primary being that Dev and Ops should talk regularly rather than being isolated in corporate silos. Other items for improvement were the inclusion of Agile methodologies, the need for continuous integration and delivery through automated software pipelines, version control, common software repositories, lightweight service management with individual responsibilities, and consolidated incident management.

The next step was publishing the first 'State of DevOps' report by Alanna Brown in 2013 through Puppet software.[12] It highlighted the many benefits accessible through implementing DevOps as captured by the DevOps Research Association metrics: deployment frequency, lead time to change, change failure rate and mean time to recover. These elements focus on how fast one can accurately deploy and the time to recover from a published or newly discovered bug. These reports continue to be one of the yearly tools useful in measuring DevOps, although several organizations now publish yearly DevOps reports from different perspectives. One example is the DevOps Institute, now under PeopleCert, which publishes yearly 'Upskilling IT' reports highlighting the skills humans need to continue their DevOps transformation.[13]

Following the initial collection of DevOps-related data, the next advance for DevOps was the publication of *The Phoenix Project* in 2013.[14] The book relays a fictional story about an IT manager called upon to perform a long-suffering project. It introduces some of the first alignments to the Three Ways and is recommended reading for anyone interested in DevOps success. The book was followed in 2016 by *The DevOps Handbook*, which broke down many of those initial concepts into more practical approaches, and which remain highly useful.[15] These two books form the foundation of many DevOps practitioners' work libraries.

Since those initial steps, DevOps has only continued to grow. In 2015, a Gartner report predicted that DevOps would transition from a niche strategy to a mainstream ideal employed by more than a quarter of the Global 2000 organizations.[16] In 2017, Forrester's research called for 'the year of DevOps' and reported that up to 50 per cent of surveyed organizations were practising DevOps.[17] As of 2021, up to 83 per cent of IT decision makers use DevOps practices to unlock higher value, 99 per cent report DevOps as having a positive impact and 61 per cent state it has helped to reach higher-quality deliverables and reduce time-to-market for software.[18] These positive statistics then align with Gartner's predictions about most companies adopting cloud computing by 2025, with almost 100 per cent of new digital workloads occurring on the cloud. Each of these suggests DevOps is growing, and expanding individual confidence can be a key to unlocking success for many teams. However, the question remains: who uses DevOps today and how do I apply it to my organization?

Applying DevOps today

DevOps integration into software development and other indus-try areas today emerges directly as a result of the problems it can solve if a full cultural transformation occurs. The concept addresses the fact that the biggest problems in software develop-ment occur between the different silos that have emerged in IT. Companies segregate development teams from operations teams from customer response from product development and sales. Each of these silos then creates its own priority scheme and its own solutions. Those solutions do not translate across teams and each silo then solves its own problem rather than solving the business problem to increase revenue.

The first step emerges from aligning the work processes that successful DevOps addresses. A DevOps team must represent development needs from coding to test, driven by a product-owner person who represents business needs, and then build something easily operated at scale. Operations depends on newly implemented platform technologies and infrastructure-as-code. At a minimum, these two options relate directly to increasing business value by reducing expensive IT operations resources. DevOps accelerates the demand signal from the customer to produce some value quickly, allowing a constant iteration of product quality by increased functionality and aligning business expenses with the most profitable areas.

Modern technology often uses a subscription model to ensure revenue past the initial construction of the thing. One example occurs in Planet Fitness, a US gym franchise. The company's mission is to offer large, affordable and non-judgmental areas where one can work out based on the theory that over 50 per cent of Americans found gym membership either initially stressful or were intimidated when they reached a location. Planet Fitness makes 50 per cent of its money from direct franchising (those who initially purchased the product), 28 per cent from corporate revenue (those who subscribed to access regardless of daily use) and 22 per cent from new equipment sales (upgrades to the product).[19] If one looks at this from a software development perspective, most of the revenue comes from having an initial delivery and then having continued licence access to that the software, such as a Microsoft 365 offering, generating almost 80 per cent of the revenue. That next piece then comes from continuing to offer new options through a standard chain.

Microsoft's strengths are its core Office 365 products, Windows and software-based implementations. In the DevOps mindset, Windows is the basic platform and Office 365 provides the expanded functionality.[20] While the need for a licence may be seen as a weakness, it also keeps end-users tied to the product and willing to pay continual subscription costs as long as the product continues to improve. The key to continuing use is quickly delivering to the customer and offering continuous, valuable deliveries.

Numerous DevOps success stories follow a similar pattern. In many cases, this cultural transformation is the 'secret sauce' to their success:[21]

- PayPal, financial – 4,500 developers working on a 50-million-line code base with days to create a new application, weeks to deploy to test and months to production.
  - Adopted a self-service model accelerating creation to production in under two weeks.
- Kaiser Permanente, healthcare – six big-batch releases per year struggled with scope creep and siloed communications.
  - Implemented DevOps in 2017, service request time 47 per cent faster and change requests 53 per cent faster than industry standards.
- Starbucks, retail – moved from Waterfall to Scrum in 2015 to reduce work-in-progress bottlenecks.
  - Reduced steps in application development 41 per cent from 189 to 111, and cycle time 74 per cent from 86 days to 22 days.
- Amazon – use of dedicated servers wasted capacity and moved to Amazon Web Services with continuous deployment initiative.
  - Within a year of the move, deployment times were at 11.7 seconds, reducing the number and duration of outages.[22]

DevOps implementation advantages for software development are numerous. Each of the above companies faced different problems and different cultural challenges. Many companies regard their DevOps process as the secret ingredient to value, happy to share the new production numbers if not the underlying path. Understanding how to build your own path to success is one of the primary reasons for this book.

Growing confidence in DevOps requires constant learning from implementing different solutions, obtaining feedback and making the experiment to grow an individual implementation. DevOps is not simply the purchase of a technology stack that promises benefits like pipeline and CI/CD automation but working those changes into individual success. Each of the above companies faced different challenges but each were able to implement DevOps and make changes that improved their long-term revenue. Throughout this book, I will address how to identify those problems and implement changes regardless of the challenges faced with a DevOps cultural transformation.

Notes

1 Elshaikh, E M (2023) Standing on the Shoulders of Invisible Giants, Khan Academy, https://www.khanacademy.org/humanities/big-history-project/big-bang/how-did-big-bang-change/a/standing-on-the-shoulders-of-invisible-giants (archived at https://perma.cc/B9UT-FQ8V)

2 Bento, F, Tagliabue, M and Flora, L (2020) Organizational silos: A scoping review informed by a behavioral perspective on systems and networks, *Societies*, **10** (3), 56, https://doi.org/10.3390/soc10030056 (archived at https://perma.cc/Y3MH-BN8J)

3 Management.org (archived at https://perma.cc/F7G2-P2L5) (2023) 'The history of programme management', https://management.org/history-of-project-management (archived at https://perma.cc/H5WC-GREV)

4 Kwak, Y (2003) 'Brief history of Project Management' in E G Carayannis, Y H Kwak and F T Anbari, *The Story of Managing Projects: An interdisciplinary approach*, Quorum Books, 2003

5 Lean Enterprise Institute (2023) A brief history of Lean, https://www.lean.org/explore-lean/a-brief-history-of-lean/ (archived at https://perma.cc/TYZ9-2UG9)

6 Lean Enterprise Institute (2023) Toyota Production System, https://www.lean.org/lexicon-terms/toyota-production-system/ (archived at https://perma.cc/XN7J-7KB9)

7 Sacolick, I (2022) A brief history of the Agile methodology, Infoworld.com (archived at https://perma.cc/9K2B-3FQ8), https://www.infoworld.com/article/3655646/a-brief-history-of-the-agile-methodology.html (archived at https://perma.cc/9SQ8-JTFX)

8 Agilemanifesto.org (archived at https://perma.cc/59Y6-YLL2) (2023) History: The Agile Manifesto, http://agilemanifesto.org/history.html (archived at https://perma.cc/M8AP-EL6H)

9 Anand, B (2023) A Brief History of DevOps, Knowledge Hut, https://www.knowledgehut.com/blog/devops/history-of-devops (archived at https://perma.cc/9YJM-YVQJ)

10 Allspaw, J and Hammond, P (2009) Velocity 09: John Allspaw and Paul Hammond, 10 + Deploys per Day at Flickr, YouTube, https://www.youtube.com/watch?v=LdOe18KhtT4 (archived at https://perma.cc/5ZBN-NH27)

11 Kim, G, Humble, J, Patrick, D and Willis, J (2016). *The DevOps Handbook (2nd ed)*, Portland, OR: IT Revolution

12 Brown, A (2013) State of DevOps, Puppet.com (archived at https://perma.cc/H2MP-85WL), https://www.puppet.com/resources/history-of-devops-reports#2013 (archived at https://perma.cc/ACL5-5DTU)

13 DevOps Institute (nd) SKILup IT Learning, https://www.devopsinstitute.com/skilup-it-learning/ (archived at https://perma.cc/AW3Q-6ZA3)

14 Kim, G, Behr, K, and Spafford, G (2013) *The Phoenix Project*, IT Revolution Press

15 Kim, G, Humble, J, Patrick, D and Willis, J (2016) *The DevOps Handbook (2nd ed)*, Portland, OR: IT Revolution

16 Gartner (2015) Gartner Says By 2016, DevOps Will evolve from a niche to a mainstream strategy employed by 25 percent of global 2000 organizations, https://www.gartner.com/en/newsroom/press-releases/2015-03-05-gartner-says-by-2016-devops-will-evolve-from-a-niche-to-a-mainstream-strategy-employed-by-25-percent-of-global-2000-organizations (archived at https://perma.cc/H5HW-L6X6)

17 Stroud, R (2017) 2018: The year of enterprise DevOps, Forrester, www.forrester.com/blogs/2018-the-year-of-enterprise-devops/ (archived at https://perma.cc/9Q9Y-945P)

18 Todorov, G (2023) 40+ DevOps statistics you should know in 2024, httpSs://www.strongdm.com/blog/devops-statistics (archived at https://perma.cc/QD8R-U9XT)

19 Goel, S (2022) How does Planet Fitness work and make money, The Strategy Story, https://thestrategystory.com/2022/09/29/how-does-planet-fitness-work-and-make-money-business-model/ (archived at https://perma.cc/EU96-CKXZ)

20   Periera, D (2023) Microsoft Business Model, Business Model Analyst, https://
businessmodelanalyst.com/microsoft-business-model/ (archived at https://
perma.cc/YE76-R3UL)

21   Kanaracus, C (2023) How they did it: 6 companies that scaled DevOps,
TechBeacon, https://techbeacon.com/app-dev-testing/how-they-did-it-6-
companies-scaled-devops (archived at https://perma.cc/ZV8S-VHX8)

22   Null, C (2023) 10 companies killing it at DevOps, TechBeacon, https://
techbeacon.com/app-dev-testing/10-companies-killing-it-devops (archived at
https://perma.cc/QNQ4-YWBC)

CHAPTER TWO

Comparing DevOps methods

Understanding how DevOps enhances software development value requires a broader perspective for the comparative analysis options available. While the previous chapters addressed historical growth, this chapter explains functionality and compares the various models of a software development lifecycle:

- Waterfall and Spiral
- Extreme Programming and Agile
- Modified DevOps versions

Each step uses the SDLC framework to address how the model supports or misses the DevOps solutions through Strengths-Weaknesses-Opportunities-Threats (SWOT). Most business use cases include SWOT analysis, which is our basis for comparison. Frameworks are an essential tool for effectively choosing a transformational DevOps solution.

The software development lifecycle (SDLC)

The SDLC concept appears frequently in business planning. Taken simply, it means the cradle-to-grave approach to managing software. This lifecycle model emerged from physical manufacturing processes. At the simplest state, the SDLC includes planning, analysis, design, implementation and maintenance (Figure 2.1). More traditional versions align multiple steps under each while modern approaches like DevOps focus on shortening step time to increase how often the entire cycle can execute. One common organizational problem is creating different departments for each process step, greatly increasing silos as well as the difficulty in smoothly linking steps.

This chapter uses the SWOT model to better understand SDLC challenges. This business case model helps provide a comparative assessment between methods.

The SWOT model

SWOT analysis is a strategic management tool to identify organizational assumptions and uncover hidden truths. Careful SWOT planning can find needed improvement areas and allows for quick comparability to outperform marketplace competitors. The whiteboard approach to SWOT draws a two-by-two matrix with four quadrants, one for each model element. In this matrix model, list strengths in the upper left, weaknesses in the upper right, opportunities in the bottom left and threats in the bottom right. This pairs strengths and opportunities on the left and weaknesses and threats on the right.

STRENGTHS

Strengths identify items done well and range from technical skills to the cultural environment. These items allow a company to stay competitive. Strengths directly tie to the proposed business model. Strengths bring clear advantages and should be compared to competitor strengths. If one considers high-speed production a strength but cannot crack the marketplace top 10, it may not be a strength. For example, if one looks at Google's market leadership, strengths are brand knowledge, brand valuation, rapid growth and an ability to rapidly respond to marketplace changes.[1] Each strength puts Google in a market-leading position.

WEAKNESSES

Generating weaknesses relies on a comprehensive strength category. A market leader's strength might pair with an inability to change quickly as a weakness. The best weakness assessments consider how others in the marketplace see the organization. Many personnel systems use a 360-degree assessment where individuals are rated not only by managers but also by peers and subordinates. This also applies to weaknesses, as competitors will actively try to attack your position or gain market share. Returning to Google, their weaknesses are privacy policies, unfair business practices and failures in the social media revolution.[2] These outside perceptions turn inward as Google has lost personal data, fought to prevent other organizations from entering the marketplace and failed to launch a viable social media platform. Not all weaknesses need fixing to remain competitive but acknowledging weaknesses helps one to prepare.

OPPORTUNITIES

Opportunities are the areas where you can gain an advantage over competitors. While a company may not yet be moving towards an opportunity, recognition allows change before others seize those advantages. Changes in technology often become a major opportunity source. These can often be devastatingly overlooked – one historical example of this is Thomas Watson as President of IBM in 1943 stating, 'I think there is a world market for maybe five computers'.[3] While IBM still maintains consistent revenues, their chance for exponentially higher numbers may have disappeared by not recognizing the opportunity earlier. Returning to Google, some recognized opportunities might be the wearables market, recent remote work increases and non-advertising revenue sources. In non-advertising revenue, while most Google revenue comes from platform advertisements, new options include Google Cloud, selling apps under the Google Play logo, expanding services to emerging markets and home hardware such as Nest.[4] Each shows movement Google is taking to leverage opportunities as a market leader.

THREATS

Threats deals with what competitors are currently doing to influence your marketplace position. These items negatively affect the business from market shifts, inability to gain and retain needed talent, or supply chain issues. In 2020, the chip shortage caused by the pandemic was a major threat to many businesses. The global supply chain meant chip manufacture became distributed and required aggregating multiple products. Threats might be as simple as cash-flow problems or poorly managed debt that prevents moving on new opportunities. Google faces market share threats from competition with Facebook, Amazon and Instagram, antitrust controversies and lingering post-pandemic economic uncertainties.[5] Each clearly appears as a threat but can be difficult to address without comparing other SWOT elements.

Traditional SDLC

Each stage of the standard cycle appears in Figure 2.1 with various definitions. After years of working with project management, these steps will become embedded in your understanding. Knowing stage requirements intimately allows for adjusting and implementing those stages in best-fit, targeted models. While each stage is distinct, sometimes one stage's answers may solve the next without requiring process reversion.

FIGURE 2.1   The software development lifecycle (SDLC)

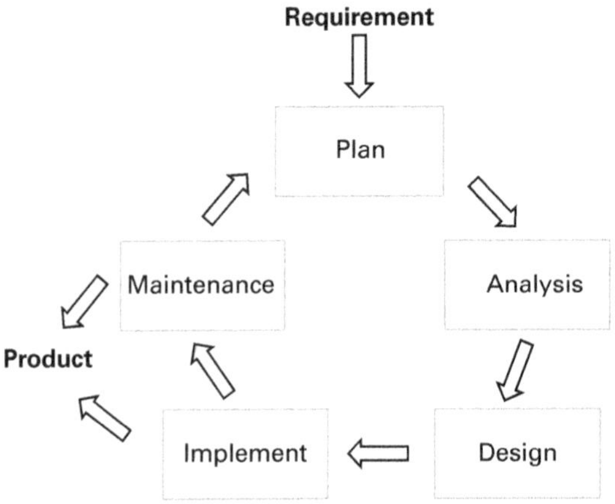

This image depicts each stage sequentially, but steps may be parallel depending on requirements and team involvement. For example, one may build limited software functionality and deploy while still building later interface or plug-in improvements. These basic steps relate to physical manufacturing where, for example, an incomplete automobile, such as one missing a tyre and an engine, could not be delivered to a customer. In software, one can often separate these pieces and still deliver functional products. Even if every car part requires distinct cycles, all components are needed to successfully manage delivery.

PLANNING

The first cycle stage is planning, starting with receiving requirements. In this cycle, requirements emerge from planning and are adjusted to the larger context. Planning allows the opportunity to solidify requirements from good, high-level ideas to concrete requirements. Planning requirements can be selected through various value criteria such as value chain analysis, company strategy alignment, resource availability or technical

TABLE 2.1   Weighting factors

	Weight	Security Patch (Raw)	User Login (Raw)	Security Patch (Weighted)	User Login (Weighted)
Resource	2	2	1	4	2
Mission Impact	1	1	3	1	3
Time	3	2	1	6	3
Totals		5	5	11	8

Fibonacci					
	Weight	Security Patch (Raw)	User Login (Raw)	Security Patch (Weighted)	User Login (Weighted)
Resource	3	3	1	9	3
Mission Impact	1	1	5	1	5
Time	5	3	1	15	5
Totals		5	5	25	13

difficulties. While this basic list comprises some common comparison items, in any model, planning's importance is connecting initial requirements to prioritization. Without prioritization there can be no guarantee that completed products will deliver value to the company.

One planning challenge is that many organizations spend a long time planning without effectively connecting delivered value. The tools embedded in the planning stage allow for direct comparison between different assessments based on resource commitments, value and required time elements. No one assessment should be used, but a variety of assessments, each weighted for the organization's goals. In a software example, fixing a recent security patch might be a medium resource requirement, important to the company's stated security mission, and take a medium amount of time. The next item, changing the user login screen, might be a low resource requirement, not important to the overall mission and take very little time. If one scored resources from low (1) to high (3), mission from important (1) to not important (3) and time required from low (1) to high (3), then the first element would be a 5 (2,1,2) and the second may score a 5 (1,3,1). The importance of distinguishing the weight would be another factor. Then the factors could be weighted as mission is most important (1), resources are second (2) and time is third (3) as shown in Figure 2.2. Allowing multiple teams to assign weight and average can be an effective tool as well.

The table shows that, if the lowest score is prioritized, then the user login is a clear planning winner despite the professional instinct to prioritize the security patch. One useful tool appears in the bottom half of the figure where the rankings are converted to a Fibonacci sequence rather than straight numbers. This allows a broader gap to appear more quickly. Fibonacci is a mathematical sequence where every number is added to the one before (1,1,3,5,8,13) and allows for rapid growth. This accentuates the difference between any two items.

My preference is for scores where the lowest wins, like in golf. Another tip is ensuring any weighting or scores appear as a 1 to n ranking where n represents the total number of set items or the highest Fibonacci score. For an item in a three-element set, the scoring would be 1,3,5 and in a set of five elements it would be scored as 1,3,5,8,13. One can see how quickly complexity grows but DevOps emphasis relies on prioritizing a small number of things often, and finishing the intended items. Experience and practice are the best ways to succeed at planning elements. One must create effective categories and efficiently score various options.

ANALYSIS

From planning, the SDLC moves into the analysis phase. Analysis takes the approved requirement and includes users to fully understand the customer ask. This builds specific use-cases. In the previous security patch example, a use-case might state, 'As a user, I want to know that the system I use has been patched and that my personal data is not easily available to those outside the environment or for malicious purposes.' Correctly defining the use-case allows for determining where and how an organization addresses goals. In this case, the following requirements might be a team familiar with security warnings, the current system status, fix implementation and integration.

After breaking out the requirement, analysis continues by eliminating redundancies between this requirement and others. For example, the new user login might require the security patch before the login can be integrated. If the patch stated all login information should be encrypted on transmission, then new logins should include patching requirements. This deconfliction helps assure alignment. If one understands dependencies and redundancies, this creates feedback in rapidly moving cycles to add dependency resolution as part of planning.

DESIGN

The third SDLC phase is design. At this step, the teams begin to take the task and work through proposed solutions. In design, logical and physical requirements are essential for success. For a software solution, logical designs are the first step. Logical requirements establish linkages between computer processes, reports, databases, stored information and internal or external sites.

Next, the design phase requires analysing physical require-ments. While most software does not require physical components, the possibility remains. In some cases, a security patch implemen-tation might require all users to have a key fob that generates a random software synchronized number to provide multi-factor authentication. In this case, not only would the security patch be installed but key fobs must be produced and distributed. In the traditional cycle for this change, adding a key fob might constitute a different requirement and require returning to Stage 1 or Stage 2.

IMPLEMENTATION

The fourth phase is implementation. When delivering software, implementation requires coding and testing and delivery. Each aspect helps refine the product to meet defined needs as well as offer a stable, supportable delivery. Sometimes SDLC models go offtrack if coding solutions vary significantly from requirements. In remote organizations, sometimes even the code basis may vary between common standards such as Python, JavaScript or even Cobalt. In later DevOps models, consolidated pipelines help resolve these issues as differences in linters, scanning tools, testing models or integrated builds for each user could signifi-cantly slow implementation. Another gap between requirement and coding can exist if the customer asks are so detailed as to remove developer creativity, for example if the requirement for one aspect of a parking application requires Apache integration and another explicitly requires an architecture not supported by Apache.

MAINTENANCE

Once implemented, the cycle is not complete. The final SDLC consideration is maintenance – how to fix and update a distrib-uted thing. DevOps solves the maintenance problem by continuous delivery and continuous integration rather than distinct elements identifiable as repairs. More traditional IT Ops employ large, heavily manned divisions whose sole purpose is keeping code and systems running. Sometimes this means maintenance fixes are not communicated back to implementations for quick solutions but instead re-enter planning as new requirements. These approximations affect how quickly you can deliver new value and maintain a positive return on investment.

Overall, the output from a carefully planned, traditional SDLC approach is often a business plan with hundreds of pages, multiple documents and communication gaps between decision makers and implementation. Aligning all needed individuals can be challenging, especially if the decision authority resides separately from those enacting decisions. DevOps tries to reduce this cycle, shorten the paperwork and push decisions as low as possible, similar to some effective military operations.

Traditional SDLC SWOT

Traditional SDLC strength lies in its well-known and documented approach. Every decision can be traced to every other decision. It is highly familiar to most participants and stage roles are well defined if not always fully understood. The weakness appears as the strength's downside. Since the roles are well defined, innovation can disappear. While tasks may be understood, the reason to accomplish those tasks may disappear over multiple iterations. A solve made to fix a particular aspect, for example a need for a specific integration test outcome, may be added as a required task. One sees this in government software planning, where an engineering plan becomes a requirement, even when that engineering appears as delivered pipeline. Similarly, the exhaustive nature means quick opportunities and small fixes take the same time as large decisions spanning the company. DevOps solutions will shrink the paperwork while maintaining decision trails and broadening roles to expedite innovation. If large and small changes require the same work to initiate, then an example would be that moving 200 tons 2,000 miles requires the same preparation as moving 100 pounds around the block. You can quickly see how that adds additional work without additional value.

The SDLC opportunity appears in that no aspects of any solution will be missed. Design and implementation are well-structured and fully aware of all hurdles, especially in static environments. When considering broad-ranging technical implementation or items for highly regulated industries, sometimes longer and more detailed plans are more efficient. An old friend worked on software for nuclear submarines and there was an inherent cultural mindset against accepting any technology that had been tested for less than six months before installation on the submarine. Six months was a required timeline, even if the change could be built and delivered in less than two weeks. Customers understand the long timeline but then plan for how everything is delivered in at least six-month increments, never thinking faster. The high risks and need for additional surety create a requirement that prevents moving quickly, regardless of the problem.

The threat to this mindset arrives from DevOps organizations. A traditional SDLC cannot move quickly or adapt to changing technology. Moving to a cloud-native approach, implementing containerized software or changing requirements can drastically short-circuit development. An example occurs in HashiCorp's 2023 move from a Mozilla Public Licence v2.0 to the Business Source Licence in all future releases.[6] Terraform was a strong pipeline creation option and the change will prevent future improvements from reaching past implementations without purchasing a new licence. While everyone using Terraform will have to pay, the change creates an incentive to find less costly alternatives. Lacking quick reactions can influence market share and quickly run a cashflow-inhibited corporation out of business.

- Strengths: Formal mindset, captures all requirements, well documented.
- Weaknesses: Lacking innovation, difficulty in reacting to market shifts.
- Opportunities: Highly regulated items with required audits.
- Threats: Inability to adapt, new technology, shifting requirements.

The DevOps SDLC

It would be remiss to travel further without reviewing the DevOps SDLC model. The 'Three Ways' framework in the next chapter handles fundamental DevOps concerns but the double helix often appears in literature as the DevOps SDLC. Expanding here allows us to compare the remaining SDLC models. The main difference between this and other models is the commitment to single teams conducting all functions to deliver flow, feedback and improvement along the chain. The DevOps SDLC is shown in Figure 2.2.

FIGURE 2.2   DevOps SDLC

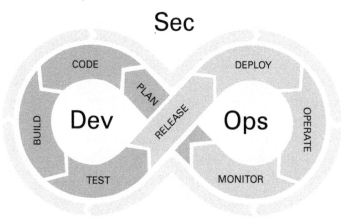

The first element noticed in comparing the DevOps SDLC is the lack of a defined beginning and end. The process can start anywhere and be delivered anywhere. Every cycle feeds into another stage and another cycle. Each element's arrows indicate overlapping functions. This overlapping nature allows for effective feedback in garnering the best approach. Many companies use the DevOps SDLC as a basis for creating pipelines and align software recommendations with each step. One of the most important comparisons between the DevOps SDLC and others is that every step executes with all teams for every feature. This means that when Waterfall hands off items, they are left undescribed in Agile, or individual roles are defined safe; all items are done for each DevOps feature.

Every cycle item completes for every section. This cannot be emphasized enough and is the single greatest DevOps strength when applied correctly. One anti-practice happens when organizations create handoffs between Dev and Ops while allowing security to remain a distinct sequential or parallel track. Some exceptions occur for Infrastructure as Code (IaC), platform teams and highly specialized teams where their outputs enhance the overall flow.

Platform teams focus on the internal customer rather than the external customer, building products that advance the overall DevOps SDLC speed. For example a platform team creates the toolbox, enabling the DevOps team to start with the necessary tools, service blueprints and configurable working spaces. Despite that, the most important cultural takeaway exists in recognizing that any DevOps team should be able to independently handle all the SDLC functions. One excellent example is the ability for each Dev to run an independent sandbox, mimicking the larger system, where they can test and integrate items without impacting overall performance

The Dev cycle portions are plan, code, build and test, while the Ops side addresses release, deploy, operate and monitor. Security plays consistently in the overlapping loops through static and dynamic testing. In other approaches, Dev and Ops, as well as individual stage components, occur as different teams. In a DevOps team, all of these functions execute in the same group. In later chapters, you will see how scaling to larger customer sets may require operational separation and automation but the fundamental aspects will remain. This core aspect allows any team to operationally run their code directly to the customer.

Scaled operations allow focusing on individual skill sets. If we use a car analogy, the developers are the engineers and the operators are the mechanics. We want engineers to design the best model off the line and we want the mechanics to fix it. Mechanics can design new features and engineers can fix operational failures but as user levels grow, specialization becomes important. While engineers can fix problems, we do not want to spend engineering cycles on fixing common operational issues like oil changes. These changes are standardized and automated to the point where others can complete the task without affecting the overall design.

The most important aspect for technical features is that all features occur in every lifecycle element. An automated pipeline allows a single DevOps team to move features from planning to deployment and on to operations without pauses or breaks. Other approaches lack observability between elements but DevOps elements and tasks can be observed by any team member at any point in development or delivery. Essential to this approach is the concentration on delivering quickly and not just satisfying all requirements before delivery. If one requirement can be fixed, delivery is approved, even if you could wait for a solution to everything. This ensures the customer has some value now, as opposed to a potentially higher value at a future date.

DevOps SWOT

The DevOps strength lies in agility and versatility. Each step appears as formally defined even without formal execution. A

DevOps pipeline can handle any project and a business designed with the DevOps cultural underpinnings can break down even the largest project into small, valuable steps. The DevOps weakness can be in the lack of specializations. While each team can handle code, highly specialized items may still revert to a preferred team. Since every project uses flow and feedback at the lower levels, highly specialized applications may be difficult to achieve as the amount of time to gain proficiency in the specialization delays customer delivery. Similarly, businesses preferring to dictate technical solutions may have difficulty incorporating DevOps processes.

One example appears with some legacy systems where the goal is continuing the current process rather than adaptation. During the pandemic, some older systems based on the COBOL programming language required changes to adapt to remote working systems that needed help.[7] The system design prevented a Java refactor or a cloud migration, making it a poor target for DevOps-style implementations where technical possibilities generally remain wide open for best-fit solutions.

The DevOps opportunity lies in the free-flowing approach. A DevOps team can take any problem, at any stage, and integrate through the double-helix for improvement. This allows brown-field and green-field approaches to be solved with a DevOps SDLC. A brown-field approach is where an application exists and requires modification while a green-field approach describes where the initial requirement does not have any pre-determined technical specifications. In addition, DevOps typically has a shorter time flow to deliver working software than other models and allows quicker return on investment than a Waterfall approach.

The threat faced by a DevOps SDLC is the traditional or highly regulated industry. These approaches can quickly disrupt and delay a DevOps SDLC and leave customers complaining that DevOps failed them. Examples of this threat appear in government solutions where an acquisition programme adopts

DevOps but requires all the traditional documents produced including system designs, maintenance plans or five-year road-maps. Another example appears when customers fail to understand DevOps basics, challenging why multiple pipelines are required, or wanting to build a customized toolbox based on their favourite applications. Some organizations think pipelines are distinct items rather than flexible components and fixate on the idea that one tool should provide all solutions. The common analogy to this is that if all I have is a hammer, then every problem should become a nail. These threats can be overcome through shared understanding.

- Strengths: Agility, versatility, constant feedback.
- Weakness: Lack of specialization, legacy requirements.
- Opportunities: Free-flowing approach, value now.
- Threats: Traditional industry, structured processes.

The Waterfall SDLC

The Waterfall approach is a traditional, programme management-based system. This worked well for legacy systems but the speed at which tasks occur is insufficient to be competitive in the modern environment. Any slowdown reduces the time to market between idea and delivery and subsequently detracts from end-user value.[8] Each Waterfall step, from planning to maintenance, occurs in a separate silo with individuals depending on other steps to complete before moving on. One primary objection to Waterfall design appears in the downhill flow, which minimizes feedback and eliminates any return to previous steps. Normally, each step occurs with a different team. A sample diagram of the Waterfall process is shown in Figure 2.3.

Waterfall systems approach the SDLC from an explicitly defined path. The typical Waterfall project plan can run to hundreds of pages for a single task or thousands of pages to

FIGURE 2.3 The waterfall process

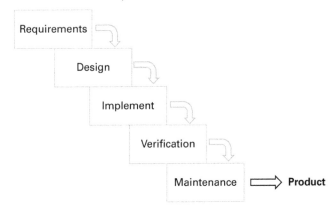

cover integrated tasks. Planning pages are exhaustively checked and error-corrected, ensuring all parameters are technically correct and formatted properly. One example is if a planning document described a function as delivered in less than .1mg, when the element was meant to be in microseconds. A flaw like this might result in a lightweight application but not in the manner intended. Although this example illustrates a typographic error, similar discrepancies are common in Waterfall programmes.

Some modern companies conducting software development processes have merely attempted to accelerate Waterfall. Analysing across 462 research studies showed that most corporations focus on initial management concepts, and then assessment without considering value-based elements such as customer satisfaction or time to market.[9] Waterfall shows high success in highly regulated, well-defined functions such as building a bridge or a house. When Waterfall concepts are applied to rapidly changing elements, success is less certain. Moving away from structured approaches is the essence of DevOps and Agile success.

The basic Waterfall steps reflect the traditional SDLC approach while substituting a requirements phase for planning and analysis cycles. However, the typical Waterfall plan remains five steps with a later verification element. Sometimes software verification may be split into integration and deployment within a Waterfall model. In many Waterfall approaches, you may find that each individual approach splits into multiple sub-elements, requiring documented completion before advancing. When you work in government or highly regulated industries, these approaches become even more complex, with tracking and management rapidly escalating.

In decomposing Waterfall steps to ensure full comprehension, Waterfall systems start with requirements, gathering all possible or needed items. These items are then summarized in a requirements document, which would list all the material needed during the process instead of allowing bilateral communication between users. A missed item would be built around rather than procured at a later date. The design phase follows requirements, using the requirements listing to build design-focused documentation. Again, designs are summarized, recorded and usually indexed in a large document describing explicitly the options available for the implementation phase. Complex problems might result in many design documents that may not be tied to an overall design plan. For example, each app interface might be designed, but the high-level linkages to reach each interface might follow a different model. The strict requirement and design nature removes the innovation potential as the product gets gradually closer to user delivery.

The implementation phase in DevOps approaches normally includes some user feedback. However, when using Waterfall, the implementation goal will be assessed as how closely the delivery matches the requirement and design elements. For example, if one requirement was for the system to be in Python, require less than 4GB of memory and return an answer in .1ms, those will be the tested requirements during the implementation phase. Notice these might leave out any assessment of user satisfaction, or ability to handle the planned task. Simply making it out of implementation rarely allows delivery as Waterfall adds an additional verification step.

Verification phases conduct user-based tests. One primary use for verification is in correlating requirements from technical satisfaction to user integration. The above technical requirement stated some elements but others include qualitative measures such as easy to use, low cost, repeatable or capable of working in digitally disconnected environments. In previous work, I saw programmes shut down here because users did not receive software training even though the training design required software to reach a final form. Another example occurred when the specialized verification testers were testing multiple systems simultaneously. Blockers can occur in lacking integration, or if testers cannot maintain pace with software implementation. In our case, the testers worked on a Waterfall schedule and our team used Agile so rapid deliveries flummoxed the verifiers. DevOps solves many of these problems with automated testing, covered in Chapter 7.

The maintenance phase remains similar to traditional and addresses how a product gets fixed once released. Waterfall has difficulties with small releases, wanting to consider the entire system before making a change such as a patch or an upgrade. This does not allow small integrations between stages for minor changes. Fixing things in Waterfall entails describing actions projected to break, rather than solving new problems. As an example, the USAF experienced problems with the newly deployed F-22 when pilots experienced frequent oxygen deprivation. After an exhaustive look at the aircraft systems, it was found that system inflation in the pilots' life support gear at high altitudes crimped the aircraft's oxygen supply hose.[10] To determine the cause, all the aircraft's systems had to be examined rather than implementing a simple fix.[11] Waterfall design took the problem as a new step, then compared all potential systems rather than working backwards from the problem.

Waterfall processes are generally used because they are simple to understand, easy to manage and clearly show progress as processes are completed. This works well for projects with clearly understood requirements and well-understood milestones. As mentioned earlier, Waterfall can work effectively with architectural solutions, some basic mechanical designs and even basic programming. While simple software can be produced such as internal controllers to run air conditioning or power systems, user interactions with software should remain a primary consideration. The less user interaction matters, the better the design is suited to Waterfall. This theory is contrary to most modern software delivery.

Waterfall's simplicity becomes disadvantageous when desired solutions do not require the process weight that Waterfall assigns. Despite thorough documentation, the process injects high risk as products are only produced at later stages. This makes it a poor choice for ongoing projects as it is difficult to measure progress within stages and integration is held until the process ends. The delayed integration prevents early identification of bottlenecks. For example, if each team was developing a business process micro-service, those pieces would lack integration until the final steps, and then only after every micro-service was completed. A more flexible design could continuously integrate and deploy those pieces with changes made along the way.

One variation of Waterfall is the Spiral approach. This approach varies from Waterfall in that instead of committing to a single cycle, it works through multiple, cyclical approaches.[12] Each of these spirals can be repeated forever until the project delivers a final item or runs out of money. This design was an early iterative-style application, and is shown in Figure 2.4.

One Spiral challenge is that each cycle segment is projected for similar time commitments. This means the risk analysis portion takes the same time as identifying requirements, building and releasing, or conducting the progress review. Weighting each similarly means those planning phases are as important as those building functions. Communication between elements is devalued and adding extra layers increases the overall risk in deploying a successful product, even if risks do not appear until after testing. As a continuing theme, in software, the more group separation, the less likely the end product will reflect the customer requirements.

Another inherent issue is that user feedback only occurs after product delivery. Despite focusing on smaller deliverables to manage cycles, the early feedback benefit disappears. Delivering early creates an opportunity to learn more but the Spiral approach delays learning. When learning emerges, the focus is typically on better leveraging requirements rather than fixing design or verification phases. DevOps considers each of these elements to be equally important.

FIGURE 2.4   The spiral approach

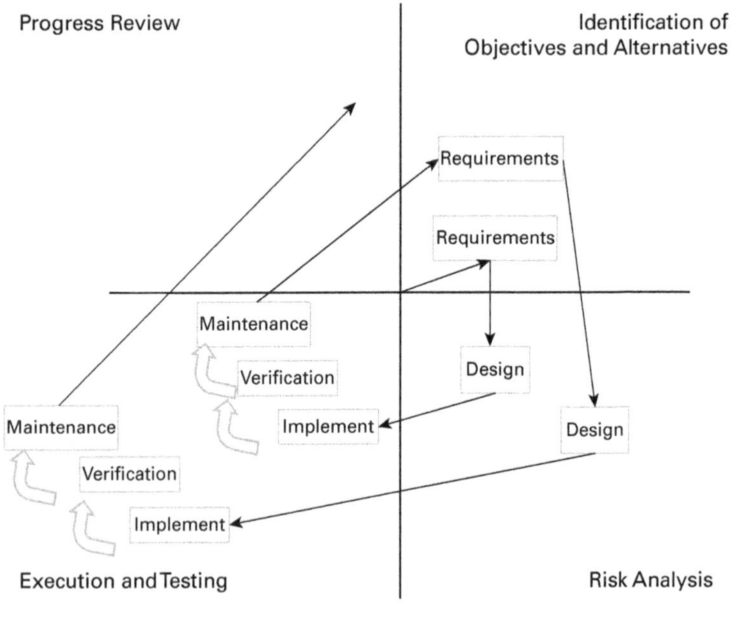

Waterfall SWOT

In analysing Waterfall with the SWOT matrix, several elements stand out. The strength of the waterfall method is the concentration on every element. Each individual instance is categorized in the plan, and must be accomplished before moving to the next segment. This allows for clear progression from one area to the next, as long as progression is defined in the plan. Managing a Waterfall system is also a strength as every step is documented and recorded. A project manager can clearly show where the programme is at and what steps occur next.

The same stability providing strength creates weakness if unexpected changes occur. Changes not addressed in the plan are neglected or plans returned to earlier stages. This serial Waterfall approach may then require cancelling a project to return to the beginning. For example, if building a house, material shortfalls such as lumber may require an alternate material solution that might not have been considered in the requirements and design phases. This could cancel the project. In a software cycle, a new patch in dependent software, vendor shortfalls or moving to an alternate cloud environment would have the same impact. The changes most developers handle through version control systems like GitHub are anathema to a good Waterfall programme. There are no early offramps in Waterfall allowing for good ideas to succeed; the programme runs to completion or fails.

The opportunity offered by Waterfall is planning well into the future. Waterfall can recognize and plan for strategic opportunities in longer timelines than Agile methods. However, not all those timelines are achieved. The Waterfall outline appears as if removing risk but the uncertainty with every element often adds significant project risk. Clear planning offers resource investment at a known cost, and early procurement but external shortages and changing markets can derail those planned goals. Organizations advocate Waterfall to accurately portray resource needs and commit company resources consistently. The challenge then becomes that stability poses a threat to responsiveness.

The threat faced by Waterfall SDLC approaches is lacking change opportunities. Projects must be clearly defined and resources may need to be scheduled early in the cycle. This makes it difficult to deal with rapid market changes and innovation. If another company can produce faster, the longer Waterfall cycle inhibits response and decreases business success. A good example could be any security patch required by modern systems. The Log4J vulnerability, a zero-day exploit against an open-source logging framework, required rapid identification and response across a variety of industries.[13] If those solutions had needed to wait for a Waterfall approach, the first fixes might still just be rolling out years later.

- Strengths: Well documented, easy to manage.
- Weaknesses: Highly prescriptive, no early offramps.
- Opportunities: Clearly defined, stable process.
- Threats: Inability to adapt to new technology or shifting requirements.

Extreme Programming and Agile SDLC

Moving to more iterative SDLC approaches requires looking at Extreme Programming (XP) and then Agile. XP was one the first implementations of iterative SDLC philosophy.[14] XP started before Agile, developed by Kent Beck in 1999 for a long-term Chrysler Corporation project to refactor payroll applications.[15] In grouping Agile and XP, one can see where XP working practices correspond closely with later Agile developments. Overall, XP offers an iterative SDLC approach but fails to be as universally applicable as Agile.

TABLE 2.2   XP and Agile

XP	Agile
1. Simplicity	1. Individuals and interactions over processes and tools
2. Communication	2. Working software over comprehensive documentation
3. Feedback	3. Customer collaboration over contract negotiation
4. Courage	4. Responding to change over following a plan
5. Respect	

XP suggests five values and 13 practices to accomplish goals while Agile uses four statements and 12 principles. Commonalities include a focus on communication, simplified design and moving work quickly. As opposed to covering each practice individually, this section comparatively evaluates the statements and values and then principles and practices. Table 2.2 compares the XP values to the Agile statements with each segment presented in the approach's preferred order.

Clearly, the system creators had different goals in mind. The XP values align better with the DevOps CALMS approach than with the Agile statements. One add to the Agile statements is the concept that although the items on the right side of the statement have value, the ones on the left are assessed to have more value. One other trend appears in that Agile solutions present as conceptual understandings rather than a declarative path to the goal.

The XP values aim to overcome traditional software barriers with simplicity, communication and feedback. The last two values hit emotional intelligence targets with courage and respect. On further consideration, one cannot have effective communication and feedback without courage and respect between team members. Individuals who do not respect each other are unlikely to have effective communication and at the same time, those without courage may be reluctant to present the honest feedback needed for group success. These values support the later 12 XP practices.

The Agile statements follow the XP call for simplicity, communication and feedback. Each item comparing one item to another during active development requires communication and feedback about inherent values. Early DevOps thoughts appear in the constant evaluation of how and why you select a practice. Further, the clarifying statement valuing the two approaches means showing respect in never leaving any individual out of the conversation. The Agile values are interwoven without the explicit statements made through XP.

As an example, one common challenge emerges between working software and comprehensive documentation. The user representative will often insist on early documentation and training when a new software version is delivered. Agile enthusiasts often argue against writing any documentation when emphasizing functional software. The more correct reading should be that functional software must be built before finalizing documentation. Some documentation is always necessary but writing the entire description before the journey can be ineffective. If one is writing a travel documentary, it might be effective to outline visits prior to departure, but writing about the experience before the trip would be ineffective. Reality causes change and action then reduces the overall entropy. Industry professionals must realize the difference between some instructions and complete documentation, especially if no software model exists to validate documents.

One other common struggle with the Agile statements is in responding to change over following a plan. Just as with documentation, the statement does not suggest one does not plan, only that the plan must allow changes. As with the previous travel example, a trip plan may be prepared but if planes are cancelled, or one of the locations experiences a hurricane, it is wise to have change options. An Agile approach allows planning but infers that all plans are flexible and subject to change. Adherence to a plan above all else can create delay in achieving functional software. At the point that sticking to a plan introduces more risk than a change, avenues for change must exist.

A similar discrepancy appears when comparing XP practices and Agile principles. XP intends to provide set items to accomplish when creating code and Agile gives generic statements subject to user interpretation. The two appear in Table 2.3 for comparison; however, because of the increased numbers, I attempted to pair the XP practices with what I saw as the best-fit Agile principle.

The first call-out should be for items at the top. XP defines the whole team concept as a team working together daily, in a collocated site, where business representatives and developers can communicate freely. Agile defines this broadly through team interaction and innovation to obtain functional delivery. On the other side, customer tests, collective code ownership and coding standards have no direct comparison to an explicit Agile principle. The thought appears instead through multiple principles focused on design, self-organization and reflection. Again, the primary difference is the Agile desire to propose thought guidelines appropriate for multiple situations while XP offers a more dedicated approach.

One of the unusual XP terms is metaphor. Here, metaphor means relating a program function towards a visual approach, such as describing a search program function like a hunting owl – it finds prey at night by rapidly discriminating between multiple distractions and captures only the wanted item. While metaphor approaches the Agile simplicity desire, simplicity expands beyond initial capability statements to remove work not required to focus on functional software quickly.

TABLE 2.3   XP items and Agile principles

XP	Agile
Whole Team	Our highest priority is to satisfy the customer through early and continuous delivery of valuable software.
	Businesspeople and developers must work together daily throughout the project.
	Build projects around motivated individuals. Give them the environment and support they need, and trust them to get the job done.
Planning Game	Welcome changing requirements, even late in development. Agile processes harness change for the customer's competitive advantage.
Small Releases	Deliver working software frequently, from a couple of weeks to a couple of months, with a preference to the shorter timescale.
Customer Tests	(Intentionally left blank)
Simple Design	Continuous attention to technical excellence and good design enhances agility.
Pair Programming	The most efficient and effective method of conveying information to and within a development team is face-to-face conversation.
Test-Driven Development	At regular intervals, the team reflects on how to become more effective, then tunes and adjusts its behavior accordingly.
Design Improvement	The best architectures, requirements, and designs emerge from self-organizing teams.
Continuous Integration	Working software is the primary measure of progress.

(*continued*)

TABLE 2.3 (Continued)

XP	Agile
Collective Code Ownership	(Intentionally left blank)
Coding Standard	(Intentionally left blank)
Metaphor	Simplicity – the art of maximizing the amount of work not done – is essential.
Sustainable Pace	Agile processes promote sustainable development. The sponsors, developers, and users should be able to maintain a constant pace indefinitely.

The close correlation between XP and Agile appears throughout the table. One sees indecision in the XP model as failing to determine whether it wants to be practical implementation or overall guidance. Agile clearly lands on the overall guidance preference. This makes Agile more universally applicable to model SDLC through the cultural emphasis on delivering functional software. In any approach, if you consider implementing XP, it should probably be done within an Agile framework. The variance means one can run XP within Agile but has more difficulty in applying Agile to an XP culture.

Extreme and Agile SWOT

Agile's strength builds a culture framework to deliver software. This strength addresses each SDLC stage in parallel rather than sequentially. In addition, Agile routes phases as effectively communicating to teams rather than passing completed items between teams. As a weakness, Agile does require cultural implementation. Just as with DevOps, cultural transitions are more difficult to achieve than a technical or process approach. Some processes are addressed in Agile but not explicit enough for universal success without cultural understanding. The Agile principles drive implementation but lack sufficient outcome orientations to be successful in the same manner as DevOps. Again, one can run DevOps as part of an Agile framework, or Agile approaches within a DevOps framework as long as the differences are understood and communicated through cultural understanding. The key Agile weaknesses are an explicit requirement for cultural emphasis and lacking principles addressing metrics or automation.

The Agile opportunity is the first SDLC change highlighting cultural needs. In words accredited to Peter Drucker, 'Culture eats strategy for breakfast'. Unless the business culture aligns with overall goals, success is difficult, if not impossible to achieve and sustain. The opportunity continues in building a development business initially as Agile rather than transforming later. Agile businesses are likely to remain Agile whereas a business advertising as Agile may fall short of the full cultural integration. Agile opportunities appear in handling a wide project range and delivering quickly.

The threat to Agile emerges from those same cultural leanings. Fast-moving and development-focused businesses are often quick to assess Agile from their process approach. They attempt to implement underlying practices without adopting the high-level, cultural conversion. The business then attributes these failures to the Agile system rather than their cultural implementation shortcomings. Outside viewpoints can see Agile as limited successes in one field or location rather than the underlying strengths, especially if their transformation failed. One common strike against Agile is the lack of explicit testing protocols.

- Strength: Creates a cultural frame for delivery.
- Weakness: No explicit process guidance.
- Opportunities: Cultural and strategic alignment, wide opportunity.
- Threats: Difficult to define success, lack of testing protocols.

SDLC implementation processes (SAFe, GitOps)

Other methods also attempt to resolve traditional SDLC, Waterfall and Agile perceived problems. Each appears here for review and reference, although they better fit as DevOps SDLC options rather than distinct elements. The Scaled Agile Framework (SAFe) is a proprietary system designed for allowing transformation. GitOps offers a partially proprietary system focusing on technical implementation. Each alternative states that the entire SDLC is addressed with SAFe in an extremely detailed manner and GitOps in a surface-level consideration grounded in continuous delivery.

Each also depends on already having an Agile or Agile-receptive culture within the business environment. These link high-level DevOps with additional fixes. Neither are complete models, with SAFe being the most descriptive and GitOps the least, but each offers perspectives to incorporate SDLC concepts. Instead of offering stages, the concepts suggest technical processes to accelerate the DevOps SDLC.

SAFe model

The Scaled Agile Framework (SAFe) was first advertised in 2011 and has undergone six major version changes since then.[16] SAFe offered exactly that for big companies – what felt like a safe transition from traditional Waterfall formats to a DevOps model. Each version offers more diagrams, a further expansion and more explicit charts defining individual roles and responsibilities. The system currently states they have more than 20,000 organizations and one million people using their system worldwide.[17] Most SAFe profit originates from continuing training classes associated with every step, distinct classes for every role in the process and the need to update to the newest version every two years. I personally have been certified at multiple levels with SAFe as I worked for different organizations.

From the analogy sense, SAFe, much like the DevOps SDLC, offers a basecamp for those seeking a DevOps summit. It provides detailed plans built on themes such as organizational agility, lean portfolio management and agile product delivery. Each theme then divides into levels for portfolio, solution, Agile Release Teams (ART) and team flows. The disconnect from SAFe and DevOps appears in the way each step hierarchically flows and connects into the next step. Critical assessments and success stories all emerge from the SAFe stack based on the organization's ability to adapt.

Throughout the process, SAFe makes use of sound DevOps approaches, Agile transitions and the Waterfall documents, which makes large organizations comfortable. The system advocates value throughout but only by fully adopting all hierarchical methods. The portfolio level encompasses high-level business strategy, solutions deliver products, the ART offers features and the individual teams complete the stories necessary for each feature. At every level, one sees a responsible manager, an architect and an engineer. These individuals are supplemented by the teams at every level. These levels suggest a DevOps flow exists and can be split through levels. SAFe designates individuals rather than accepting collaborative responsibilities.

One unique SAFe implementation occurs in the Programme Increment (PI) design. Programme Increments are designed as approximately 12-week sessions to organize delivery. This matches some DevOps thoughts but too many organizations take the opportunity to build a Waterfall delivery model based on 12-week increments. At the planning sessions, all members of each team are intended to sit together, plan design and resolve issues associated with dependencies and delivery. These allow each level to observe lower-level actions, and build their own plans from those. This best mimics the DevOps Feedback elements.

The part lacking in the SAFe model is that the structured delivery inhibits flow, feedback and improvement. Flow occurs but must progress through every level rather than directly to delivery. An item that satisfies a business strategy, no matter how big or how small, must progress across the multiple levels. For example, if a security change requiring new encryption standards is needed for the portfolio, it must be integrated as code, feature, solution and then portfolio even if a simple code change would solve the problem. Feedback disappears between levels and only occurs at the scheduled interactions. Experimentation also disappears in the structured models and the commitment to the planned PI deliveries.

The SAFe strength is that large corporations can buy a model advertising a DevOps philosophy without fully committing to cultural change. One weakness with SAFe is the cost required to fully train and develop employees inside the explicit model. The other weakness is that the rigid approach prevents the flexibility DevOps incorporates. An opportunity exists with SAFe as it allows larger organizations to begin a DevOps approach without total commitment. Some soon learn that the rigid nature prohibits the desired end goals. In fact, in 2019 the US Air Force released a memo advocating Agile practices but specifically discouraging the use of the SAFe model.[18] Finally, the threat from SAFe is being locked into a delivery model. While looking at the surface like a DevOps transformation, it falls short of that success.

- Strengths: Move to DevOps, similar model.
- Weaknesses: Cost, rigid approach.
- Opportunity: First steps for large organization.
- Threat: Delivery model lock-in.

GitOps model

GitOps offers the opposite approach to SAFe – a minimal approach designed to reach DevOps SDLC results. Instead of linking high-level strategy, GitOps links low-level commitment to a software model delivering quickly. GitOps depends on the common Git command framework in the command line inter-face (CLI) using either GitHub or GitLab. GitHub is an open-source approach to managing code versions while GitLab is the proprietary model. GitLab offers a wide range of options designed to help reach DevOps goals.

GitOps builds on three main DevOps best practices: Infrastructure as Code (IAC), Merge Requests (MR) and Continuous Integration/Continuous Delivery (CI/CD).[19] IAC basics appear in the next chapter as infrastructure but it states that any item required for software to function appears at the coding level. Merge requests are how one pulls code from forks and branches to the main code delivery elements. CI/CD states the flow process never stops; every improved item goes straight from development to delivery based on integrated automatic testing and promotion.

And that is all there is to the GitOps model. The system does attach four principles, each at least partially embedded in the GitLab/GitHub software. The first is that the Git repository acts as the sole source of truth for all software, and all changes must be present somewhere in those repositories. Next, the CD pipe-line builds, tests and deploys all applications. This links software in that no applications can be manually promoted; all must use the GitLab technology to progress. Third, deployment steps monitor resource usage and fourth, monitoring systems track performance to provide feedback. More on the third and fourth elements appears in Chapter 5 on observability but the feedback essential to DevOps is core to the GitOps process.

This process is not a DevOps cultural transformation or a full alignment to the SDLC. Instead, it explains how to use a tool to mimic the DevOps SDLC benefits without the cultural transfor-mation. The underlying gap is that to appreciate GitOps benefits, those cultural transformations should already exist. GitOps works best for DevOps organizations that are looking for some custom tools rather than as an approach one could start without the underlying DevOps culture.

The GitOps strength is in apparently containing all tools to nominally complete DevOps SDLC requirements in a single space. In a library analogy, GitOps provides the catalogue and shelves but still requires the user to bring the books. The weakness is that the underlying factors associated with DevOps success appear in resource management, delivery and planning. These can be done with GitOps but lack the automation advertised until you build local pipelines, i.e. bringing the books to the completed system. The opportunity is that all potential tools seem to appear in one box. In Chapter 6 we discuss pipeline solutions and, later, platform solutions. GitOps is an early step to incorporate pipeline and platform solutions quickly. The threat to GitOps emerges from the proprietary lock-in. For example, if feedback suggests experimenting with other platforms or pipelines, it may not be possible for those devoted to GitOps.

- Strength: All the tools in one place.
- Weakness: No planning, resource structure or guidance outside CI/CD.
- Opportunity: All in one platform.
- Threat: Vendor lock-in.

Summary

Starting with the DevOps model, all of the above SDLCs offer potential benefits to pursuing an organizational transformation to quickly deliver software. One can see how different cultural organizations prefer different approaches and why those might be chosen. The SWOT comparison allows an understanding of those business advantages and approaches. As software development requires faster delivery and more comprehensive processes, one can understand how the various SDLCs emerged, from the traditional to the GitOps and SAFe approaches today.

The next chapter takes the assumption that as you are reading this book, you are primarily interested in current DevOps success or conducting a cultural transformation. The various cultural components that guarantee success in the DevOps SDLC are explained to show how integrating cultural transformation into organizational practices poses a confident route for one's journey into DevOps.

Notes

1   Parker, B (2023) Google SWOT analysis 2023, Business Strategy Hub, https:// bstrategyhub.com/swot-analysis-of-google-2019-google-swot analysis/

2   Ibid.

3   Strohmeyer, R (2008) The 7 worst tech predictions of all time, PC World, https:// www.pcworld.com/article/532605/worst_tech_predictions.html (archived at https:// perma.cc/WZ3W-47S9)

4   Parker, B (2023) Google SWOT analysis 2023, Business Strategy Hub, https:// bstrategyhub.com/swot-analysis-of-google-2019-google-swot-analysis/ (archived at https://perma.cc/CBP4-X7TJ)

5   Parker, B (2023) Google SWOT analysis 2023, Business Strategy Hub, https:// bstrategyhub.com/swot-analysis-of-google-2019-google-swot-analysis/ (archived at https://perma.cc/YUA8-PYNH)

6   Vizard, M (2023) Rebellion against changes to open source Terraform license mounts, DevOps.com (archived at https://perma.cc/MA8D-4BPR), https:// devops.com/rebellion-against-changes-to-open-source-terraform-license-mounts/ (archived at https://perma.cc/UH8W-WSR3)

7   Lawton, G (2020) How COVID-19 created a demand for COBOL basics, TechTarget, https://www.theserverside.com/feature/How-COVID-19-created-a-demand-for-COBOL-basics (archived at https://perma.cc/EE6J-K3JB)

8   Banica, L, Radulescu, M, Rosca, D and Hagiu, A (2017) Is DevOps another project management methodology? *Informatica Economica*, **21** (3), 39–51, https://doi.org/10.12948/issn14531305/21.3.2017.04 (archived at https:// perma.cc/S7ES-HHS8)

9   Meidan, A, García-García, J, Ramos, I and Escalona, M (2018) Measuring software process: A systematic mapping Study, *ACM Computing Surveys*, **51** (3–58), 1–32, https://doi.org/10.1145/3186888 (archived at https://perma. cc/78LD-HC6P)

10 Airforce Technology (2012) Root cause of F-22 Raptor hypoxia identified, confirms USAF, https://www.airforce-technology.com/news/newsroot-cause-f22-raptor-hypoxia-identified-usaf/ (archived at https://perma.cc/2UXW-3FST)

11 House Hearing, 112 Congress (2012) F-22 Pilot Physiological Issues, https://www.govinfo.gov/content/pkg/CHRG-112hhrg76215/html/CHRG-112hhrg76215.htm (archived at https://perma.cc/875T-D5QC)

12 Martin, M (2023) Spiral model: When to use? Advantages and disadvantages, Guru99, https://www.guru99.com/what-is-spiral-model-when-to-use-advantages-disadvantages.html (archived at https://perma.cc/FVH9-F8AK)

13 Gallo, K (2022) Log4J vulnerability explained: What it is and how to fix it, Builtin.Com (archived at https://perma.cc/CAJ8-639A), https://builtin.com/cybersecurity/log4j-vulerability-explained (archived at https://perma.cc/5NKN-SZFT)

14 Jeffries, R (2011) What is Extreme Programming, https://ronjeffries.com/xprog/what-is-extreme-programming/ (archived at https://perma.cc/ZS35-JNMP)

15 Copeland, L (2001) Extreme Programming, Computerworld, https://www.computerworld.com/article/2585634/extreme-programming.html (archived at https://perma.cc/76TG-G5SK)

16 Boswell, T (2022) A brief history of the Scaled Agile Framework, Medium.com (archived at https://perma.cc/LBH6-V98R), https://medium.com/lean-agile-mindset/a-brief-history-of-the-scaled-agile-framework-633665a73a37 (archived at https://perma.cc/R9FP-UM7H)

17 Scaled Agile (2023) What is SAFe? https://scaledagile.com/what-is-safe/ (archived at https://perma.cc/HY2F-VT5N)

18 Chaillan, N (2019) Preferred Agile Framework, https://software.af.mil/wp-content/uploads/2019/12/CSO-MFR-on-Agile-Frameworks-12282019.pdf (archived at https://perma.cc/8DJM-EM2H)

19 Gitlab (2023) What is GitOps? https://about.gitlab.com/topics/gitops/ (archived at https://perma.cc/R6NV-UY7T)

CHAPTER THREE

Beginning with DevOps

Paraphrasing the beginning of one of my favourite fiction books, *The Eye of the World* by Robert Jordan, at the start of the *Wheel of Time* series, some points are neither the beginning nor the end, but they are a beginning. To start any journey, you must identify those beginnings. Learning about DevOps and becoming conceptually familiar can be a beginning for many people but just learning DevOps should not be the end of your journey. DevOps is often not the beginning as most individuals only find it after either several jobs or several years working in development. Frustration leads to seeking answers, and at some point that usually leads to DevOps. Similarly, DevOps is not the end. It will not immediately solve all problems, largely due to the need for cultural transformation supporting DevOps tools.

Most individuals discover DevOps at a personal low point, frustrated by slow deliveries and organizational processes and unhappy with delivering low-quality code. The initial DevOps experience might be an individual interaction, a conference presentation, a podcast or an organizational change. However it occurs, DevOps addresses common problems: slow product delivery, complex issues, inability to scale, poor resource utilization and minimal observability. DevOps solutions are designed to increase delivery speeds by ensuring smaller value increments reach the customer regularly. Of course, the customer can define 'regular' as daily, monthly, quarterly or other time windows. These types of solutions sound simple but implementation is challenging not because it is complex but because these programmes require constant diligence for success. This chapter takes a detailed look at understanding the Three Ways:

- Flow
- Feedback
- Improvement

Vendors today often offer technical DevOps solutions without considering the underlying organizational issues. Despite focusing on the best technology, DevOps remains a cultural solution to software development. Changing the culture changes the box for software delivery and enables continuous improvement versus simply installing new tools without changing the foundational focus. Each of the Three Ways is explored from the cultural to the process perspective.

The Three Ways explained

Everyone likely has a favourite martial arts movie where the student struggles to learn and apply various principles until a certain scene reveals unexpected truths. These truths help the student relate the studied techniques to realistic mindsets such as wind blowing through the trees, human interactions or animal movement. The learning epiphany results in the student internalizing those previously repeated approaches without understanding. In the original 1984 *Karate Kid* movie, Daniel repeats various manual chores without realizing they duplicate karate motions until his epiphany occurs. From this point, the student becomes unstoppable. Learning to be confident in DevOps follows a similar path. One must learn and internalize the Three Ways to achieve the needed success. Simply repeating the motions is insufficient; one must understand why those actions need repetition. The Three Ways are flow, feedback and improvement.

My own introduction to DevOps occurred later in my career. For years, I had worked as a US Air Force intelligence officer. Completing various field tasks entailed gathering and processing intelligence quickly, passing the knowledge on to someone else for actionable outcomes, taking their feedback and then preparing a way to gather improved intelligence for the next mission. I moved into the cybersecurity and software development fields when I finished my military career. In my first role as a contractor, I was informed they were using DevOps processes and I needed to learn those essentials before beginning any critical roles. I resolved to learn as much as possible and become an effective worker.

I started reading books about DevOps and soon noticed various similarities to my previous intelligence work. In each intelligence task, I flowed to produce as much value as possible quickly, sought feedback from my users as pilots and senior officers, and then improved for the next task. For me, this meant I had already internalized many concepts and was able to apply them to my new field. My epiphany occurred quickly.

A quote from a German field marshall, Moltke the Elder, states, 'No plan of operations extends with certainty beyond the first encounter with the enemy's main strength.'[1] This highlights a DevOps strength with smaller plans delivering smaller value increments to allow quick changes. Any small software delivery plan can be changed to allow adaptation. Recognizing necessary changes rather than simply committing to a given plan requires culturally incorporating DevOps principles and organizational management to implement and support those principles. At the top level, those principles are flow, feedback and improvement.

Cultural synthesis

The culture concept remains important to every organization. A well-known quote attributed to Peter Drucker, a widely influential contributor to management thinking, states 'Culture eats strategy for breakfast'.[2] Deconstructing the quote suggests it is impossible to succeed with a strategy running counter to the company's culture. One example occured when Rollerblade, a business with a free-wheeling past, was bought by Benetton in the mid-1990s. The loose culture at Rollerblade, with employee exercise breaks and independent approaches, was countered by the stricter retail company.[3] Accompanied by employee cuts, Benetton went from $5 million annual US income to losing $31 million in the first year. The underlying culture must support desired outcomes and this remains true to implement DevOps.

Cultural designation elements remain similar whether the culture is national, ethnic or organizational. Those elements are symbols, language, norms, values and artifacts.[4] DevOps flow, feedback and improvement are best expressed through those organizational norms. The shared common structure is not just part of DevOps success but the key reason behind success and failure at different organizations. Without a common shared framework, companies are unable to adapt to the 'deliver value now' DevOps aspect, relying on traditional approaches and often unsuccessful paths, similar to the Bennetton example.

Culture is defined by the shared attitudes, values, goals and practices characterizing an institution. These concepts are reflected through chosen leadership, decision-making styles and strategic architecture. The DevOps practice starts off emphasizing the Three Ways. Many DevOps practices further explain this with the CALMS concept: Culture, Automation, Lean, Metrics and Sharing. The Three Ways and CALMS shape how you implement a DevOps culture regardless of location, company role or assigned work. Culture appears first as integral to the other four factors succeeding. A shared learning culture creates belief patterns to drive organizational decisions.[5]

- C – Culture
- A – Automation
- L – Lean
- M – Metrics
- S – Sharing

One frequent challenge in implementing a DevOps culture deals with shifting from a local, in-person model to the partially or fully remote operations necessary for global organizations. Modern companies may use more remote work with independent contractors, temporary employees and regular employees. Regardless of corporate attachment, culture drives the basic foundations for success. Measuring individuals occurs across three dimensions of work: status, content and conditions.[6] The gap between the fully and mostly employed can create divisions detrimental to a cultural establishment.

Many companies use various subcontractors as individual teams or sub-contractors within existing teams. Small variations among teams can cause stressful cultures. One example appears in the practice of taking government holidays. If working for a government customer, one may find the government takes all federal holidays such as Labour Day, Martin Luther King Day or other designated holidays as downtime with optional down days added to create longer weekends. As a local team, one may prefer to work on holidays, accentuate flow and perhaps skip regular meetings to prevent contextual shifts. This discrepancy can create organizational friction which can increase as operations scale.

The growing translocality cultural problems appear in a qualitative Agile practice study on Agile circa 2011–2014. Many of these issues have yet to be resolved. The study finds that coordination, temporality and communication all suffer in a diversely cultured environment with geographic boundaries.[7] Studies and use-cases show that despite an original ethnic or locale-based culture, you can implement successful DevOps cultural transformations. In implementing the DevOps culture, one depends on close human communication as a key factor in building value through a bottom-up approach. These integrations promote a sharing culture and further DevOps strategies by avoiding organizational silos.[8] Establishing an effective culture can help prevent future challenges.

Addressing stress and creating cultural synthesis at the early level occurs through developing team working agreements. These are standard within Agile practices and often lead to increased success. The basic agreement foundation dictates that every team member agrees to a consensus, facilitating flow. These agreements occur at the team, management and higher levels to communicate cultural role understanding. While team agreements are discussed later in this chapter, the basic concepts provide knowledge of roles, responsibilities, communication expectations, feedback mechanisms and change processes. Early identification of flow, feedback and improvement mechanisms within a team agreement is vital to creating effective DevOps cultures.

The DevOps model creates a cultural process based on flow, feedback and continuous learning that interacts with other business processes, even when considering compliance. One way many teams improve communication is by adopting elements like the Unified Modelling Language (UML) baseline to detail business and development standards within a common framework. An individual's experience with standards leads to first interactions in conforming to corporate culture and improving standards for continuing success. These cultural elements identify synthesis needs but cannot happen without implementation direction from management.

Management implementation

No culture can be complete unless alignment between management and workers occurs on the agreed-upon standards. The goal in sound cultural implementation is creating value alignment on delivery and ensuring steady value delivery to the customer. There are many management texts describing the difference between top-down and bottom-up activities and DevOps requires adopting a hybrid approach. The workers must want to go faster, develop effective products and feel empowered through success. Management must agree that adopting DevOps creates some uncertainty and risk in previous long-term plans. The risk occurs at the delivery level rather than the strategic level as small, valuable deliveries ensure continued success but are not aligned to the Gantt charts and standards management may have previously favoured. The key element link lies in recognizing how groups communicate. As the basis for this communication, I prefer thinking through the social exchange theory.

Social exchange theory determines if an exchange will occur when profit, defined as reward minus cost, reaches a sufficient level for the involved groups to see beneficial exchange.[9] The core essence states, 'Social behaviour is an exchange of goods, material goods but also non-material goods'.[10] The theory originated from George Homans' 1951 work, *The Human Group*, exploring the behavioural decision theory with activities, interactions and means defining the group.[11] These areas are a model for everything occurring within DevOps software development. Activities are coding, merging and producing to create customer value as well as including the observability created through using task boards such as Scrum and core repositories like Git. Interactions describe value transfers within daily team meetings, product demonstrations and accepted deliverables. Means implies the entire Three Ways and CALMs implementations.

Social exchange addresses individual interactions to interpret the meaning others hold about the world. The expansion to social exchange provided a more precise definition of how groups determined which behaviours were acceptable, understanding the multiple perspectives of how one uses experience as the lived-through events to guard against the cliché, conceptual and predetermined. This allows moving from the overall meaning to the moment where the individual reaches their intuitive grasp. Collecting the shared success within those intuitive mindsets focuses on the smaller elements driving DevOps implementation.

Converting to any process takes time. Management implementation should not be considered a one-day change but a cyclical process. Most transformations typically take three to six months to move from a previous standard to a new change. These changes should be preceded by training for new standard elements. This is where generating the team working agreement (TWA) typically occurs. In this space, those TWAs can also be shared to help eliminate silos and emphasize flow across multiple elements. In creating a new team, it typically takes three months for the forming process and initial capability. The next three months allow the team to find their speed and lock in elements. Then, at that point, the DevOps benefits begin to occur, and velocity will gradually increase. It should be noted that any change to teams such as new members, product shifts or organizational changes can reset these teams to the initial forming phase. This restarts the three- to six-month process. Many management implementations constantly change teams without realizing the structural impact.

Studies show how social exchange behaviours affect corporate practices by aligning direct cost models to social responsibilities.[12] Most important are the experiences that link cost models to social responsibility. One social exchange interpretation brackets conceptual, empirical and technical information technology aspects through three aligned case studies.[13] Again, one sees the connection to DevOps through

formulating the idea, converting the idea into code and then testing the code through product implementation. If one has
frequently dealt with engineering professions, one finds that
teams often jump from the idea to the preferred solution and
work backwards into the code. Unfortunately, this can derail the
feedback element and while code might be developed, it will not
be the best solution but only a solution that fits at the time, and
future solutions may become more difficult.

Decomposing these ideas returns one to the human experience aspect as the core of DevOps, that DevOps is for humans
and not a technical solution. Social exchange standards integrated into industrial settings show how decision-making costs
and rewards, the economic individual decision principles and
relationship levels between teams affect the overall outcomes.
These core concepts demonstrate social exchange utility standards to the DevOps cultures. From the thought perspective,
Heidegger offered an underlying proof through the unique
term, *enframing*, as the process by which the individual orders
and is, in turn, ordered by technological processes.[14] This
provides a philosophical foundation for the flow and feedback
aspects of the DevOps experience.

Understanding these interactions from the management
perspective allows for describing experiences and interpreting
the interaction across multiple teams within the organization's
cultural flow. A step-by-step process would first create a sound
ontological assessment for common issues, capture first perceptions, identify parts and wholes inside the data and finally a
deeper understanding that captures the textual essence of the
global process. This approach contributes to how the DevOps
culture experiences valuation processes.

DevOps constitutes not just another project management
methodology but a conceptual method to break organizational
silos. Some functional answers to creating value appear infre-
quently in research, such as value-based software engineering,
but still fall short of determining any value-based approach

towards the entire development cycle.[15] A key DevOps attribute must be to increase speed and stability while delivering but again the question remains implementation.[16] Delivering value as the end goal should be the desired aim for all organizational participants.

The practical management question becomes not 'What is DevOps?' but 'How do I lead a team into adopting DevOps processes and methodologies?' Before one gathers requirements, begins an architecture and forms teams, the system must be understood. Perceptions need management at every level when a transformational topic appears. These perceptions lead to understanding the process parts and wholes to create conceptual understanding. Those understandings allow our DevOps practice to grow, just like the martial artist at the start of the chapter, into an organically supported whole.

In the rest of this chapter I will use the CALMS approach to show how DevOps grows through the Three Ways into a fully functioning whole. CALMS becomes a useful approach as ideas and values associated with DevOps are expressed. These first steps build the basis for your understanding to grow as you proceed.

Flow

Flow always appears as an easy process. All that has to happen is work needs to be done. Good flow sets the path for the DevOps journey. The word 'flow' fills parts of speech as a noun and a verb. The dictionary defines the noun as 'a smooth, uninterrupted movement or process' and the verb as 'to move in a stream'.[17] Both apply when using flow as the First Way. The teams should offer an uninterrupted action creating value moving in a stream. Every stream has a beginning and an end, even if the end is simply in a larger body of water, i.e. product. This increases the relevance for value streams to represent

DevOps flow, beginning with the customer requirement, delivered into the customer's hands, and allowing the next iteration with continued flow. As in every element, the opportunity to create flow begins in culture.

The culture around flow should support constant movement from idea to done, usually within a sprint cycle. The difficult part for teams when adopting flow is not to allow themselves to derail delivery. The best practice should be identifying blockers as a positive when they impede flow. Too many teams see a blocker and avoid discussing those issues with management to prevent negative responses. As an example, if one identifies a dependency for a third-party software mid-sprint, it often becomes a solution quest without visibility. If the solution does not readily appear, that interruption then slows other pieces, much like trees falling across a stream. A team hitting blockers needs to communicate those aspects, so everyone knows when each stream will hit the reservoir as the end state.

Building a flow culture requires management and teams to emphasize what work needs to be accomplished. Critical to accomplishing work is deconstructing requirements to complete the smallest work elements possible. While work often starts with grand ideas, the company must ask what should be done first, and what can be done most quickly. If the idea is to construct a new mobile app to accelerate public parking, the first element may not be a completed app but recognizing users, a second element to accept secure payments, and the third as scanning existing parking databases to find spots. Rather than build the elements in silos, each should be simplified and incorporated into the flow.

Automation expedites flow. Any flow is good but fast flows are markedly better than slow progression. The first step in automating flow is recognizing what slows you down and the next accepts that automation does not remove job needs. A common example is grocery shops moving to automated checkout lines. Where before, every item required multiple interactions, the overall grocery process to deliver value through selling goods improves if every customer can scan their own groceries. This then enables the employees to focus on stocking shelves and improving the overall value of the shopping experience.

In the same manner, automating flow is accomplished through pipelines, planning boards, high observability, version control and other DevOps-associated tools. Each tool takes a manual process and passes it to a machine to allow humans to focus on creativity. Pipelines are an excellent example as the typical pipeline can incorporate multiple processes that would take hours individually but aggregated are much faster. In addition, process automation allows a developer to move on to another task while waiting for pipeline results. Automation also improves flow by allowing management to see progress directly rather than stopping a developer to ask about progress or require an update meeting.

Lean, of course, gained its beginnings from flow. Lean eliminates waste to focus on product delivery. We saw Lean in the Andon cord, in understanding the SDLC and in the struggle to make delivery faster. Some Lean flow elements can include daily standups of ten to fifteen minutes rather than an hour-long meeting, asynchronous communications such as Slack or Mattermost, and remote work versus daily commutes. One way to accelerate Lean in organizations is to strictly timebox all meetings and then apply common communications. Timeboxing refers to setting a desired time and then stopping the meeting there, regardless of outcome. Some communication formats for DevOps involve meeting calls, of which several are listed below:

- 'LMO' (pronounced 'elmo') – let's move on. We think we have reached the useful end of discussion on this topic and are moving to the next one.
- 'Weeds' – the topic is too far from the initial subject and may deal with solutions rather than characterizing the current issue.

- 'Parking lot' – that point is necessary but does not relate to the subject at hand so will be captured for later discussion.
- 'Shiny' – the topic is interesting and merits discussion but is not relevant currently.
- 'Thumbs' – call for consensus, used to verify group agreement. A thumbs requires a positive up or down from every meeting participant, no abstentions allowed.

Flow-based communication calls are based on creating alignment rather than consensus. Agreeing to a parking lot or a shiny call does not mean that you always agree, just that you agree for now. These calls build alignment to move an idea forward in the flow even without complete consensus.

Metrics are an important topic that I'll raise throughout the book. Any metric used must not impede flow and must address automation needs in accelerating flow. The DORA (DevOps Research and Assessment) metrics are a good spot for starting to recognize flow with deployment frequency, lead time to change, mean time to recover and change failure rate. These convey how fast code moves to production, the time an idea requires to become code, how much bad code passes the pipeline and how long fixing bad code takes in operations. The most important part of flow metrics measures observable events within normal progress and highlights items impeding flow with unusual starts and stops.

The last element considers sharing. Sharing returns to observability and reminds us that all DevOps events should be universally visible. Enhancing sharing requires coding in common repositories rather than individual silos to support shared learning practices. Sharing also extends to processes, working through retrospectives to acknowledge issues and sharing knowledge forward through active demonstrations about delivered features. Like many of the CALMS elements, sharing ties to other levels through culture, metrics and automation.

The best method to enhance flow resides in using Scrum or Kanban boards. A Scrum board focuses on story points and only commits a team to completing assigned items, while a Kanban board uses the work-in-progress structure. Work-in-progress limits the total items underway at any one time, ensuring every item reaches completion before new work begins. Ideas in Kanban can be pulled from the backlog at any point while Scrum limits pulling work to items assigned to the sprint. While both boards can use columns to show the state in which work occurs, I always advise limiting those areas to 'backlog', 'good ideas', 'to do', 'work that has yet to be assigned', 'in progress', 'work assigned to individuals' and 'done, all items complete'. A secondary tip here – every item should at least have a use-case and acceptance criteria. Being aware of the problem and potential solution helps drive flow.

These boards put all items in a common area, allow everyone to visualize problems and actively track the progress of work being done. Having work displayed commonly allows shared judgments about whether work items are large or small. In addition, it commits the culture to the pull requirement of constantly moving work across boards. This allows flow across multiple teams as all participating can visualize any other team's work at any point. Flow is maximized not by directly counting work or story points accomplished on a board but by how well each team completed the items planned. High completion rates demonstrate flow occurred.

Returning to a SWOT approach, the strength of flow is in the constant production of value. The weakness is that a high flow rate does not lend itself well to long-term or ongoing projects. Opportunity emerges constantly through flow, allowing quick failures to drive learning without overcommitting to resources. Threats to flow occur when you allow flow to be driven from a push rather than a pull approach. In the push approach, you generate and complete new ideas but these can become disconnected from the end-state value.

Feedback

Feedback, the Second Way, provides the fuel behind successful DevOps implementations. Feedback means that once an item flows, information flows back to workers and forward to customers. Without regular feedback, DevOps becomes just another project planning tool.

The DevOps feedback mechanisms should emphasize constancy and continuity. Every element drives discussion, which eventually leads to the Third Way, improvement. When you inspect automated DevOps pipelines, you see feedback's essence. Every step in the pipeline returns feedback, not based on success or failure, but on step functions. An item can be evaluated based on either the high-level success or the results from an individual line of code within the progress. In connecting with observability, feedback allows anyone to see results and interpret.

Using feedback does not require a set format but DevOps accepts all feedback as valuable. One of the DevOps keys is constantly having blame-free discussions about what occurred. Normal organizational action tends toward ordered processes. Feedback, from the initial definition, creates a corrective action requiring energy. Too many organizations devalue negative feedback, wanting to hear only positive results while ignoring negative feedback despite similar opportunities for change. From this feedback, you can derive that while all action creates change, inaction can create disaster. The continuous feedback mechanism attempts to avoid disaster.

Culture describes the organizational context and determines if a highly ordered state is preferential to the culture favouring strict processes with low entropy. Order here means the static process the organization has adopted. Some organizations thrive with high-entropy cultures and some with low-entropy cultures. If you place a space heater into a cold room, you'll notice the results sooner than if you placed one in a warm room. DevOps feedback is the space heater, constantly injecting more energy. Regardless of the initial state and whether you notice it or not, the energy injection always takes place. Organizations should seek a culture of accepting feedback. This reflects Conway's Law, 'Any organization that designs a system will produce a design whose structure is a copy of the organization's communication system'.[18] Feedback culturally follows an organization's communication system.

Automation allows quick feedback on repetitive processes. The goal here is to create mechanisms that rapidly provide the necessary information to make adjustments. This typically includes the dashboards common in modern software engineering. An automated dashboard can provide details such as the current security state, bandwidth consumed, memory in use, lines of code committed and many other factors. Organizations should seek to automate as much as possible within their delivery cycle to provide improvement opportunities.

Lean directly emphasizes feedback. In the previous chapter we saw takt time as flow, the difference in planned versus actual production. This is an example of feedback automated with a dashboard to create feedback. Lean also drives the impetus behind all feedback to eliminate waste. Feedback attempts to create an optimal First Way flow by implementing feedback. Just as with my prior experience in the intelligence field, Lean suggests feedback should be actionable. Feedback without suggested actions becomes a wasted effort.

In an example, feedback stating that this quarter's work was terrible and we made less money is not actionable feedback. Feedback stating that production was unable to meet demand and our customers turned to an alternative product becomes more actionable. Then, if we dig into the feedback further, we may find we were unable to meet demand because there was growth from 200 units per quarter to 400 per quarter. This then becomes a difference in the communication between the sales funnel and the production element. Further discussion between those two areas should create feedback to drive experimentation and improvement, aligning better in the future.

Metrics are equally essential to feedback. They provide the initial source of truth to determine if actions can be undertaken and then measure the impact of those actions. One key to feedback is understanding the baseline. Baseline means creating the standard for any action measured. One common DevOps transformation problem is when many organizations believe adopting DevOps creates success. Most organizations require three months to adapt to a new change, and then an additional three months to start producing with the benefit from that feedback. In a small organization this applies to any change, including changing team members, altering product strategy or even changing company snack policies if they affect team morale. Metrics show a historical record of what has happened and allow comparison to the current output as feedback.

Sharing, the last element of the CALMS structure, is equally key in feedback. Feedback must be shared at all levels. DevOps requires management involvement from the top and suggestions from the bottom to be successful. The interaction through these elements improves through constant sharing. One can implement sharing through bulletin boards, open meetings, suggestion boxes and open file structures. Traditional organizations often adopt a process of locking files, managing internal business in silos and not sharing processes. When these silos occur, one can not baseline events. In the previous example, if the sales team never shares the new business funnel, there is no method for developers to observe demand change prediction. On the other side, if the production experience is mired in secrecy, the sales team does not know where to share their information to drive production.

Although metrics and measures occur across many dashboards and automated processes as feedback, there are two common tools to verify answers. The tools I prefer are the sprint retrospective (retro) and the feature demonstration (demo). In software development, retros occur after a sprint or product cycle. At this time, everyone gathers around and discusses what went well, what went poorly and what needs to improve. Another version uses the terms keep doing, stop doing and do better. Both tend to reach the same point. The most important part is that the feedback here resembles a brainstorming session; no ideas should be discriminated against. The other essential part requires revisiting the retro on a regular basis to ensure previous issues are being addressed rather than recreated during the following work cycles.

My other favourite feedback tool for software development is the demo. The demo is a key software development function as it confirms a feature has been accomplished. Regardless of the feature size, DevOps' Agile background emphasizes functional software. If functional software is the goal, then those functions should be demonstrated. Sprint features that cannot be demonstrated should not be considered complete. This can range from showing slides about research to demonstrating a new interaction in logs or presenting a new capability. Demos should be presented to a stakeholder or user and allow feedback between what was promised and what was delivered. This is one of the best ways to ensure everyone stays on track.

From the top level, the main strength of adopting feedback systems is the very nature of the feedback. Strong feedback means every action produces information that can be looped back to improve the action itself. Organizations with good feedback tend to improve and organizations without feedback tend to fail (the progression of the early generations of Apple computers is good evidence of this). As a weakness, one must ensure that feedback creates a chance for further discussion. Just because feedback exists does not always mean the feedback is beneficial. A good example here would be prioritizing feedback for availability when the company only has one customer who logs in for 15 minutes a day. The feedback would be all positive but if the company trusted only that availability feedback, they would be unlikely to improve.

Feedback creates an opportunity to get better. Good opportunities address that the best feedback leads to an opportunity for more feedback. The best feedback may not necessarily be positive – the important factor is that it answers the intended question. The threat from feedback comes in a similar path to the weakness. You must always seek to expand feedback and gain more breadth or depth on issues. The company must also not stop the feedback process by believing that all useful questions have been answered. There is always a need for more feedback.

Improvement

If Flow sets the path and Feedback fills the tank with fuel, then Improvement is the engine for DevOps success. If a commitment to continuous improvement does not occur, the DevOps journey ends. Flow and feedback create the necessary data to move forward. Improvement does not commit to big changes but to small incremental changes over time. On our journey, we want to look to the destination, then our feet, taking one step at a time, overcoming current obstacles and being careful about the next step. Then, over time, we can look back on the path and realize that the start point is so distant because all those small steps occurred at the proper place and time.

Starting with the definition, improvement is 'the act or process of improving'.[19] We add that improving is 'something that adds value or excellence' to become the act or process of adding value or excellence. Then we have improvement as the act or process of adding value or excellence to a product or process. Improvement cannot be isolated but must link to experimentation. Third Way experimentation allows one to quickly try alternatives and then use the feedback to create flow. The actions improved are not isolated and removed from daily processes but organic growth from what needs to be changed.

In that nature, every improvement starts with a question: Why do we do this? Can the numbers be better? Where can the code be refined? What other elements should be considered? Key to those experiments is the ability to set up a trial and test alternative methods. Traditional SDLC models examine those alternatives only during early planning phases but DevOps allows for experimentation to occur continuously to drive improvement. All experimentation starts with a question and builds to an answer. The scientific method appears below for a quick reference on how to build any experiment:

1 State the question
2 Analyse existing research or data
3 Form a hypothesis
4 Perform the experiment
5 Analyse the results
6 Form a conclusion

Each step can be done continuously but understanding a method allows one to make comparisons between different experiments. A successful experiment is one that answers the initial question. Not all answers are successful but all answers have value in contributing to improvement.

Three types of experiment can be conducted: qualitative, quantitative and mixed method. Each is suited to a different type of question. Qualitative answers questions about interaction, such as 'What was the customer's best experience with this software?', 'Do employees like working with the company?', 'What common experiences do developers share when working with a feature?' These are geared towards feelings and experiences and are difficult to quantitatively analyse. Quantitative research looks for a numerical answer: 'How many did we produce?', 'What is the uptime?', 'How many users returned for a second visit to the website?' These are useful for statistical data. The mixed method, as the name suggests, includes elements of both to provide better alignment. An example might be, 'Why did customers return for a second website visit?' or 'How does a high uptime (over 80 per cent) relate to the customer's experience with the site?' The key element should be understanding what questions will be asked by the experiment and how the answers will be conveyed.

A culture driven by experimentation is an inquisitive one, one that believes the only sin is the unasked question and devotes time and resources to finding answers. A common practice in experimental cultures is instituting hackathons. A hackathon is where an organization proposes a problem, allows developers a set time to create solutions and then integrates those solutions into the business strategy. Another experimental approach appears with Google, where employees are allowed research time to spend 20 per cent of their time learning new skills and trying new solutions.[20]

Driving automated improvement through experimentation is more difficult to assess. As experiments are driven by creative questions, most automated solutions will fall short. The answer lies in not automating the experimentation but automating experimentation environments. DevOps teams using Infrastructure as Code (IaC) can rapidly deploy multiple environments mirroring the production environment. This simplifies testing and allows experimentation with multiple options. Another method appears in using chaos engineering principles. This experimentation technique attempts to predict where faults occur. Successful prediction allows the team to work on solutions before problems emerge.

Lean does not consistently reference experimentation. The experimental idea appears as the Andon cord when you stop the entire production line until a solution can fix the issue. That solution is experimental. The part left out would be structuring experiments into a regular process. Experiments lead to improvement, and those continual improvement cycles do appear in

Lean. DevOps tries to structure experiments into a more regular frequency.

Metrics are an essential part of improvement through experimentation. Linking to the quantitative and qualitative measures early, all experiments should tie answers to metrics. At the same time, these metrics are likely to be explicitly tied to the question answered. The goal in experimenting to reach improvement is to achieve an answer. Those answers may not always create direct improvement but should result in future discussions about what to implement.

Finally, sharing improvement creates growth across the team structure. Members should build cultural links to sharing growth. We see these improvements shared through feedback processes and through team interaction. Sharing experimental results benefits the team in communicating results and enhances the overall culture in demonstrating management and team support for experimentation.

The best methods to advocate improvement were mentioned earlier with the hackathon and dedicated research time. Describing the best way to implement experimentation can be difficult. An employee's nature and cultural alignment play a central role in whether they are receptive to experimental leanings. Even if the hackathon is in place, many employees are not motivated to learn and experiment with new technology. In those cases, your business should always seek to advance and promote those who show those qualities.

The strength in the Third Way is that continuous improvement and growth allows rapid adjustment to a changing marketplace. The weakness is that when employees expect constant improvement and experimentation, they can quickly grow dissatisfied with static environments. As an opportunity, if you adopt an improve and adapt workplace, as with Google, the workforce is constantly prepared and planning for changes. These changes can create rapid growth, or just better connections to marketplace trends. Finally, the threat posed by improvement means management needs to be prepared to find and offer opportunities to advance and experiment, in line with the Third Way's weakness.

Summary

Understanding the Three Ways, their interaction with CALMS and the fundamental characteristics of each allows one to journey deeper into DevOps solutions. The Three Ways are the cultural pillars for all of DevOps. Here, you saw flow as the central path to set the journey, emphasizing the need for quick and continuous delivery above all else. Those deliveries only become continuous when you can integrate regular feedback. Returning information makes sure the flow proceeds in an iterative fashion, constantly adapting to small changes. Finally, improvement and experimentation allow one to concisely determine those areas that are not small changes and then implement an iterative approach.

In the next section, the concepts change from a broad, cultural understanding of DevOps to a technical one. The following chapters will build out the technical underpinnings behind successful DevOps and allow the creation of infrastructure, applications and environments that support the Three Ways. Throughout all the following chapters you should remain focused on these Three Ways and how technical solutions enhance those opportunities.

Notes

1 Bergeson, D (ND) Strategic Planning: Moltke the Elder, Dwight Eisenhower, Winston Churchill, and Just a Little Mike Tyson, connect2amc.com (archived at https://perma.cc/DG4A-WCVN). https://connect2amc.com/118-strategic-planning-moltke-the-elder-dwight-eisenhower-winston-churchill-and-just-a-little-miketyson (archived at https://perma.cc/F2NC-Q9RR)

2   Guley, G, and Reznik, T (2019) Culture eats strategy for breakfast and transformation for lunch, *The Jabian Journal*, https://journal.jabian.com/culture-eats-strategy-for-breakfast-and-transformation-for-lunch/ (archived at https://perma.cc/2X9X-DN7T)

3   Bridges, W and Bridges, S (2016) *Managing Transitions*, Lifelong Books, pp 4–5

4   University of Minnesota (2016) Sociology, https://open.lib.umn.edu/sociology/chapter/3-2-the-elements-of-culture/ (archived at https://perma.cc/42LB-L7LN)

5   Walton, P (2020) The limitations of decision-making, *Information*, **11** (12), 559, doi: https://doi.org/10.3390/info11120559 (archived at https://perma.cc/N5MM-2ZSL)

6   Pichault, F and McKeown, T (2019) Autonomy at work in the gig economy: analysing work status, work content and working conditions of independent professionals, *New Technology, Work & Employment*, **34** (1), 59–72, doi: https://doi.org/10.1111/ntwe.12132 (archived at https://perma.cc/U7ZF-UFR8)

7   Bjørn, P, Søderberg, A-M and Krishna, S (2019) Translocality in global software development: The dark side of global agile, *Human-Computer Interaction*, **34** (2), 174–203, doi: https://doi.org/10.1080/07370024.2017.13 98092 (archived at https://perma.cc/Y94K-NVRN)

8   Bento, F, Tagliabue, M and Flora, L (2020) Organizational silos: A scoping review informed by a behavioral perspective on systems and networks, *Societies*, **10** (3), 56, doi: https://doi.org/10.3390/soc10030056 (archived at https://perma.cc/T6QQ-TPNM)

9   Homans, G C (1958) Social behavior as exchange, *American Journal of Sociology*, **63**, 597–606

10 Ibid, p. 606

11 Homans, G C (1951) *The Human Group*, New York: Routledge

12 Carroll, A B (1979) A three-dimensional conceptual model of corporate performance, *Academy of Management Review*, **4** (4), 497–505. doi: https://doi.org/10.5465/amr.1979.4498296 (archived at https://perma.cc/HU84-2LCM)

13 Friedman, B, Kahn, P H and Borning, A (2008) Value sensitive design and information systems in P Zhang and D Galetta, *Human-Computer Interaction in Management Information Systems Foundations*, Armonk, NY: M.E. Sharpte, pp. 348–72

14 Heidegger, M (2013) *The Question Concerning Technology and Other Essays*, Harper Perennial

15 Mendes, E, Rodriguez, P, Freitas, V, Baker, S and Atoui, M A (2018) Towards improving decision making and estimating the value of decisions in value-based software engineering: The VALUE framework, *Software Quality Journal*, **26** (2), 607–56, https://doi.org/10.1007/s11219-017-9360-z (archived at https://perma.cc/9BZJ-9NBH)

16 Forsgren, N (2018) DevOps delivers, *Communications of the ACM*, **61** (4), 32, https://doi.org/10.1145/3174799 (archived at https://perma.cc/M4N3-7MZ5)

17 Flow, https://www.merriam-webster.com/dictionary/flow (archived at https://perma.cc/55Z2-8LJQ)

18 Conway, M (1968) How do committees invent? Melconway.com (archived at https://perma.cc/5AGL-FN94), www.melconway.com/Home/Committees_Paper.html (archived at https://perma.cc/4QRK-246A)

19 Improvement, https://www.merriam-webster.com/dictionary/improvement (archived at https://perma.cc/H39A-H29S)

20 Clark, D (2022) Google's 20% rule shows exactly how much time you should spend learning new skills-and why it works, CNBC.com (archived at https://perma.cc/4384-6NZZ), https://www.cnbc.com/2021/12/16/google-20-percent-rule-shows-exactly-how-much-time-you-should-spend-learning-new-skills.html (archived at https://perma.cc/2QXA-3X8B)

PART TWO

Fundamentals of DevOps

.

CHAPTER FOUR

DevOps architecture

One common element between the world's manmade wonders – from the Giza pyramids to the Great Wall of China – is that none of them were built without careful planning. Too often, DevOps implementations focus on delivering quickly and leave out architectural components. Architecture frames construction, allowing expert craftspeople to deliver confidently. Without architecture, you can deliver quickly but lose continuous integration over the long term.

Architecture constitutes a modern system's core. It includes everything from conceptual design to the interacting software and hardware. Software and hardware create the computer system supporting user interaction. Whether one works from Windows or Linux, or codes from Python to ReactJS, each obeys architectural prescripts. This chapter focuses on communicating architectural basics for the planner or the programmer and ensures success in building a common perspective. The chapter covers the following:

- Architectural basics
- Communicating about architecture
- Best architectures for DevOps
- Implementing architectural standards

Each topic will include key takeaways to guarantee creating a confident architecture for your DevOps deliveries.

The basics of architecture

As always, starting with a definition creates a foundational discussion point. The dictionary definition of architecture offers multiple explanations: 'The art or science of building; formation or construction resulting from a conscious act by unifying a coherent form; how components of computer systems are organized and integrated.'[1] The most relevant is the third definition, and the widest the first; the middle section should be our focus. The architectures we design and employ must fill a coherent form. These coherent forms create synergy for developers, operators, managers or any organizational mix. Coherent forms create clear communication, maintainability and allow rapid value delivery.

The first architecture sets a foundation for all functions and applications. Architecture for information technology (IT) requires three central steps: fetching information, decoding into a usable state and executing commands. A straightforward architectural example is the contact list on your personal phone. Contact lists have various formats, but a central architecture exists to link data – the individuals – to the operations – making a call. One selects the phone contact by fetching data from a memory location and decoding that information for the user to select 'John Smith'. The John Smith entry contains email addresses, phone numbers, perhaps a picture and associated notes. Then, one executes commands by selecting a contact method and connecting to John.

These architectural interactions often become complex, but the core resides in fetching, decoding and executing commands. These three areas resolve to three essential architectural functions in the DevOps solution. The first is System Design, how the hardware, firmware and software interact. Next is the Instruction Set Architecture (ISA), the embedded programming code allowing interaction. And finally, Microarchitecture, data paths for processing and storage. One of the hardest architectural design elements lies in distinguishing overlapping items.

When evaluating DevOps architecture, one must learn the four Cs: cloud, cluster, container and code. These four levels describe organization for any cloud-native or cloud-migrant architecture. Every architecture can mirror or change as operations shift levels. Cloud covers the top virtual space as AWS, Azure or private cloud instances. A cluster details where users operate in cloud segments, virtual private clouds (VPC) or virtual machines (VM). Containers are the cluster-resident, individual applications and pods. Code is the lowest level as the ISA directs communication. Moving between levels requires abstracting commands and interpreting. Abstraction remains important as any element at these or changing levels should offer observability regarding inputs, outputs and processes. The fact that they are abstracted requires translation between levels.

System design starts with the basics. Despite various complexity layers, all systems follow one of three approaches: the Von Neuman, Harvard or Hybrid architecture.

Von Neuman was the first approach (1945) for computing machines and derived from the Electronic Discrete Variable Automating Computer (EDVAC). The basic design has an arithmetic logic unit (ALU), processor registers, control units containing instruction registers, memory including data and instructions, external storage, and input and output designs.

FIGURE 4.1   Von Neuman architecture

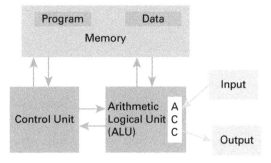

FIGURE 4.2   Harvard architecture

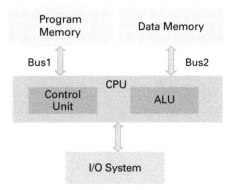

Today, a Von Neuman design suggests any design in which data fetching and operations occur sequentially because the two commands share a common bus. A bus describes any design, including connection and communication.

Starting from the external, input and output describe where users enter problems and receive answers. The ALU converts into a computer-readable format, then retrieves data or performs an operation. The central processing unit (CPU) then executes a command to access program or data memory. This leads to the central architectural problem, the Von Neuman bottleneck. As CPU speeds have increased, units frequently wait for data to move from memory in either direction, preventing full resource utilization.

The Harvard architecture attempts a solution by separating the memory stores. This architecture allows for either retrieval or programming to occur simultaneously. Since the Harvard style can access data and program memory, it requires only one clock cycle to act, while a Von Neuman requires two clock cycles.[2] In this case, a clock cycle is the function's unit of time. The memory separation increases computer speed and performance. Von Neuman architectures are preferable where speed is not a concern, such as with personal computers, while Harvard types appear with speedy multiple locations such as microcontrollers. One can visualize this as the difference between a traditional home thermostat that only regulates temperature based on user inputs and modern smart home systems incorporating multiple options.

The hybrid model incorporates the two architectures to improve functionality while retaining an architectural design. In the hybrid, the processor uses cached memory distinct from the main memory unit to handle functions. Cached memory supports many current designs as each item processes independently. The main concern arises when cached memory differs from the main memory store but most modern applications can resolve those

FIGURE 4.3   Hybrid architecture

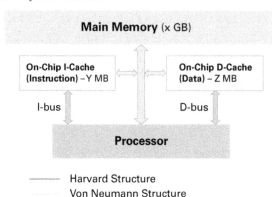

97

differences. In most cases, the processor only calls for changed memory, resulting in faster applications. For example, if a sales list date changes from 7 September to 9 September, the processor may use a key identity to look for only the date rather than all associated product data.

Considering the benefits and limitations of each architecture, it is an excellent time to discuss SOLID architecture. SOLID is a mnemonic device to remember certain core principles detailing architectural characteristics: single responsibility, open-closed, Liskov substitution, interface segregation and dependency inversion. These principles are tied to object-oriented programming (OOP). A quick detour through OOP will help explain further. Though other options exist, modern languages deal almost exclusively with some object-oriented programming form. Object-oriented programming states that all data or code items are handled as a defined object with abstraction, encapsulation, inheritance and polymorphism.[3]

- Abstraction – only provides the essential details. As an example, asking 'What is the area of a circle?' gives an output, not the underlying math formula.
- Encapsulation – wrapping data under a single unit with variables or data of a class hidden from other classes. A user may need to know if a system is operating but not all the operational functions, so they see a green light on a dashboard versus detailed sub-process descriptions
- Inheritance – allows code reuse through using previously defined properties. If our circle area formula was part of a larger geometric tabulator, it could use the circle code from a defined object rather than rewriting the code.
- Polymorphism – the ability of a message to be displayed in multiple formats. In the circle area case, that area may be the sole output, or may be a basis for further calculations

While each element may seem inherently complex, as you use them in the DevOps approach, they garner increased meaning.

These principles are more important as we delve into the SOLID discussion.

SOLID principles interpret each coding element as an object. Single responsibility means that each object in an architecture has only one reason to change and thus only one purpose. In the above architectures, the memory element held a single responsibility to provide data elsewhere. The open-closed principle states that all objects should be open for extension but closed for modification. When considering container-based architecture, this becomes extremely important. One can extend the container to perform a wider range of functions, such as handling circles, squares or hexagons, but not modified to provide a change such as evaluating the diameter of the same object. Area and diameter would be different modifications and require a new object code.

The Liskov substitution states that every class derived from the parent should be substitutable and provide the same answer. The best example appears in organizational guidance. If one applied Liskov to organizational guidance, it would state that lower levels could be more strict than higher-level guidance but not less. If your company has a dress code requiring a collared shirt and tie, your team might add a colour, but not change to uncollared t-shirts. The t-shirt would no longer fill the collar requirement and not be inheritable to the parent class.

The next principle, interface segregation, states that users should not implement or depend on an unused interface. In the dress code example, this means the parent class should not include an option for the daily temperatures if the dress code is unchangeable. This prevents memory from encountering errors for functions without bearing on the overall output. Finally, the dependency inversion principle relates to the abstraction concept from OOP. It states that the objects within the class depend on an abstraction rather than concretion. Returning again to the dress code, the organizational guidance (architecture) depends on whether the shirt and tie are worn but should not depend on the size, collar or style of that coat and tie. Following the SOLID principles in architecture helps prevent relationship errors between various elements.

Understanding architecture and principles is fundamental to compiling a useful architecture. The next step, and a required element, should be how one communicates about architecture and practices. Being confident in DevOps requires understanding and communicating about requirements. While many methods exist to discuss architecture, two common standards are the Unified Markup Language, and The Open Group Architecture Format (TOGAF) discussed in the next section.

The language of architecture

While language is a verbal and textual process, we extend those concepts into visualization when we talk architecture. The textual discussions that correlate best to architectural designs are the Unified Modeling Language (UML) and The Open Group Architecture Framework (TOGAF). Each has benefits; the most important aspect is finding a language you can be comfortable with. I find UML slightly less prescriptive but equally valuable.

Unified Modeling Language

I first ran across UML while researching an academic paper and its simplicity rapidly converted me. UML is simple to explain, easy to visualize and the basics are quickly assimilated. UML, as the Unified Modeling Language, provides a general-purpose system design notation to visualize any system design. UML was created by Grady Booch, Ivar Jacobson and James Rumbaugh while working at Rational Software and adopted as a member standard by the Object Management Group (OMG) in 1987. The International Organization for Standardization (ISO) published UML in 2005 and the most recent update to 2.5.1 in December 2017.[4] This system can explain broad concepts or detailed implementations. One UML benefit is rapidly designing in any graphics editor. Important to remember is that UML uses rectangles and lines for all interactions. These are labelled by interaction but allow room for rapid identification and change.

UML analysis centres on 14 diagrams in two broad categories: structure and behaviour. The structural diagrams, with quick definitions below, include class, profile, component, composite, object, deployment and package. While each diagram includes rules and instructions, they are simpler than the TOGAF descriptions in the next section.

- Class – models object-oriented through inheritance, interface and relationship.
- Profile – extension mechanism to adapt to machine or platform with stereotypes.
- Component – complex system view with interfaces and relationships.
- Composite – demonstrates internal classifier with parts, ports and collaboration.
- Object – describes system or parts at a point in time, especially with data.
- Deployment – shows artifact location on physical nodes.
- Package – illustrates dependencies between packages.

The structural diagrams allow one to rapidly communicate interactions between different architectural areas. One can start at any point and share the interactions between elements. One example is when you might design a mobile application to model available parking spaces.

One can see how easy it is to rapidly configure and begin working on the various levels within a proposed deployment. Switching from one architectural element to another makes it possible to inform the right individual at the right time with the right information.

Behaviour diagrams can be an activity, use-case, state machine or interaction diagram. Interaction contains a subset for

FIGURE 4.4 UML

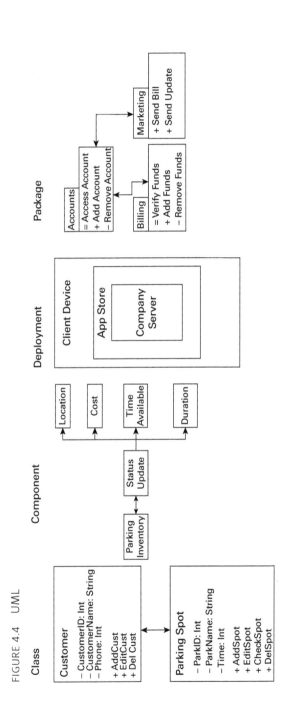

Class

Customer
- − CustomerID: Int
- − CustomerName: String
- − Phone: Int

- + AddCust
- + EditCust
- + Del Cust

Parking Spot
- − ParkID: Int
- − ParkName: String
- − Time: Int

- + AddSpot
- + EditSpot
- + CheckSpot
- + DelSpot

Component

Parking Inventory

Status Update

Location

Cost

Time Available

Duration

Deployment

Client Device

App Store

Company Server

Package

Accounts
- = Access Account
- + Add Account
- − Remove Account

Billing
- = Verify Funds
- + Add Funds
- − Remove Funds

Marketing
- + Send Bill
- + Send Update

sequencing, communications, interaction overview and timing. Short descriptions appear below. These two types allow one to capture every system aspect. The behavioural diagrams show the initial interaction leading to structural component design.

- Activity – flows of action such as sequence, conditional decisions, branches and loops.
- Use-case – the various roles and relationships for user interaction.
- State machine – an entity's state and transition between states.
- Sequencing – communication between objects with vertical for time and horizontal for messaging.
- Communication – objects and parts as messages occurring anywhere.
- Interaction overview – high level for system or subsystem highlighting process over specific activities.
- Timing – illustrates change in a classifier over a timeline.

Returning to the parking application, our use-case would show customer need to obtain timely parking, the activity select an available spot, sequencing would demonstrate from the parking request to fulfillment and the state machine might show changing a spot from empty to filled and vice versa. Building the structural and behavioural models establishes clear links between elements.

UML SWOT

My favourite part of UML is the lack of declared definitions in building architecture, which feels more comfortable from a DevOps perspective. While diving into the ISO standards gives detailed answers, the initial requirements can be addressed anytime. This makes the core strength the system simplicity. However, as a weakness, the lack of explicit requirements mean a less mature team might skip necessary steps. UML presents an opportunity in that you do not require extensive training to communicate effective architectures. Most professionals have designed flowcharts and sequencing diagrams but UML offers a path to add missing steps. As a threat, one can see where designing in UML and missing a step could delay or derail a planned delivery. The next section explores how TOGAF offers an alternative method to architectural descriptions

- Strength: Simplicity.
- Weakness: Lack of explicit requirements.
- Opportunity: Easy to learn and implement.
- Threat: Potential for missing needed steps.

The Open Group Architecture Framework

TOGAF was first introduced in 1995 as an outgrowth of a US Department of Defense project. The intent was to achieve four goals which are:

- improving ROI
- using more cost-effective resources
- avoiding being locked in to specific vendors
- establishing a common language

These DevOps goals align closely with wider business goals: they increase profit, improve effectiveness and create efficient transitions. TOGAF is simple enough for anyone to use, but training and certifications are available, like many other solutions.

The TOGAF goals are based on three pillars: an enterprise continuum tracking from highly individual solutions to generic industry standards, an architectural development model (ADM) and establishing enterprise architecture domains.[5] These domains are business, data, applications and technical architecture specifications. Each domain can incorporate multiple individual architectures in a web-like design of more webs. As an example, if one sees the business domain as maximizing parking within a geographic location, the data domain could hold

FIGURE 4.5   TOGAF

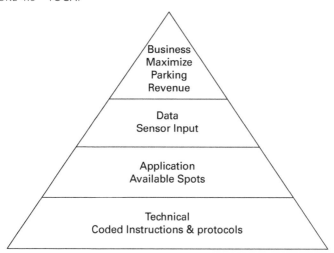

multiple sensors to show filled and available parking. Those data architectures interact with the application domain to interpret the data and present customer-available parking slots. The technical domain holds code as instructions, compiled services and communication protocols. Our discussion focuses on the ADM with the associated steps adjusting to meet system and business requirements, defining the work scope, managing development and implementation, and addressing necessary changes after implementation.

Starting with TOGAF requires designing four architectural areas within the ADM: vision, business, information systems and technology. The framework is based on ISO/IEC/IEEE 42010, an international standard expressing how different items are documented. The basic use-case is as a stakeholder who is interested in a system within an environment to display an architecture captured in descriptive terms.[6] These descriptions include an area of concern, the view angle, the particular view, input and output communications and a rationale. While this seems overly detailed, using this checklist emphasizes each architectural design item. Communications here are critical as when mapping you can readily identify which elements actually contribute to the overall design rather than being orphaned.

Building on the previous example, each architectural level includes multiple descriptions for every level's items. If we choose the application domain then the determination for available spots could be from multiple applications for street parking, garage parking, private parking and temporary parking. Each would link to the above sensor input domain to report and record data about parking places and to the technical level in the exact instructions executed. TOGAF then expresses that every architectural element has four aspects: active, passive, behaviour and motivation. Selecting an application element for street parking might look like this:

- Active: When sensor data reports a car moving out of a parking spot, report status as empty.
- Passive: If no data received, parking status does not change.
- Behaviour: Constantly running and waiting for data.
- Motivation: Maintain current status of available spots.

This might connect to a parallel element reporting status as filled, or an element checking for whether parking is allowed during the timeslot. This helps provide an initial architectural web to begin design. A comprehensive design with TOGAF would provide the initial resource awareness and requirements necessary to achieve the overall business strategy. Figure 4.6 shows an initial layout for a parking layout.

One notices a couple of immediate and intentional discrepancies that would resolve in the architectural description. First, no sensors exist for Vernon Street, suggesting a gap in initial planning. One also notices that the check time code does not apply to the City Garage; this could be an oversight or due to 24-hour parking where a legal parking time check was not required. One other unusual item appears between Vernon Street and the City

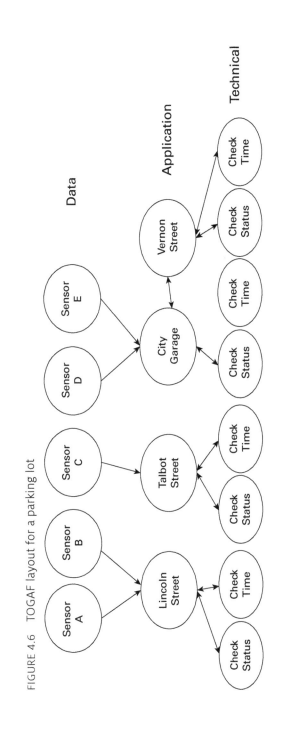

FIGURE 4.6   TOGAF layout for a parking lot

Garage. If the garage was on Vernon Street, it might make sense to redirect users from one full location to another. These technical schematics could rapidly get more detailed but this offers an initial sample. It would also allow a DevOps team to choose the most valuable place to start work based on the most available parking spots, the easiest technical integration or other factors. None of that would be apparent without a starting architecture.

TOGAF SWOT

The strength associated with TOGAF is that it is commonly understood and globally available. TOGAF provides an excellent format, especially with more detailed SDLC models such as Waterfall or Spiral development. The weakness is the depth required to perform a full TOGAF analysis. The numerous steps and training required can make it difficult to implement on time. When using software, the opportunity presented in using TOGAF is the ability to rapidly scale up and down across multiple domains with full explanations. Any changes can be incorporated into the overall pattern. The threat occurs in the technical detail required and the tendency to allow teams to specialize in domains or areas rather than understanding the entire architecture.

- Strength: Commonly understood, global format.
- Weakness: Depth required to perform initial analysis.
- Opportunity: Rapid scaling with software to incorporate changes.
- Threat: Technical detail, tendency to specialize in areas.

Servers and serverless, monoliths and microservices

When discussing architecture, some terms appear more often than others, although they are less high-level architecture than technical decisions related to connectivity. At a high level, having a server means that one physically owns the technology while serverless relates to using someone else's server, and most cloud implementations. Monolith structures tend to be legacy systems where everything from the human relations tools to new development occurs within the same domain. Microservices separate commands and applications into smaller units to better manage resources. Each of these approaches may belong somewhere in your architecture – the question becomes where and how to implement it.

The most important part of a server-based architecture is the technology ownership. Customers and employees may still experience a serverless technology implementation through virtual machines or private clouds, but the company still owns the hardware. Typically, most serverless implementations use a third-party cloud implementation to accomplish tasks. Owning your own server offers the benefits of full accessibility, controlling data and physical access, and working without needing internet connectivity. The drawback appears in the high technology cost of installation, upkeep and the IT staff. We generally see server-based architecture in companies with unstable internet or a need to maintain high levels of security surrounding development.

Conversely, serverless technology brings us to the familiar cloud-native approach. Cloud-native translates to high internet availability and minimal IT staff. One only pays for the time used so serverless system cost tends to be lower. Scaling on serverless systems is easier as one can request the additional resources rather than purchase them. Cloud-native also allows opportunities for hardware emulation in business, such as telecommunication or small hardware deliveries, when one can simulate the projected hardware rather than owning it. Simulation pays dividends for supervisory control and data administration (SCADA) systems that gather and control real-time data to drive system outputs. SCADA systems typically appear in industrial applications or distributed networks such as power and water utilities.

Serverless implementations also offer global data access. As many DevOps companies found during the pandemic, remote work only becomes viable with cloud-native and serverless architectures. On the downside, serverless architectures tend to lack control and observability. The three As of cloud transition are access, availability and abdication. Consumers believe they will gain broader access, have availability whenever needed and abdicate security and maintenance responsibilities. True success in serverless management requires treating the virtual instance almost as physical location other than the initial purchase.

A monolith is a large, tightly coupled architecture. If one thinks of a large stone piece such as Mt. Rushmore in North Dakota or the Statue of Liberty in New York, the picture of a monolith becomes clear. The monolith is a single defined unit where every part must be changed to adjust any smaller part. Netflix was one of the first public companies to manage a successful monolith-to-microservice transition in 2015. The company realized they could segment user demand into smaller sections and run multiple instances, increasing runtime and decreasing the overall resources. Some projects often start as a monolith and then make later transitions as they scale, just like Netflix.

There are benefits to monoliths in some approaches. Monoliths are easily deployed as one file can kick off the entire architecture. Performance and development also benefits as a single application programming interface (API) can be used rather than different service instances. Additionally, a single instance allows for a single code base. This single code base then allows, theoretically, for easier debugging and testing since only a single thread exists.

Reading through those benefits, you are likely wondering about the connection to DevOps. Those benefits in unifying a code base and API create a negative in taking nearly forever in

DevOps time (six months or more) to approve a single change. Scalability, reliability and flexibility all suffer in the monolith, as any change must reflect through the entire structure. These problems also occur when it is time to shift to a new technology or language, as rather than refactoring a small element, the entire system must change. Monoliths are best suited for areas where data and technology do not change quickly, in some cases the aforementioned SCADA constructs for power and industrial systems. Another excellent spot for a monolith is the geographically isolated edge deployment, where it is difficult to make timely updates.

Architecting through microservices offers a loosely coupled approach where every service in a system runs independently, calling for data or commands through other microservices. The best builds enable each microservice element to have its own business logic and processes. It is important not to confuse microservices with containers. Containers are the function packages containing all the information to run, but the microservice, even if built with Kubernetes or Docker, can contain multiple containers. Testing, deployment, scaling and all other software functions occur within each microservice element. In the previous section's parking app, building a microservice for separate elements such as available parking, sending out space notifications, billing and other services would be possible. Each might pull from common data stores and share information but each element could be maintained differently.

Microservices are often perfect for DevOps implementations with flexibility, reliability and testability. These factors all support the need for continuous deployment. The architectural challenge is knowing what segments to bundle within the microservice to minimize those API calls while increasing quality. On the negative side, one can often see development sprawl with microservices with any poor architectural choices. Functional items are often made too small and lack standardized development, thus increasing infrastructure and maintenance costs. Lacking code standards or establishing clear ownership means different microservices wind up managed by specialized teams that only understand their microservices. One architectural key to microservices can be establishing effective service mesh designs.

Service mesh offers a dedicated infrastructure layer to control network communication. The mesh can provide service discovery, load balancing, failure recovery and encryption. Software controlled by the mesh manages through APIs rather than direct interaction, making it perfect for a microservice design. The design uses a sidecar alongside the primary service. Rather than allowing elements with different microservices to communicate directly, the mesh interjects a control plane that manages those interactions. These designs are common in the control and observability mechanisms that appear later in the text.

Regardless of the design choice, none are possible without supporting architectural choices. When one proposes an architecture, moves into some basic technology approaches and prepares to develop, one of the continuing steps is ensuring the right people, processes and technology to support the overall architecture.

Architecture people, processes and technology

A common position for software development organizations is that of the software architect. While most engineers can do architecture, and many managers feel they understand architecture, hiring a person for architecture can increase outcomes. The two positions typically have similar education backgrounds with degrees in computer science and field experience. The largest difference between hiring these two positions is that architects should be prepared to communicate design requirements to stakeholders and engineering teams. The designed architecture should be easily communicated to multiple individuals.

TABLE 4.1

Utility	Function	Priority	SLI
Stability	File Handling	High	Within 24 hours
	Sensor Ingest	High	Within 5 minutes
	Data Comparison	Medium	80% accuracy
	Throughput	Low	5 MB/S

Once a software architecture design appears, the next step is dealing with how those architectures are communicated to the team. The team must be aware of the central architect on the project and understand how their development supports that architecture. At the same time, those teams must feel free to raise issues about where changes are needed. DevOps means a commitment to flow, feedback and improvement; architectural designs must support those continuing changes. One of the processes used to support those changes is the Architectural Tradeoff Analysis Method (ATAM).

ATAM allows one to take the design built with TOGAF or UML, then select lower-level details based on specific requirements. This is where one can return to the design model qualities, such as the stable, secure, adaptive and scalable characteristics I prefer. The basic analysis says three teams execute analysis but in actuality, one needs only the architect, the stakeholder and the development team. The analysis uses three phases: first, presenting the architecture, second, matching the architecture to design components through a utility tree, and finally, analysing where changes may be made.

Each architecture item would be matched against those issues, for example matching a cloud provider to the stable element. The technical elements connected below that might be the communication between the sensor and the application. While a full utility tree would compare every element, we will keep it short here. For the stability element, we might want to consider file handling between the sensors, sensor data ingest, comparing sensor data and throughput. Each of these would then be assigned a service level indicator (SLI) stating the specific level of input desired. Table 4.1 demonstrates an initial approach.

While the full table would include all five of our primary characteristics, this sample shows requirements and priorities. Then, one can change and evaluate to trade different modelled technologies for each step. One may decide that files to update sensors must occur sooner, or with a lower priority. If the priority decreases, one could see how comparing data between the sensor and the tabled input within the application might increase in priority. One could also address user input that parking spaces were no longer available when they reached the location so a higher-priority comparison might be needed.

Trading the architectural elements allows feedback in how the design flows through the process. Remember, architecture provides the plan to develop functional software. Changes in the architecture change the priority to develop different parts of the system. The stable architectural models may require different coded elements to reach overall success. So, if the right people and a design to modify the architecture are in place, the last step becomes the technologies to support integrations.

A technology list can be exhaustive, but two critical elements can help expedite those challenges: first, one should have a software-driven modelling tool, and second, one should understand the system language for expressing architecture. In this case, the specific examples are the ArchiMate tool for TOGAF architectures and JSON as a system language. For other cases, with UML some common options are Lucidchart, Microsoft Visio Pro or Gliffy. Alternatives to JSON can include YAML, XML, SCALA and Rust.

ArchiMate offers an open-source alternative to some of the more expensive options. The software uses a GUI to design the architecture, incorporate the utility tree options for a tradeoff and quickly match between technical and functional interactions on a common platform. Using a tool such as ArchiMate increases design observability and allows improved feedback across multiple layers. One advantage of ArchiMate is that it allows the opportunity to create viewpoints within the system to examine an architectural flow from different perspectives.

ArchiMate is a tool based on Open Group modelling, which follows the TOGAF standards. The system offers a design based on layers and aspects. The pre-built layers are strategy, business, application, technology, physical and implementation, while the associated aspects are passive structure, behaviour, active structure and motivation. These are all the same requirements one uses for TOGAF modelling. As well as these items, the tool allows construction of relationships between various items, including structural relationships describing the static construction, dependency relationships with event-driven and time-based requirements, and dynamic relationships where one event can trigger another.[7]

Sometimes challenges exist in converting an approved diagram into a technical coding language. The coding language ensures that those architectural models for communication, message handling, event-driven triggers and other factors remain expressed in code. Despite the name, JSON (JavaScript Object Notation) is a language-agnostic tool supporting communication between an application and the architecture. JSON approaches are relatively common within many DevOps pipelines and subsequent implementations.

JSON is a language standard with a text-based format to represent structure and is human-readable. It establishes a lightweight format for storing and transporting data, such as moving elements between a server and a web page. An example based on the parking structure appears below:

```
{
'Parking' :[
{'Location' : 'Vernon', 'ParkID' : 1},
{'Location' : 'Vernon', 'ParkID' : 2},
{'Location' : 'City Garage', 'ParkID' : 3},
]
}
```

This basic example shows the core syntax that data is contained in name/value pairs and separated by commas. Then, curly braces hold objects, and the square brackets hold the array. The data and arrays can then be called within other coded options to ensure the right connections exist. In this case, parking spots identified at two locations will link to sensor data or other factors. JSON allows the same notation as many other formats with numbers, strings, Boolean, array, object and null data. One downfall with JSON is that it does not allow commenting; however, calls from other languages support returning to those comments for the item requested.

Summary

This chapter introduced the basic architectural design concepts, including using SOLID principles to support designs. From there, the discussion compared the UML and TOGAF standards as a basis for communicating architectures. Since any architecture establishes a design that others must follow, communicating those standards must happen. Without a common language, those architectures become nothing more than noise for developers.

Establishing that common language led to discussing UML and TOGAF approaches to designing an architectural model. This moved us from a thought- and narrative-based structure to the expressed design where developers and project managers can compare deliveries to planned architecture. With all these steps established, we then discussed the importance of hiring an architect and their team interactions and the Architectural Tradeoff Analysis Method (ATAM) for comparing architecture to requirements during those interactions. Finally, we touched on a modelling tool (ArchiMate) and a programming language (JSON) to convert all the architectural knowledge into digital diagrams and expressions. In the next chapter we discuss how to observe and ensure that a confident DevOps architecture appears in delivered applications.

Notes

1 Architecture (2023) https://www.merriam-webster.com/dictionary/architecture (archived at https://perma.cc/4VQL-PREW)

2 Kann, C W (2023) Von Neuman and Harvard Architectures, Eng.libretexts.org (archived at https://perma.cc/TT3F-RTRV), https://eng.libretexts.org/Bookshelves/Electrical_Engineering/Electronics/Implementing_a_One_Address_CPU_in_Logisim_(Kann)/01%3A_Introduction/1.03%3A_Von_Neumann_and_Harvard_Architectures (archived at https://perma.cc/9X2Y-VE5H)

3 Sambhav228 (2023) Introduction to Object Oriented Programming, https://www.geeksforgeeks.org/introduction-of-object-oriented-programming/ (archived at https://perma.cc/CMN9-6XL9)

4 Gliffy.com (archived at https://perma.cc/ZBT4-V598) (2020) What is UML? https://www.gliffy.com/blog/what-is-uml-everything-you-need-to-know-about-unified-modeling-language (archived at https://perma.cc/NEY4-23UD)

5   MindMajix (2023) What is ToGAF? https://mindmajix.com/what-is-togaf
    (archived at https://perma.cc/F8A2-MDRH)
6   A conceptual model of architectural description (nd) http://www.iso-architecture.
    org/ieee-1471/cm/ (archived at https://perma.cc/FX7D-XS4A)
7   LeanIX (2023) What is ArchiMate? https://www.leanix.net/en/wiki/ea/
    what-is-archimate? (archived at https://perma.cc/WRJ5-9LNQ)

CHAPTER FIVE

Managing observability

As children, many people experience the hidden picture model. A common picture is shown with other shapes hidden within its structures. The goal is to identify hidden shapes within the main picture. *Where's Waldo?* (or *Where's Wally?*, depending on where you are) has been popular for the past 30 years, offering books that hide the iconic character within a variety of pictures. This same methodology applies to software development. If given the full listing of logs, traces, scans and other development outputs, it's a similar challenge to rapidly isolate the needed areas to provide actionable data to improve software development. This chapter outlines how to build those observable items into your confident DevOps practice. We will cover:

- Basics of observability
- Observability metrics
- Advancing metrics
- People, process and technology

One of the fundamental differences between DevOps and other methods concentrates on observability. It is impossible to identify bottlenecks for removal to streamline value delivery without understanding how a process works, where new contributions emerge and what has been prioritized. This chapter identifies the basic concepts associated with software development observability. Then, basic concepts are converted into metrics to measure initial success. Once the basic metric concept structure is implemented, the next step modifies those metrics for crown jewels, the items your business needs for success. Finally, the chapter concludes by identifying the people, processes and technology necessary to make observability work.

Basics of observability

Observability basics start with understanding the word's derivation word and software development applications. The Merriam-Webster dictionary defines observe as 'to conform one's action or practice to something'.[1] This shows the strong DevOps connotation in suggesting that all actions observed must be about changing an action to another action. In DevOps, observing's purpose is to emphasize feedback to improve flow, confirm experimentation and drive future actions. Three standard implementations apply when discussing DevOps practices with the terms observable, observing and observability. One frequently hears these terms interchanged but all reach a different end state. Understanding these frameworks requires the three pillars of observability – logs, traces and metrics – to which one should add a fourth category for measurements.

Before deconstructing the terms, a brief step to align understanding of the observability pillars is necessary. A log is a computer-produced output that lists all system actions chronologically. A trace again appears as a computer-produced output in chronological order but one following specific system actions.

A metric performs calculated analysis combining numerous inputs and outputs to allow rapid decisions such as a table or graph showing all security vulnerabilities on a product. A measurement assesses raw numbers such as the number of features produced, work hours or other products possibly contributing to metrics. Logs and traces are normally included in standard system features. Some metrics and measurements are organic to the system, while others must be created or included from third-party software for unique tasks.

Observable actions are functions producing data in manipulatable formats. When we watch a sports event, from football to cricket, we're watching actions that produce data as a score. While those scores are not generally manipulated, they can be reported in a manipulated sense through multiple sources. The score could relate to the individual game, collective scores for a group of games, or how that score translates into a broader league standing. From the software context, any action producing data is defined as observable. The output might be as simple as a 'Hello, world' response, or a more complicated answer considering a customer's cloud usage. The data typically includes computer-produced functions like logs, traces, metrics or measurements.

Observing actions means interacting with data at specified points. This incorporates the individuals and collection tools used for gathering data. Those observing the actions in the previous sports match could be scoreboard operators, referees and assistant coaches. Each individual observes actions such as offence or defence and records a specific data point, a hit, a steal or a pass in the relevant format. Some individuals may collect multiple aspects but the data all compiles to a single point. Observing software actions occurs through an individual or function designated to collect at a certain point, or through a tool such as OpenTelemetry (OTel) or Prometheus. The tools can be configured to collect data singularly and then modified for multiple reports to contribute later. Observing software means reporting an individual output in a trace, knowing where logs are stored or establishing test coverage.

Observability emphasizes observing outputs from software development tools and functions. We expect the coaches and managers to exemplify observability in a sports contest. They correlate multiple actions, assess the results and create actions to attempt to modify feature results in the desired way. This returns to the initial 'observe' definition that one attempts to conform to a standard by observing. In DevOps, an observability state generates continuous feedback. Numerous logs, traces, metrics and measurements provide useful data contributing to observability. When observability is achieved, you can manually adjust inputs to provide better outputs or automate to manage routine corrections. An excellent example is AWS cloud monitoring; the system monitors cloud usage and adjusts to predicted usage by making relevant changes. This predicts cloud space needed and can rapidly scale to customer demands.

The key is the ability to find points to observe. When watching sports, we already understand the needed observation points: the batter, the forward, the goalie or the interaction at a designated space. These may seem more difficult to find in software development but the same initial thought governs point selection. Observation points are anywhere something happens, whether in the system, like pipeline runs, or external to the system, delivering a completed product. The more observation points, the more likely it is to find actionable data. Observation points can help find where the development process has stalled and then generate flow-improving feedback. Some common examples of observability through metrics are in security scans, measuring lead time to change in submitting fixes to production, or time needed to recognize and fix a bug in deployment.

The basics are summarized by one of my favourite hacking stories. The year was 1834, the place was France and the hackers were François and Joseph Blanc. The goal was to beat the current-day stock market and the hacked system was the optical telegraph system. Optical telegraph uses semaphores, a flag system controlled by manual pulleys, to pass messages within the line of site. At the time, the stock market in Paris controlled the pace for other trading cities such as Bordeaux. This information was communicated through the telegraph but normal investors only received messages by standard channels such as horseback, which would take closer to five days than five hours.

The target was the market rate on federal obligations, futures for the government investing in livestock or other commodities, which traded in Paris and Bordeaux. It seemed impossible to subvert with humans at every messaging stop, but the Blancs had a plan. Normally, messaging errors would be detected and corrected in subsequent transmissions but the error was not removed from the message until they reached the final station in Bordeaux. The Blancs bribed an operator at the Paris station to add notable errors to the messaging, then hired an accomplice to observe those errors through binoculars at the last stop before reaching the Bordeaux station. This allowed them to purchase with advance knowledge of the stock prices. The hack lasted for two years before the bribed operator became sick and tried to convince his replacement to follow the hacked plan. The replacement had a crisis of conscience and turned all of them in. At the time, Paris had no law against using the telegraph for private purposes but did have one against government officials taking bribes. The operator went to jail for years and the Blancs went on to own a casino.[2]

The key here was the lack of system observability. Corrections only occurred at the endpoints with corrections included with the error during messaging. The intermediate operators were not trusted sufficiently to make changes. The official telegraph could be observed at multiple spots due to the optical relay. Those noticing the errors and adding corrections observed the system but lacked the observability for understanding. Lacking observability meant that errors could be found and noted but not remediated until the end. When one thinks DevOps only observes at designated points to create a metric, the cultural foundation disappears. DevOps observes everywhere to create an observability state that increases value delivery. There are some common observability metrics recommended in the next section that can help in building the preferred observability state.

Observability metrics

The first step in observability metrics should be identifying what requires measurement and how. In the previous section we discussed establishing observability points. For this section we will break out collected elements and some initial metrics. Then visual models and interpretation are discussed to take initial metrics and create useful actions. Metrics create feedback to discuss required actions. In many cases, one uses tools to visualize feedback beyond the raw data and create graphics summarizing numerous levels. Important throughout is focusing on metrics creating opportunities for action. Metrics that are not actionable are merely noise.

System data generally appears from four points: logs, traces, metrics and measurements. Most sources only count the first three but that leaves out the DevOps flexibility required for improvement. One cannot make effective metrics without understanding measurement. Logs are time-sequenced reports of system activity. A log sample appears below.

```
Thurs Mar 07 20:21:08 2022: NAR-VG-EGF300 NAR-VG-EGF300
/box_Firewall_Activity: Info NAR-VG-EGF300
Remove:
type=FWD|proto=UDP|srcIF=eth1|srcIP=192.168.30.10|srcPo
rt=35119|srcMAC=08:00:27:da:d7:9c|dstIP=8.8.8.8|
dstPort=77|dstService=domain|dstIF=eth0|rule=InternetAc
cess/<App>:RestrictTim|info=Balanced Session Idle
Timeout|srcNAT=192.168.70.7|dstNAT=8.8.8.8|duration=211
```

```
32|count=1|receivedBytes=130|sentBytes=62|
receivedPackets=1|sentPackets=1|user=|protocol=|applica
tion=|target=|content=|urlcat
```

This can include startup messages, system changes, planned and unplanned shutdowns, errors, warnings and alerts. All operating systems such as Windows, Mac and Linux generate a syslog containing a log file and expressed textually. All logs include three general information elements: a timestamp, user information and event information. The above sample shows the time stamp, with the Mar 07 date, and the user ID as NAR-BG EGF300, likely as both the terminal identification and associated activity. In this case, one sees the request to remove a firewall and then access from an internet IP. This shows the difficulty when finding information by manually sifting through hundreds of log entries unless one knows exactly what to hunt for.

Traces follow a single event throughout the event lifecycle such as login information, system connections as website touches or following an alert. Most traces are managed through a software implementation offering either a command line interface (CLI) or a graphical user interface (GUI). Trace output then appears as either a text-based option or a graphic.

Each trace consists of spans and segments, denoting where one action might interact with another function or resource. Traces are not typically shared and processed in real time. The trace occurs and then passes data for interpretation. Traces can be automated for known functions. Since a trace follows an entire function from start to end, they are typically used to assess end-to-end performance.

Metrics combine data from logs and traces using time-based events through software-driven filters to extract required information. Many who begin with DevOps first encounter the DevOps Research Association (DORA) metrics. These metrics commonly appear as the first step to DevOps measurement and are listed below:

- Deployment Frequency (DF): How often does the team commit code?
- Lead Time to Change (LTC): How long from an idea reaching the team to a developed feature?
- Change Failure Rate (CFR): How much bad code reaches production?
- Mean Time to Restore (MTTR): How long to fix a bug that reached the customer?

One can quickly see that three of the four metrics are time-based and all could combine traces and logs to acquire data. For example, with deployment frequency, one could trace an individual user and find the number of their commits over time. Commits are when a developer submits code to the repository, either as an individual or when the code is merged as a commit with the main branch. It typically shows the team's skills in completing assigned work.

Teams can sometimes game or manipulate metrics by committing smaller, less effective code elements to raise production numbers. For example, if the individual commits every time they write two lines of code, the DF metric will increase significantly. This points to why you use multiple metrics. If the DF is extremely high but the LTC is lengthy, one could assess that though the team commits, they are not committing effective code. Using multiple metrics allows for initiating discussion and showing actionable interaction.

Metrics can be combined with other measurement points. A measurement assesses a point in time of a thing, not necessarily the multiple metric points. A favourite example is measuring the cups of coffee consumed in the company kitchen. One could convert it into a metric by measuring cups over time and comparing to the DF. This would theoretically show whether more coffee creates more productivity and when.

FIGURE 5.1   Metrics and measurement chart examples

Histogram of monthly salary

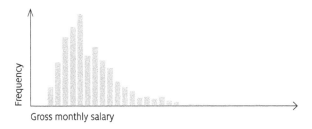

Pareto chart

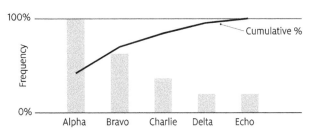

The empirical rule: sigma

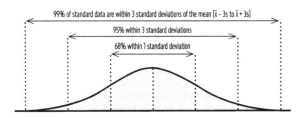

UCL control

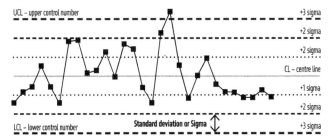

Another useful measurement element would decompose existing metrics. Suppose company leadership wants to see quarterly customer deliveries. The initial measurement is how often software features reach customers. Decomposing requires one to know what is in a software feature, the coding elements within that feature and the success rates. Each of those comprises a metric or a measurement for comparison.

Once you've started making these assessments, it can be useful to have a tool to compare various interactions. The charts in Figure 5.1 offer four samples sometimes used to demonstrate metrics and measurements.

The first chart shows a control chart, typically used in manufacturing. This standard line for development appears as the centre line, perhaps showing 100 commits per week. An upper limit would be set to show the maximum expected or possible, and a lower line for the minimum accepted. These lines can be used for quality control standards and defect rates.

The next chart shows sigma deviations, the standard normal deviation with one sigma being within 68 per cent of expected and six sigmas being within 99.999999 per cent. This explains why you often hear six sigmas or six nines related to system availability. Six nines applies to the five sigma standard at 99.9999 per cent of the mean. Companies will state they want 100 per cent system uptime with a five sigma standard. This would equate to less than one minute of unplanned downtime annually. A three sigma standard equates to seven hours of unplanned downtime. At each step, increasing the sigma level requires additional resources.

The third chart depicts a histogram dividing individual segments by frequency. In the DF coding example, the horizontal labels could be commit ranges and the vertical axis would show the number of times the team hit that mark. The final chart shows the Pareto measurements arranged in decreasing occurrence frequency. If you use the DF analysis, the goal would be assessing team failures to reach the required performance standard. The horizontal access might be security problems, not enough developers, lack of coffee or other elements. The vertical shows how often the instance occurred, and all the columns add up to 100 per cent on the top, curved line.

With all these tools in your pocket, one can begin to understand how metrics comprise the delivery core. Metrics make interactions in the software development lifecycle understandable and explainable. Observing each metric might be enough to confidently deliver DevOps but one should also understand how to advance metrics. Metrics, to be truly effective, should be constructed and aligned to your business needs. The next section discusses advancing metrics to continue building confidence in DevOps observability.

Advancing metrics

When working with consulting groups, one constantly proposes new solutions to problems. One of my pet peeves when offering those solutions is that teams frequently respond, 'Well, how does that affect my metrics?' This question wholly opposes the entire concept of metrics. Metrics exist to measure action at a point in time, creating observability into interaction points that are difficult to assess intuitively. If instead you plan activity to only show the best metrics, you lose all sense of the benefit effective metrics offer. This section looks deeper into the purpose of metrics and suggests methods to enhance and improve results.

Metrics appear in two forms: organic and created. Organic metrics are measurements contained within purchased software. Many software options, especially in security and networking, come complete with ways to measure performance. When you open a laptop's system performance logs, you typically see metrics such as system speed, internet connectivity and memory used. With a security scanning tool, you might see connections, software vulnerabilities or firewall status. These tools are excellent starting places for observability. The change happens when one makes the next step to using created metrics.

Created metrics use system tools to focus on observable factors impacting your performance. These use embedded functions to expand beyond an initial purchase or configuration. DevOps depends on feedback and improvement, and organic metrics offer an initial approach to success within a framework. Created metrics provide the opportunity to create your own success criteria. As within the last section, while the organic metric may provide a deployment frequency, a created metric can add comparison factors such as coffee consumed, team leadership direction, time of day or other variables. This knowledge allows for conducting structured experiments for continual improvement.

Metrics all start with what is being measured: a time flow, action steps from initiation to completion or any other quantitatively measured function. Remember the metric goal is to drive action, as non-actionable metrics are merely noise. Noise reduces the ability to effectively communicate by obscuring the intended message, thus restricting flow and impeding communication. In creating new metrics, I have used the following rubric with success throughout my career.

- How do you know?
- If the first is true, what happens next?
- Do any assumptions have to be true for the first to be true?
- Do the conclusions follow when I include assumptions?
- Are there any premises needed for the assumptions to be true?
- Compare apples to apples and not oranges to elephants

The first element is the most important. It requires asking yourself what source collects the data. Some of the normal applications to route data are those like Prometheus, Grafana, ElasticStack, Splunk or OpenTelemetry (Otel). Each requires specifying where the data originates. Metrics observe a point in time so knowing which sensor acquires which data is essential. If we return to modifying the deployment frequency metric, we ask how we obtain information. Questions include if deployment means code reaches production, if code counts when first submitted, or if some other measure corresponds to deployment. You might measure other elements such as the coffee consumed, which day is the most productive, which hours of the day are more productive or how team meetings affect deployment. This first step builds the foundational knowledge for advancing metrics.

The remaining items are self-checks ensuring you understand the internal thought process advancing the metric. This starts with asking what happens next. When collecting a metric, leading to the action requires asking yourself about the next steps. If collecting on deployment frequencies, one should ask the initial question about whether numbers should go up, should they decrease or are you seeking consistency? Establishing expectations lets you begin to shape potential actions.

Once the collection point and the expectations are set, the next step to advancing a metric will be identifying assumptions. Here, and elsewhere, in discussing assumptions, an assumption is a thing that must be true in order for the main metric to be successful. Returning to the deployment frequency example, an assumption might be that all submitted code appears in GitLab. One would then examine associated team processes to ensure teams were not writing code in other IDEs, consolidating in other environments and only committing to GitLab when finished. This would show delivery but lack the information about how long something was in progress before completion. Moving code between different environments and then submitting in an alternate could create large differentials.

The fourth question addresses those differences. If the assumption remains true that all code is in GitLab, then the conclusions about the metric would hold true. If you discover that teams are using other means to commit code and deploy code, then the first conclusion that deployment frequency is a useful metric might not be accurate. In another variation, if we expand the metric to report coffee consumption related to code production, the true assumption may be that all coffee is consumed from the company kitchen. If developers obtained caffeine from Starbucks before reaching work or preferred energy drinks, we may need to include multiple measurements to advance the metric.

Obtaining multiple sources of data, and alternate locations, leads to the fifth question: are all the premises around the conclusions true? Similar to identifying initial assumptions around collected data, those same considerations then apply to the second level. This verifies that we are advancing the metric correctly. From a DevOps perspective, this question creates feedback for our metric flow. Having reached this point, you can be confident that the metric is stable, supportable and creates an actionable result.

The final question should be a comparison: apples to apples, not oranges to elephants. This means the compared metrics must evaluate equivalent processes. Apples are similar to other apples, even if the colour, shape or taste is different. Substituting one apple for another apple yields roughly similar outcomes. When starting with oranges and elephants, both have rough skin, possess a navel and are wet on the inside but after that, the differences expand exponentially. The equivalent comparison is the most important part of comparing an advanced metric. One can draw together multiple metrics that complicate comparison, but at the base level, comparisons should be equivalent.

In our example, if we are gathering deployment frequency data, comparing deployments to revenue generated may be a step too far. Revenue has multiple elements involved, and simply comparing rough code, or even production code weekly, to revenue generated weekly might incorrectly evaluate. An effective comparison might be deployment code frequency to coffee consumed or errors submitted into production to show effective correlation. One might see that more frequent deployments of larger code elements result in more errors or more frequently deploying smaller elements results in fewer errors. In this case, we ensure apples to apples and not oranges to elephants.

The last thinking element when considering metrics should be two statements:

- correlation does not equal causation
- absence of evidence does not result in evidence of absence.

In the first, when two or more metrics appear to be tracking relatedly – increased caffeine consumption results in higher deployment frequency – we should not assume one causes the other. The two may be correlated, but the causation may not be accurate at a certain point. If I simply increase the caffeine consumed, at some point I will likely be sending developers to the hospital, which ultimately delays code deployments.

The other statement, absence of evidence is not evidence of absence, suggests that if I do not measure something, I cannot assume that it does not exist. In continuing with the previous example, I could assume more caffeine makes my developers more productive and thus happier. However, I should not conclude they are happier unless it is measured. In a more software sense, it could be not scanning for security because the standards require secure code to reach the same place. The evidence must be the scan, so if no scan exists, I cannot simply conclude all the code is secure.

This model for advancing metrics has worked for me for years. In the best DevOps sense, I suggest trying it out with some options. At the best stage, it provides a checklist to ensure you have adequately thought about all requirements. It even enables the decomposition of different elements. In a practical sense, when a customer asks why they are not producing effectively, they may be skipping required details or not evaluating assumptions if they are only using DORA metrics. The next section discusses finding the right people, establishing processes and implementing the technology that supports observable DevOps.

Observable people, process and technology

Measuring any DevOps process from an observable standpoint requires finding the right people who think about observable outcomes, understanding an observable process and then working with technology supporting the vision. People drive technology through a process that shapes people to change technology. Each of these elements can be critical to a successful implementation.

Observable people

Analysing observable people relies on who needs what, and when. Developers' needs are feature and deployment information, leadership tend to focus on value, cost and project success, security folks like compliance and vulnerability standards, and operational individuals see detection, recovery and task time. The important part is not just understanding individual connections to metrics but how you understand flow, feedback and improvement across multiple metrics.

Two factors can help understand how people view metrics: the first is Conway's Law and the second is the Westrum Patterns. Conway's law states, 'Any organization that designs a system (defined broadly) will produce a design whose structure is a copy of the organization's communication system.'[3] In application then, tightly coupled, highly hierarchical organizations produce hierarchical designs, while loosely coupled, collaborative organizations produce collaborative designs. Metrics allow us to observe system interactions in comparison to organizational imperatives. The first step in people interactions is understanding the organization and creating metrics emphasizing personal outcomes rather than organizational imperatives.

As an example, if a metric reflects deployment, but the hierarchical structure requires three levels of approval, deployments will always be delayed. An organization emphasizing a quicker deployment but fewer checks may deploy more bugs into production. People need to understand organizational limits and how metrics reflect those outcomes. It can be a great idea to introduce new observable points but those that create the most effect for another organization might not work for you. Thus, metrics create actionable points, having people report the known true, and the items likely to continue to be true, is not an effective measurement.

The other element for people management with observability is the Westrum patterns. In an academic article, Westrum identified three typical organizational patterns: pathological, bureaucratic and generative.[4] Examples of the three appear below:

- Pathological – power oriented: low cooperation, messenger shot, responsibilities shirked, bridging discouraged, extensive scapegoating, novelty crushed.
- Bureaucratic – rule oriented: modest cooperation, messengers neglected, narrow responsibilities, bridging tolerated, failure leads to justice, novelty creates problems.
- Generative – performance oriented: high cooperation, messengers trained, risks shared, bridging encouraged, failure leads to inquiry, novelty implemented.

We can quickly see how the preferred DevOps culture fits in the generative model. At the same time, some challenges with the other models can be identified through metrics to solve issues. For example, the bridging problem can be addressed by looking at inter-organizational communication or failure items from team retrospectives. Westrum further highlights how the models connect in response to organization inputs. These items appear below:

- Suppression – stopping messages from reaching broader levels.
- Encapsulation – isolating the messenger.
- Public relations – minimizing impacts through associating context with the message.
- Local fix – fix immediately but fail to share impacts or solutions.
- Global fix – respond to problem where it exists and highlight related problems.
- Inquiry – identify the root of the problem.

Identifying how an organization responds to messages along the path allows for assessing how observability benefits outcomes. Good DevOps people use selected metrics to track how issues occur and are resolved. Selecting the right people to manage observability requires finding ones who fix problems and inquire to prevent future problems. Chapter 10 discusses incorporating inquiry through a system reliability engineer (SRE) to provide a consistent, trained messenger, encourage novelty and manage inquiry. Having individuals who understand and implement metrics helps organizations support effective, observable processes.

Observable process

In his book *Measure What Matters*, John Doerr suggests a macro process used in conjunction with metrics known as OKR (Objectives and Key Results).[5] This process suggests every work section should identify objectives that must happen and the key result needed to accomplish the objective. This follows the first two questions from earlier: how do we know and what happens next? These OKRs flow from strategic to tactical and then down to the operational level. Every element develops its own objectives and results. A sample that includes improving deployment frequency appears below with objectives (O) and key results (KR).

- Strategic (Company) – O: Deliver more and better products than last quarter to the customer
  - KR: 10 deliveries are made to the customer
  - KR: Customer repurchases product in the following quarter
- Tactical – O: Deliver more operating systems to the customer
  - KR: 4 operating systems updates delivered to the customer
  - KR: All operating systems meet manufacturing standards
- Operational – O: The development team readies an operating system for deployment
  - KR: 6 features complete in new operating system
  - KR: Operating system meets operational benchmarks for speed and memory

One can see how OKRs can scale from one level to the next. Each key result would then be assessed as red for failed to meet, yellow for almost met and green for met. These provide a qualitative look at where one might include some metrics as a quantitative measurement. One can see how the deployment frequency at the operational level scales into the overall company. Implementing a similar process improves corporate-level messaging, demonstrates key deliverables and provides a launchpad to establish technical metrics. One other way to split these responsibilities is through using a RACI matrix.

'RACI' stands for responsible, accountable, consulted and informed. It suggests the four levels for observable individuals who drive specific metrics. The matrix highlights the four categories across the horizontal axis and the vertical axis holds the various tasks. A responsible individual is the person tagged for a specific deliverable while the accountable person holds the combination of responsible items, such as a programme manager. The consulted individuals provide guidance along the way and informed merely means those in the communication process.

Returning to our deployment frequency example, if the first item on our vertical list was feature development, the team would be responsible, the team lead would be accountable, security and platform engineers might be consulted, and informed would be management. If the task was feature security, then the security engineer might be responsible, a security manager accountable, the development team consulted and management remains informed. These matrices can be built from either an individual perspective with a marking in the column or from a team perspective where the name or position is located in the column. In either sense, it creates a process through which one can identify observable points across an organization to measure success.

Observable technology

When you consider observable technology, the first element is visualizing observability results. We mentioned graphics and comparisons earlier in histograms, control charts and dashboards but technology converts from a manual build to automated visualization. Prometheus and Grafana are two of the more popular ways to visualize network activities. These can be enhanced by functions like Open Policy Agent (OPA), Open Telemetry (OTel) or Open Worldwide Application Security Practices (OWASP) items like the Zero Attack Proxy (ZAP) and PurpleTeam.

Prometheus offers a free software application to record metrics as a time-series database with an HTTP pull model for flexible queries and real-time alerting. The core application was written on Go with source code available through GitHub and graduated from the Cloud Native Computing Foundation. An instance will use multiple exporters to transfer metrics where Prometheus then centralizes and stores the applications. An alert management tool can then notify individuals when metrics hit certain levels.

Once a tool like Prometheus has been included, Grafana, as a multi-platform interactive visualization tool, can be included. Either Grafana or Prometheus can be used in either a health check, pull for data, or heartbeat, pushing data, or configuration. The tool offers combining data at a common location rather than requiring data to be sent to third-party locations for analysis. This allows data protection across multiple deployments. The tool offers common, organic metrics with options for creating additional panels to visualize your organization's unique options.

OPA is my personal favourite for setting various monitoring rules through a side-car connection to containers and applications. It provides an open-source policy engine driven by REGO as a high-level declarative language. The side-car implementation makes OPA effective in controlling microservices, CI/CD pipelines and API gateways. The end goal decouples decision making from enforcement. Any service or event request communicates through JSON to OPA and then activates the Rego element to evaluate and return JSON data. This data then triggers alerting services.

OTel offers specialized protocols for collecting telemetry data and exporting to target systems and is also a CNCF project. The tool instruments code through various APIs to inform system components about what and how to collect metrics. The system pools the data, samples and filters to reduce noise and errors, and then converts for easy export. Telemetry appears in time-based batches directly, from the service, or indirectly through a combined service method. Many prefer OTel implementations as they offer a common data standard collection across applications, whether in a legacy, micro-service or containerized approach, as long as the APIs are accessible.

OWASP offers an alternative source than CNCF to obtain observability tools. Many tools are focused on either preventative or reactive security outcomes. ZAP automates vulnerability scanning and supports options to conduct manual penetration testing for deployed applications. This allows for actively tracking vulnerabilities, especially Common Vulnerability and Exposures (CVE) events. CVE is a commonly used security term to log new problems with existing software and offer fixes. The PurpleTeam option allows testing of security regression within pipelines, demonstrating results when development reverts to an earlier version to ensure gaps remain closed. Again, most OWASP tools can be used with OTel to report results, OPA to manage policy and Prometheus to gather results before displaying in Grafana.

The list of observable tools and options offered changes constantly. New companies constantly deliver new alternatives to explore market gaps. The key to observable technology should be finding the best solution for your processes and experimenting. This matches DevOps standards to ensure constant observability, drive feedback and kickstart improvements.

Summary

Observability remains key to the DevOps process. Without data, you cannot guarantee flow exists, feedback appears and improvement actually creates success. The first step for observability was understanding the observable framework for DevOps functions. Once basic observability has been solved and agreed upon, you can move towards deciding the best metrics to measure progress. Alternatives are available even when working with a basic standard, such as the DORA metrics. These alternatives depend on understanding your own progress and having a good framework to propose new measures that make the most sense.

All successful outcomes then depend on finding the right people, implementing a process and using effective technology. Observable people means knowing how individuals interact and the key signs supporting generative rather than pathological organizational cultures. Processes enhancing observability often use elements such as OKRs and RACI matrices to create visibility between layers. At the initial implementation, when humans drive technology, one must select tools to gather and display outcomes. Once selected, these tools are also subject to feedback to improve your confidence in DevOps observability.

Now that we understand observability, we can begin the journey in DevOps deliverables. Those deliverables start with understanding and building pipelines and so the next chapter explains how pipelines function within DevOps and key factors to pipeline success.

Notes

1   Observe (2023) www.merriam-webster.com/dictionary/observe (archived at https://perma.cc/R4PF-SXSY)

2   Holzman, G J (1999) Taking Stock, Inc.Com (archived at https://perma.cc/ NTG3-98U9), https://www.inc.com/magazine/19990915/13554.html (archived at https://perma.cc/C6M5-K3A6); Ducklin, P (2018) Forget VPNfilter – here's BACKLASH, a networking hack from way, way, back, Naked Security, https:// nakedsecurity.sophos.com/2018/05/31/forget-vpnfilter-heres-backlash-a-net working-hack-from-way-way-back/ (archived at https://perma.cc/FP5W-PXZU)

3   Fowler, M (2022) Conway's Law, MartinFowler.com (archived at https://perma. cc/K4MB-YAZX), https://martinfowler.com/bliki/ConwaysLaw.html (archived at https://perma.cc/L37X-PLUN)

4   Westrum, R (2004) A typology of organisational cultures, *Qual Saf Health Care*, **13** (Suppl II), ii22–ii27, doi: 10.1136/qshc.2003.009522 (archived at https://perma.cc/E4E6-VA4Q)

5   Doerr, J (2018) *Measure What Matters*, Portfolio Penguin

CHAPTER SIX

Routing the pipeline

Pipelines are critical in confident and successful DevOps implementations. While pipelines should be the easiest element, they are often the most difficult and complicated piece. Understanding pipelines requires building from initial concepts to technical implementation. This chapter integrates the concepts and brings them to a single point, much like a pipeline process. Key points include:

- What a pipeline can achieve and why you need one
- Setting up a useful and effective pipeline for confident, continuous integration and delivery (CI/CD)
- Exploring technical tools to develop and deploy pipelines
- Integrating the people, process and technological culture around pipelines

What is a pipeline?

Sometimes, the simplest concepts are the most difficult to understand. In the mathematics field, using zero took hundreds of years to develop. People understood additive processes, how to add one and one and get two and multiply two by two and get four, but multiplying four by zero to receive zero was challenging. The first recorded use of zero by a culture was by the Mesopotamians (3 BC), followed by India (5th century AD), and reaching Islamic countries to drive algebra and Arabic numerals later (7th century AD). The mathematical concept of zero as a written expression did not reach Western Europe until much later (12th century AD).[1] In the same way, pipeline processes have been around for years but the ability to implement automated pipelines continues to lag in developmental organizations.

The pipeline is a processing chain where the output of each element generates the input to the next step. A software pipeline can be used in various system places. Pipelines can help when using multitasking OS to monitor and return data compared to data rewritten by an upstream process. This pipeline type ensures users only receive accurate data; failing the pipeline would mean rejecting either the user read request or the upstream request to change data. An easy example would be a financial transaction; the user requests a purchase, the purchase is checked against available funds and then a successful pipeline promotes that purchase to the third party. The pipeline then writes back to the user account to adjust available funds. All these elements launch as a processing element chain, a pipeline, once the initial request appears.

When discussing DevOps pipelines, they focus on development and operational tasks. While pipelines can assist operations, they typically resolve development and deployment issues. This means the pipeline handles testing and promoting code to an environment as a series of artifacts. The shorthand name for these environments is dev, test and prod. Writing code happens in dev, testing for sufficiency happens in test, and prod contains the production code, the applications consumed by the user. DevOps teams typically use this schema to prepare deliveries.

Some teams use a pre-prod to conduct further tests while others employ prod as staging for user-accessible, commercially ready deployments. A typical pipeline would resolve code with initial error checks, verify dependencies, conduct automated tests, package for deployment at the next stage and provide results.

A pipeline in software development should be automated, observable and allow cohesive work across multiple logical and physical spaces. When designing, loops run in multiple directions while a pipeline moves in one direction. This benefits our pipeline process as artifacts are created at each step but cannot advance until meeting pipeline requirements. Pipeline steps are targeted through gates that enact checks for certain functions. Each gate expresses requirements that allow advancement to the next pipeline phase with more gates. The final gate shows an overall pipeline pass and allows for moving the artifact package to the next environment. This can be challenging as when discussed in metrics, requirements are set to allow faster advancement rather than verifying the best code.

In my early days as a consultant I worked with a team new to DevSecOps processes in connection with pipelines. After the initial onboarding, they called me on the following day and announced they had solved the security issue regarding pipelines, and did not understand why so many found it difficult to accomplish. I headed over to their spaces where they showed that every code processed had passed a pipeline, returned green for security and been promoted to the next phase. I expressed my enthusiasm, then asked to see the security logs verifying the improvements and risk mitigation at every step. This returns to the concept that pipelines produce artifacts at every step. At this, I received blank looks from the group.

When we looked at the pipeline, and the requirements at every stage, the security scanning tool had been set to 'True'. Testing processes can use integer, string, Boolean (like true) or other expressions to verify success based on what the artifact should return to pass the gate. This meant that as long as the security scan ran, the pipeline would approve the step. In this case, the team was not generating a comprehensive artifact such as a log, just verifying scans run with the 'true' requirement. We fixed the issue, set the logs to generate and then used a difference tool to measure current security versus the product baseline through comparing the logs. It all points to the variation one can have in pipelines. Setting every pipeline step to simplify verifying occurrence lacks depth in understanding that the step took some action, and prepared the code for the next element.

One final element to remember about DevOps pipelines is that having a single pipeline that works for some code should not be the end state. Multiple pipelines allow tailoring elements for different languages, changing environments or to sample different test parameters. Programme managers often express thoughts about having a pipeline so why would they need another? The only limit to how many pipelines one can run is the compute (processing power) and store (memory) available on your environment. Pipelines can be generically constructed to handle wide needs, promoting basic code, or specifically tailored for certain constraints such as publishing containers for use in edge environments or hardening containers for security considerations. Understanding pipeline basics helps one advance to the key points required to set effective pipelines.

Setting up an effective pipeline

Repeating from above, an effective DevOps pipeline serves as multiple steps to process code through an automated, observable process, running from start to finish, and creating continuous integration, delivery, deployment, feedback and operations. Pipelines create a one-way flow, generate artifacts and allow seamless integration from initial development through deployment and into operations. Each step creates artifacts for feedback. A failed pipeline step should cause the entire pipeline to fail, as each step's output creates the input for the following action. Failed steps also generate artifacts that allow resolving failures. The keys to creating an effective pipeline lie in managing the Work-in-Progress (WiP), controlling source contributions and managing successful versions. These steps allow making effective optimization decisions to maximize production and confidently deliver customer value whether other internal groups or external customers generate revenue.

Pipeline work in progress

WIP, or work in progress, appears when planning functions in Scrum or Kanban formats to control how much work can be handled at any one time by the team. Controlling work ensures each task section continues to completion and minimizes context switching for the team. As an easy step to show how context switching affects productivity, write down the alphabet from A–Z and numbers from 1–26 while timing yourself. Then write the same list with the letter, the opposite number (A = 26) and add a plant name for odd numbers and an animal name for even numbers. The task probably takes much longer. The difference is that rather than simply reciting a sequence, you have to pull in multiple different elements.

The change between a common format and something different requires the mind to switch and that creates difficulty. In a work context, when you start with a work task, then answer the phone and browse social media, think how long it takes to return to being effective on your primary work task. Limiting WIP with pipelines means being able to run multiple pipelines, in different environments and by either single or multiple developers. Each pipeline only takes the work it can handle; this means one pipeline, in one instance, runs one code element. A pipeline should be a static element, calling serial functions and named for particular elements such as JavaDeploy1, ParkingApp2 or even BobPipeline3. Since a pipeline is a series of commands, multiple developers can run the same pipeline at the same time. Having trusted pipelines and understanding how elements promote from pipelines is source control.

Source control

Source control means using tools and process to store and track changes over time. Everyone has seen the file labelled 'CompRevenue_Sales_Qtr3_v3_012323' which tells everyone, supposedly, what the file is, which version and when that version was committed. Source control should designate the initial item being selected compared to the changes highlighted through version control. These controls can be attached to the file as part of the artifacts rather than simply included in the initial name. DevOps pipeline techniques and tools identify sources of truth for good code, good documentation and security policies. The initial thought restricts software development source control to functional code but you should consider the advantages in multiple areas. Knowing where good code lands is important but having access to previous failed attempts can also generate learning. More control means channelling communication, not through silos but through multiple methods to allow better control and create observability.

In a corporate experience, the company used GitHub not only for code but for all company documentation. This caused an initial training hurdle for those not familiar but was adopted quickly. GitHub provides an open-source option for gathering data from documentation to code. It also provides the option for public and private repositories. The company worked merging code and submitted architectural decision records (ADR) through GitHub even for items like changing vacation policy. This allowed everyone to see both the current policy and past policies, and who committed the changes. This established a workflow with automated pipeline steps, even for organizational documentation. Source control allows accelerating bug fixes, simultaneous development and increased reliability.

Source control can also benefit your non-functional pipelines. While the primary pipeline use delivers functional code, security, platform and other teams can create a non-functional pipeline to control delivery. Examples could include a risk mitigation pipeline, tool ownership or non-functional testing requirements. A risk mitigation pipeline could be launched through questions involving personnel or technology change, test coverage standards or even technology change. Designating a pipeline highlights the steps, in a checklist fashion to resolve challenges before the next step.

A non-functional risk pipeline could ask questions about socialization through whether stakeholders were aware of issues, risk levels compared to company resources, probability standards and consequences. Each step would have a reference link and approval statuses. This allows source control over who verified the risk, what steps were taken and what impact the risk might currently have. A simple example is tracking dependencies through software asset control by knowing which systems run which third-party software and where those systems are located. The functional pipeline could then reference whether code had passed the risk pipeline through the existence of tailored documentation, and the establishment of standards. Having all teams establish a pipeline-based process improves the cultural connection through creating shared awareness about the methods and means necessary for DevOps success.

Version control and repositories

Version control highlights a more detailed aspect of source control and highlights more functional code through technical solutions. This refers to the specific aspect being developed rather than where sources exist within an external repository. Code versions highlight the initial trunk, existing branches and the merges committed over time. For example, the trunk might be Parking App, with branches for each of the garages. When examining any section you could see how many people forked (made working copies) off the trunk or branch and how many merges were complete. This leads into the previous chapter's metrics to assess development.

GitLab, as a paid option, and GitKraken, as an open-source tool, provide visual displays to manage version control. These show the linkages between the various items.

Having effective version control allows for managing repositories and leads to effective release management. CI/CD states that everything can be integrated and deployed but sometimes the customer environment requires deployment in a set state. If we are making upgrades to a customer network at version 1.4, and the current published version is 1.8, we want to know if we can directly go from 1.4 to 1.8 or if we must install 1.4.1, 1.4.2 and 1.5 before 1.8 is effective. Then we can establish a parallel process where 1.6, 1.7 and 1.4.1 are installed in parallel as we progress to bringing the entire system to 1.8. While this sounds complicated narratively, confidence in version control allows effective deployment.

Version control also applies to having trusted repositories, especially when using open-source integrations. If updates can be made globally, we want to see what those updated changes were, and what updates we can trust. Our sources and version should be managed locally for a trusted repository with access and authentication requirements. This allows for managing credentials and reviewing changes. It also provides source protection through encrypted tools to prevent non-authorized users from accessing local IP addresses, ensures protection of embedded secrets and reduces attack surfaces. Attack surfaces are those software areas where a hacker can gain access. These terms apply more to security decisions but also prevent one developer from changing the entire repository from Go to Python because of a personnel preference.

Repository control extends to databases. In the parking app previously, we were updating multiple local databases to correspond with a master at the same time. Knowing the source of truth for repositories keeps the customer from receiving erroneous data about which spaces are available. One typically sees the '-latest' command for version control in coding language. One can only ensure those verifications through strictly managing version and source control. One of the goals in developing pipelines should be to maintain version and source control for artifacts associated with tests and the code packaged by those pipelines.

Optimizing the pipeline

In creating an efficient pipeline, you should be learning optimization basics to create as much value as possible. After all, we do not just want the pipeline to run but to ensure pipeline processes maximize flow and customer delivery. There are common pipeline problems and then there are more advanced challenges. Each may require a technical solution, a process solution or cultural requirements about how technical and process items are organizationally implemented.

One common problem occurs when CI/CD and DevOps are considered similar functions. While CI/CD advances DevOps practices, not all DevOps practices call for a CI/CD pipeline. This can be a challenge solved technically through implementing CI/CD software or exhibit a cultural problem if multiple release approvals are required despite technical automation tools. A second problem appears with stuck branches due to bad pull requests, exceeding storage limits or authorization issues to promote code. Visualizing those branches also allows one to evaluate if pull requests for the code are being stopped, for example if individuals want to work on the code but are not allowed version access as they cannot move data within a space or are not authorized to work on that branch. One developer working for me experienced this issue but the root cause was that rather than forking the element being coded, they were trying to move the base code between a home terminal and a virtual terminal on a daily basis. This rapidly exceeded the server's daily transfer and drove cloud costs up. Identifying the problem allowed for cultural and technical training for the individual and returned the pipeline to optimum performance.

A third common problem is when one lacks observability. We discussed observability in the previous chapter but pipelines often get approved without verifying observability. Developers may restrict observability or, due to space limitations, restrict the produced artifacts to inefficient levels. In the security example above, we saw how limiting the artifact made the pipeline succeed, but not in a continuous manner. Limiting the artifacts early allows code to progress early only to be denied later when problems emerge with committed code. Again, one fixes this issue by ensuring observability occurs through properly produced artifacts and observable dashboards.

Advanced problems can include the lack of quality emphasis, lack of dashboards, multiple templates being used at scale or inefficient implementation. While these may seem simple, solving each requires cultural, technical and people solutions. You need to ensure the pipeline produces quality code and can be observed from multiple perspectives. The common root between these issues emerges from developing without a design and not committing to continuous improvement.

Templates at scale present a challenging problem. The number of pipelines does not matter but if those pipelines are built on a purposeful basis, altering those templates can change that purpose. In our example, we saw the change with a pipeline security scan from producing a log as artifact to setting the gate as true. If the templated pipeline included the full scan, any developer changes would highlight changes across logs with good source control. You must understand the template provided and be able to distinguish if changes are made, whether those are beneficial to the overall strategy or reduce customer value. Differential tools are frequently used to rapidly compare artifacts between subsequent pipeline runs. Templates at scale require observing more options, more often and attempting differential resolution, all hopefully in an automated fashion. These pipeline guides help but rely on understanding the technical pipeline application to create flow and feedback.

Technical pipeline solutions

Establishing the technology for a pipeline requires making some basic decisions about what those pipelines are and the purpose they serve. The typical pipeline addresses many continuous issues such as testing, deployment, monitoring, feedback or operations. Each attempts to create an environment observable through artifacts and ensure quality across multiple options. Pipelines are never a build-and-forget but should undergo the same iteration as any other DevOps practice. This means you should maintain repositories of useful pipelines similar to code repositories for known good code, third-party software, data libraries and frequently used open-source software.

Pipelines can require access to multiple repositories to be built effectively. This happens when one needs to call multiple elements, launch containers or use different services to verify effectiveness. The best technical solution is to either keep those requirements local through a Bitbucket, GitHub or GitLab, or allow internet access. When establishing container and service mesh access through Kubernetes and Docker, one can set those allow and block list parameters to connect to external services. When managing these interfaces, these items can be managed through application processing interfaces (API) or Amazon Machine Images (AMI). These provide automation to secure pipelines and prevent external, non-approved folks, like hackers, from accessing materials.

A technical pipeline requires multiple steps: identify the source, build the code, test, stage and then pass to production. Many interfaces like Jenkins, GitLab and AWS offer automated ways to build these pipelines, simply dragging and dropping the interfaces with the execution blocks into the preferred spaces with execution methods. In direct code, one of the options, especially in Azure, is using the self-referential YAML (YAML Ain't Markup Language). YAML uses an alignment to stages, jobs and steps to divide pipelines. Stages are a set of sequential jobs and steps are the processes within those jobs. One might see a YAML coding example like the following.

```
stages:
- stage: BuildCode
jobs:
- job: BuildPackage
steps:
- Build
- Package
- Publish
- stage: Deploy
jobs:
- job: BeginDeploy
steps:
- Deploypackage
```

You can see the first pipeline stage builds and the second deploys here. Each stage calls the lower-level job to handle acceptable steps. You can use multiple jobs in a stage if necessary, such as if you had to build for two different environments, or for a job that builds code, and then another to check for vulnerabilities. Most tools supporting pipelines offer multiple examples in documentation to start building first basic to then more advanced options. Most pipeline scripting tools use some variant of the stage, job and step methodology while allowing for some textual and sequential variations between versions.

One key to pipelines involves automation; each step should launch the next step, each completed job launching the next job with each set of completed jobs within a stage launching the next stage. These bring massive automation benefits through using telemetry tools to build effective metrics. Metrics can show automation efficacy through how long pipelines take and how successful are the completed deployments, software quality through passed bugs or vulnerabilities, and automation utilization through how often certain pipelines are used over manual builds. Each improves the ability to deliver customer value.

Another technical benefit to pipelines relies on adding security jobs. While success in building and deploying does not require security functionally, adding in those caveats can help verify builds. There are four basic security areas: code coverage, vulnerabilities, container security and dependency scans. Each area helps to build a comprehensive coding picture by contributing some security aspect. With any scanning tool, multiple variants exist and selecting the right tool depends on what best fits your performance and cost needs at the time.

Typical code coverage scanning employs a tool to remove critical bugs, frequently including those not known to the coder, from the early development stages through unit testing. Common examples of code coverage tools include SonarQube, Gradle, JUnit and Visual Studio Code. The different tools are normally limited to certain coding languages. Unit testing will be covered later but assesses the smallest possible element before moving to the next. The different coverage types are listed below.

- Function – the number of functions called, alignment between used and unused functions, and if all named functions are used.

- Statement – how many statements are executed in a defined program.
- Branch – the branch number executed from control structure to show streamlining in the programming process.
- Condition – how many Boolean expressions (True, False, Null) are executed in the code.
- Line – how many lines tested in the source code.

Vulnerability scanning moves from the initial test to compare against known bugs, problems with code or dependencies in the written expression. These errors can sometimes have published fixes that merely need application. Common tools used for vulnerability scanning include Nessus, Tenable and Nmap. One interesting software note – as companies move from open source to paid services, sometimes early versions get forked by the open-source community, resulting in a slightly different free version with similar properties. OpenVAS offers an example of code forked from the Nessus code with slightly different functions and properties. Many DevOps practices use multiple vulnerability scanners at different elements to establish complete coverage.

NMap also offers an interesting point in vulnerability scanning. While nominally a network discovery tool developed for Linux, the tool supports additional packages for other operating systems. Using NMap can quickly reveal the hosts, services and operating systems available from a particular device. My own early cyber security practices extensively used NMap in an isolated case to discover vulnerabilities. It also should be noted that using NMap against a system you do not own can actually violate several laws. It makes a good point that sometimes even practising with tools can require substantial knowledge. NMap's use in a pipeline would be to validate that certain required ports or areas were open or closed as the jobs built through different environments.

Container security again looks for a specialized security application. Many pipelines build multiple containers, deploying as a micro-service or within a service mesh so understanding interaction vulnerabilities can be critical. Container scanning tools should look for code vulnerabilities, network connecting, test source code before and after deployment and verify access. If you remember that the entire system runs cloud, cluster, container and code, then the container is a step up from code but does not allow for testing the entire environment for vulnerabilities.

The pipeline container check verifies that the container does not hold any inherent vulnerabilities and has not changed within the pipeline. As an example, one may want to deny access to a particular IP; however, the pipeline may change those IPs to focus on overall connectivity. In this case, the container scanning should flag the difference between the committed application and the deployment. Common container scanning tools include Anchore, Docker Bench, Twistlock, Tenable.io Container Security.

Dependency scans are a backwards-looking process to ensure everything called by packaged code is accessible and functions as required. I call it backwards as it looks from code execution to external items required to make code execute. Again, many of the pipeline tools available offer different scanning options. For example, SonarQube and GitLab both offer dependency checks. Dependency checks may also be called a software composition analysis (OCA). OWASP offers a dependency-check tool to find publicly available vulnerabilities located in dependences. The goal of a dependency scanner is to prevent any known vulnerabilities from migrating to deployed code.

Knowing the technical elements required to construct a pipeline, there remain only a few steps. Just like the stage, job and steps, the next stage requires finding the right people, establishing cultural processes and determining the technology to support advancement.

Picking pipeline people, process and technology

Similar to every other DevOps segment, effective pipelines depend on selecting the right people, the right process and the right technology. As with every other instance, these elements should emphasize flow, feedback and continuous improvement. People starts with the right skills and the right mentality to support delivery. Any pipeline process should be oriented around thinking through an effective pipeline. Finally, technology should be shaped to the best fit for your people and your process as people shape the technology, and subsequent technology development drives iterations towards improved quality.

Pipeline people

In other elements, you can hire architects and software engineers but as pipelines are pervasive throughout DevOps, selecting a pipeline engineer might not be the best fit. Instead of a pipeline engineer, the best fit may be a CI/CD engineer who focuses on CI/CD precepts instead of simply building pipelines. This individual would look not just at the current pipeline path but also at the long-term business goals to achieve success. These people should be strong communicators with keen analytic skills who enjoy decomposing complex processes. These traits lead to building teams who are proficient at optimizing multiple pipelines rather than making the pipeline better.

The duties for a CI/CD engineer should be to develop the effective CI/CD principles through automating observable pipelines for multiple functions. The title emphasizes the CI/CD aspect but this continues through operational pipelines to create feedback and maintain pipelines to automate upgrades without consuming significant developer cycles. CI/CD engineers manage tools to observe, maintain and iterate CI/CD tools and platforms. This should extend from choosing the best tool for a pipeline step or job, to those tools allowing smooth automation from start to finish. They should be constantly exploring by testing developmental and operational boundaries through technical experimentation.

There are some technical skills associated with a CI/CD engineer. They should be script-writing experts who can interpret and write source code in multiple languages. These skills then extend their ability to manage infrastructure, working with architects to establish dev, test and prod environments supporting multiple pipelines arching across the various domains. They must know when a pipeline is the best solution and when a temporary manual promotion might still advance the experiment. This requires familiarity with software packing and version control tools. Additionally, the individual should be familiar with security tools for vulnerability analysis, monitoring and code coverage. Above all, the individual should be dedicated to process observability, ensuring transparency across all CI/CD elements.

Pipeline process

Two main areas define initial pipeline processes: code quality and continuous monitoring. These two elements should define how any organization's pipeline processes are established as they lead to the third process element: continuous integration and continuous delivery (CI/CD). If your process focuses on developing these practices, you can accelerate the pipeline-provided value.

Code quality should be the first and last consideration for all pipelines. Every pipeline element depends on the previous element; if the basic code is bad, then the whole pipeline can fall apart. Extensive testing strategies appear in the next chapter but some initial tips will help focus those discussions. Code tests start with testing the smallest possible logical elements. Multiple tools offer solutions on different coding languages; sometimes using multiple tools can be helpful. You should experiment with tools to find the best fit for your teams. Effective unit-based code testing allows one to quickly accelerate to static and dynamic testing tools.

Basic code evaluation allows for establishing process metrics. Some initial metrics should be that fewer than 400 lines should be examined in a set. The realistic expectation for manual code reviews is to evaluate a maximum of 400 lines an hour. Incorporating automated tools accelerates these timelines and further advances static and dynamic testing practices.

Those initial tests lead to continuous monitoring processes. All pipelines should be observable but continuous monitoring ensures those elements do not go into a log blackhole but alertable exceptions are immediately pushed to users. Pipeline monitoring should be set for three major factors:

- when something happens
- when something that is expected to happen does not happen
- when policy requires it

Pipeline outcomes can drive each of these. In the earlier security example, the pipeline can be set to report when security scans complete, and then for discrepancies. This allows for monitoring to highlight fixes or simply note what is being released.

These quality and monitoring tools drive CI/CD success. To integrate constantly, you need to know when quality coding elements are submitted. Pipelines provide the process verification. Then, in turn, code with quality integration can be delivered with minimal risk. The pipeline process allows one to rapidly identify where the process stopped and what actions must occur next. These processes can be integrated into the overall pipeline technology.

Pipeline technology

Pipeline technology basics appeared previously when we were discussing internal processes. The next step determines what technology you should select to model pipelines. As with other tools, the right pipeline process can be done manually or represented by various options. I prefer DevOps platforms that support multiple tool interpretations and allow integration of multiple languages such as YAML, Terraform and JSON.

A key technological pipeline element should be visualization. The earlier elements showed the inclusion in code and the source integration. Those elements should be further expanded to allow for visually interpreting pipeline goals. The simplest pipeline visualization appears in Figure 6.1.

The pipeline includes the basic level steps for every DevOps required function. One could take that function and build out to similar elements in every step. Good pipeline technology allows direct code through CLI and GUI integrations to drag and drop different software interpretations. For example, in the visualization we see the high-level steps to move from one area to the next. Some technology will automatically include the necessary sub-items at every step.

FIGURE 6.1   Pipeline visualization

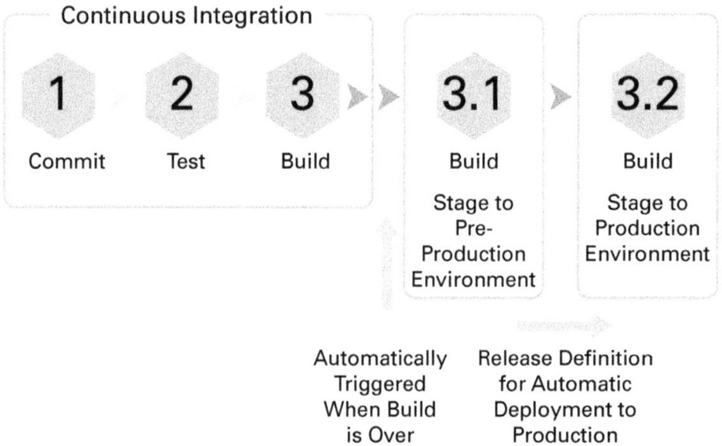

Source: DevOps Institute

FIGURE 6.2 Commit pipeline

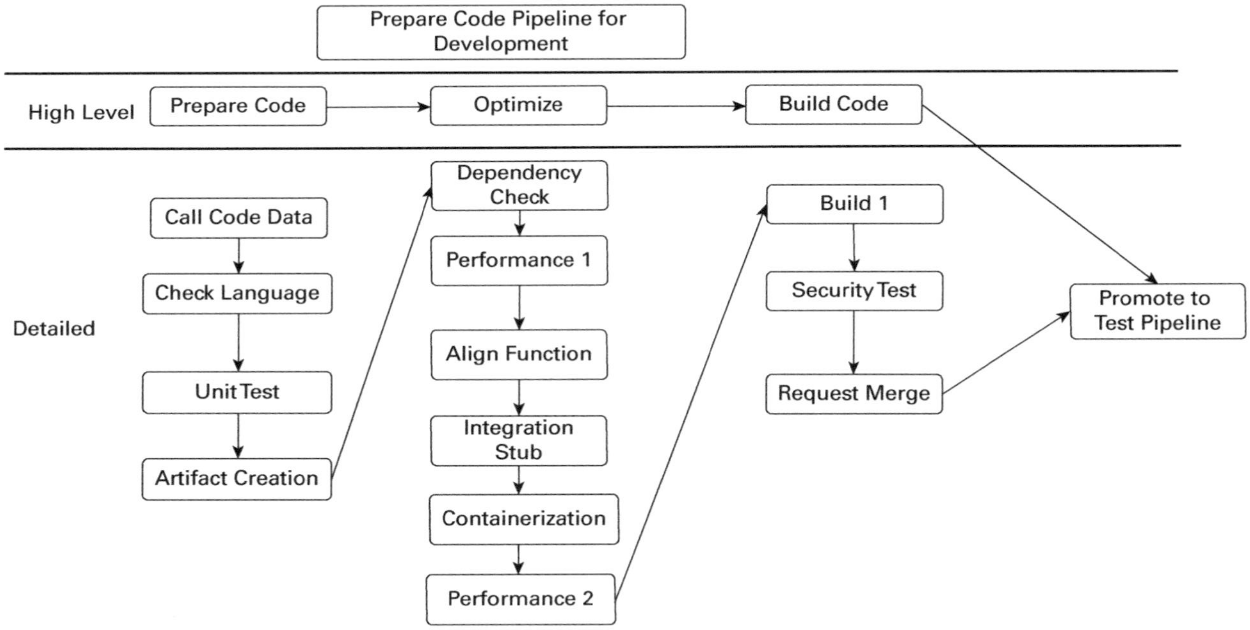

Prepare Code Pipeline for Development

High Level

Prepare Code → Optimize → Build Code → Promote to Test Pipeline

Detailed

Call Code Data → Check Language → Unit Test → Artifact Creation

Dependency Check → Performance 1 → Align Function → Integration Stub → Containerization → Performance 2

Build 1 → Security Test → Request Merge

Moving beyond the initial visualization, you might use technology to select more items and more preparation for those items. Figure 6.2 shows a potential breakout for an initial development or commit phase commonly used in CI/CD pipelines.

These break commit phases into various actions, tests and builds necessary to advance the code. In the first preparation phase, the pipeline makes sure the code arrives from an accessible repository, checks the language against known good elements, does the initial unit test against the smallest logical elements and creates a known good compilation. Those elements then advance to a dependency check to ensure all called libraries and variables exist, conduct an initial performance check, sometimes against a known baseline, and then align functions. Next, an integration stub could be held to ensure the correct API calls are in place. At this point, functions could be containerized into a Docker or Kubernetes approach and performance measured again. This would then lead to building the deployable code as a standard pipeline action.

At each step, the technology produces an artifact and adds a log depicting what occurred and the results. Any failure stops the pipeline. Backward checks can also be applied based on artifact creation. For example, one could include Performance 1 results and state that Performance 2 will not pass if the results are less overall than the previous test. At the same time, some performance results could be emphasized over others; for example, a lapse in speed might be set to pass if the memory used decreases. Each item would be technically set when creating the pipeline.

Good pipeline technology allows for automating these results. Rather than writing code for each pipeline, selecting a function at each step would apply those gates to the pipeline. As an example, when using Argo CD, one can select ingress and egress points, which are then included in code. This helps generate the manifests for systems to understand how to deploy code packages. When that compilation returns to the pipeline, checks for ingress and egress points would likely pass. Focused on automation, one common error with pipelines occurs when results are set to manually pass rather than relying on tests. For example, one might specify that any code that makes it to Performance 2 will always pass. These manual promotions can work in early samples to test certain code elements but defeat the overall CI/CD purpose.

Summary

Pipeline variations and manual promotions offer one reason why testing appropriately is a critical DevOps methodology. Pipeline processes begin with understanding the reason behind using pipelines while maintaining effective source control and methodologies. The next step lies in understanding how pipelines are built. Finally, we discussed the emphasis on selecting the right people to maintain processes through the correct skill combination. These people can be empowered by effective processes and efficient technology, especially in visualization.

Pipelines can best be optimized through effective testing procedures. While we separate tests into a different category, each pipeline stage implements one or more tests to produce artifacts. In the next chapter, the discussion focuses on what tests can be performed, selecting tests for different results and testing in operational environments to maximize security and customer value.

Note

1   Kaplan, R (2007) What is the origin of zero? *Scientific American*, https://www.scientificamerican.com/article/what-is-the-origin-of-zer/ (archived at https://perma.cc/9GHG-RLQ9)

CHAPTER SEVEN

Testing the process

Critical to building an efficient DevOps mentality is continuous testing. Testing produces artifacts and creates observable interactions. Testing different aspects and areas varies from initial unit testing to complete functional integrations. In addition to development testing, testing can be anything from security testing like penetration tests to optimizing operational methods with chaos engineering. One vital contribution offered by testing is integrating continual testing and monitoring through various tools. These tools support a universal approach to observability and creating shared artifacts supporting future development. This chapter explains testing from the basics to the most advanced levels and demonstrates some useful frameworks:

- Testing basics
- Determining testing use-cases
- Establishing continuous testing
- Driving improvement through testing

As with several previous chapters, the final section discusses people, processes and technological solutions for testing success. Finding the right individual with a testing mindset can either block or be vital to a practical test process. All testing elements are vital to confident DevOps.

The basics of testing

The first step to understanding testing clarifies our definition. If we revert to the dictionary, test means 'the procedure of submitting a statement to such conditions or operations as will lead to its proof or disproof or its acceptance or rejection'.[1] Regardless of the level, every test seeks to prove or disprove an item and communicate those results. The most basic tests check items like the correct coding format, while the more advanced ones examine connections to external software or proper messaging formats between the two items. Each testing aspect uses a different syntax and approach to obtain results. The next step defines testing types and their attached solutions.

A generic term refers to most tests. Sometimes, the term explains the function, but some cases require additional detail. A list of testing types appears below but each receives additional detail in the following paragraphs. One must distinguish between generic development tests like a unit or integration test, more specific applications like Static Application Security Testing (SAST), and performance testing like load, spike or stress testing.

- Unit – smallest piece of code
- Quality – subjective assessment
- Code review – usually manual instance of paired programming or pull request review
- Static analysis – pre-run debugging
- Data – check information with which the code interacts

- End to end – runs workflow through application from start to finish
- Regression – runs functional and non-functional tests after change to verify software
- Functional – quality assurance testing based on black box formats
- Smoke – determine if ready for the next testing phase
- Dynamic – finding errors in running programming
- Red/blue – manual tests using teams to find errors
- Operational/user – brings in users to check for human errors and usability

Types of testing

Unit testing is the first step for all continuous testing practices. These tests feature assessing the smallest possible units of codes. A common analogy would be the spell checker in a word processing program. As a spell checker, unit tests assess a specific language such as Python, React, Go or others. Integrated development environments (IDEs) often have unit testing integrated so users can correct before code reaches pipelines. Building unit tests into the pipeline ensures potential errors resolve and eliminates easy missteps.

Code quality and code review are manual practices. These remain manual as they are incredibly subjective. Code quality establishes value-based metrics, including ensuring sections are commented, that code blocks run smoothly in a determined order or that code functions only occur once. For example, if code needs to add an item multiple times rather than adding distinct components every time, good code calls the initial section. These include using libraries for standard functions rather than defining each item as it occurs. These distinctions happen as code advances, such as the machine learning libraries available for NumPy, Pandas, Scikit-Learn, Tensorflow etc.

These elements allow others to build the simple code to create a graphic display and your code to use the data.

Static analysis moves on from those initial stages to verify that the code runs as written without other inputs. These types of tests use input from previous tests and verify successful code. The most critical element would be that the code is not running during testing. Static tests ensure all identified variables are called, FOR loops end and identified functions are correct. Some standard tools that can help with static analysis are SonarQube, Veracode and Fortify.

Data testing verifies the essential information for program interaction. There are three types of data testing: standard, erroneous and boundary. Standard testing prefers an expected input to generate an expected output; when the user enters their username and password, they are checked against the database and admitted. Erroneous testing performs the opposite case and looks to ensure that if wrong input occurs, the system recognizes and rejects the request. If the same login function requires creating a password with specific character numbers, the system rejects attempts that fail to meet standards. Boundary testing looks for edge values at opposite allowable spectrum ends. A boundary testing example could be gender on surveys; if fields only allow certain values, then the system ensures only those values are possible.

Effective data testing secures software and prevents future vulnerabilities. Standard Query Language (SQL) injection is a hacking tool that can disrupt effective tools. This attack uses malicious SQl code to send database entries that can execute commands. Rather than the data reflecting the input, when systems read injections, it executes a command. For example, the query could direct a system search to delete the table rather than returning the desired field.[2]

End-to-end (E2E) testing continues to progress testing. A good CI/CD pipeline includes some E2E testing to ensure correct operations. This testing measures unit functions, conditions and test cases. E2E is essential in conducting test-driven development (TDD). TDD suggests that a test exists to verify desired functions before writing code. All TDD evaluates as a three-step cycle: red, green and refactor. First, the red tests evaluate the simplest test that could fail. Green tests solve the red problem by creating the simplest code, solving the problem and passing tests. The last step refactors overall code, going back through all material, solving any problems or trash created when solving the red problem.

Regression testing evaluates whether software can return to a previous state without lingering changes. If you think about common patching and upgrade cycles, sometimes software works well in tests but creates different errors when installed by a user. This test area ensures that regressing to a previous version does not leave new changes within user spaces. For example, if a new version calls out to new libraries, and those libraries create errors, you would verify that returning to the previous software does not repeat the same mistakes. Regression is a common solution for operational teams when errors mount after a new upgrade. Regression testing ensures that those operational practices will be successful.

As the name implies, functional tests test for functions within the programs. To run a practical test, one sets expectations for what running the program achieves. Each test should have clear inputs and expected system outputs. At this point, one uses mocks and stubs to create results. A mock creates a fake class to evaluate in surveying the interaction with the tested class. A stub functions as a database connection to simulate scenarios without live databases. If a test function involves medical data or personal information, stubs provide significant compliance benefit over using actual data.

Smoke testing applies a new practice through testing if code versions work before advancing.[3] These tests can be either manual or automated to find delivered code gaps. The process starts when a development team delivers a new application build. The term originates from physically testing equipment for approval if the equipment did not ignite when powered on. QA teams perform these tests to ensure no simple but severe failures exist by applying test cases evaluating software functionality.

Dynamic testing verifies software code's changing behaviour. Dynamic tests evaluate the software's response to changing inputs affecting overall behaviour. Code must run sequentially to pass dynamic testing. This testing typically occurs as either white box or black box testing. When the user knows the existing code, the testing is white box. Tests verify how systems perform based on the code. In black box testing, the internal configuration is unknown. Black box testing is also known as user acceptance tests. Testers attempt to enter different data types without access to code to identify errors. White box testing requires engineering knowledge but any user can conduct black box testing.

The last two testing types require active participation. Red/ blue tests occur at the system level and select an attack (red) and defence (blue) team. Red/blue reveals vulnerabilities not apparent during other tests. Operational and user tests present the software to users and identify preferences. Sometimes the system buttonology might work effectively through test cases but be ineffective for users. Examples include drop-down menus, items arranged logically but different from user preference, or commonly used items that might require selection at every instance rather than saving past requests.

The best way to assess which test to use is by writing effective test cases. Test cases define testing areas and align expectations against occurrences. These items are essential to test-driven development and critical to any continuous testing model. The next section covers developing and employing test cases.

Writing a test case

One of the keys to successful testing lies in writing effective test cases. Test cases describe what must happen for a test to succeed.

Writing successful test cases depends on looking for how others accomplished similar tasks. Some good online resources are the Practical Test Pyramid by Martin Fowler, Robot Framework learning resources or Axelrod's Complete Guide to Test Automation. Finding the right solution works differently from different solutions, and everyone must find their own test design approach.

Testing involves some similar steps to other functions. Building tests can start at the individual unit level, or top end and build down. Four common testing levels are procedure, case, design and plan. The smallest unit, procedure, details an individual test such as verifying that at least two upper-case letters appear in passwords. The next level might ask for passwords to meet all required elements. Test cases compile multiple procedures. Test design states specifications for testing across multiple test cases. An example would be mandatory password protection, which must be retrievable from an encrypted database. Finally, the test plan incorporates multiple designs and verifies the organizational strategic approach.

Testing can be unit-based for a particular language such as Python, C+, C#, Go, Ruby, etc. or aligned to different elements. Some testing software combines various tests or languages in a single mechanism. Common testing frameworks include software like Junit, Selenium, Robot Framework, Cucumber or Avocado. Software can guide one through writing the individual test case. Those first examples include assessing what will test and the expected answer. Test cases include processes for test failures. A sample outline for conducting testing is:

- analyse the requirements
- set up a test environment
- analyse any software or hardware needs
- write down how systems should respond
- list testing methods
- design individual cases

Although I am not a test expert, when I conduct tests, one option I prefer is Robot Framework. Robot Framework provides an open-source generic automation guideline for acceptance testing and supports TDD. The system uses a keyword-driven testing format supporting tabular test data for multiple languages. The open-source approach means multiple libraries are available to provide pre-built tests. Like other testing features, online tutorials are available to dive deeper into testing frameworks and reporting.

When designing test cases, one must carefully monitor for common errors. All test cases should include tool integration and the resulting fidelity should match the desired output. Once one begins testing, fixing errors should only occur after all tests run. Fixing one early error can often create multiple other problems. Waiting allows for investigating root causes where several failures link to a common problem. Once the problem resolves, rerunning tests is a must. When failure continues, the appropriate response should capture data and seek additional help.

Running tests can sometimes create some unusual but ordinary problems. Sometimes errors may only occur on one system, so you should run tests in multiple environments. At the same time, correctly duplicating environments, especially when using multiple Virtual Machines (VM), is essential. Another test error can occur if run from IDE or from the command line. One solution is to narrow the evaluated section to the specific problem and investigate influencing tests. Sometimes an earlier test might influence the results of a later test to cause unusual results.

One final unusual test case example can be flickering tests. These tests resemble a flickering lightbulb where they occur at unusual intervals. In many cases flickering is not caused by the test or the code but by external environment changes. This error identifies the need to create effective test environments. For example, a performance test might report unusual results from a production environment rather than in an isolated testing environment. The difference in test results over time are one reason continuous testing continues to be a favoured DevOps approach.

Continuous testing and monitoring

Continuous testing (CT) and monitoring means testing never stops, and testing results benefit from monitoring every development, deployment and operations phase. Good testing practices start with implementing test-driven development (TDD). One can establish testing practices by using various approaches and implementation at different pipeline stages. A sample of tests

FIGURE 7.1   Testing plan for pipeline

Testing Plan for Pipeline

Developer Branch PR	Epic/Feature Branch PR/AD-HOC	BugFix Branch PR	Devel Branch Daily/PR	Hotfix Branch PR	Release Branch Daily
Unit Testing	Unit Testing	Unit Testing	Unit Testing	Unit Testing	Unit Testing
Static Code Analysis	Static Code Analysis	Static Code Analysis	Static Code Analysis	Static Code Analysis	Static Code Analysis
	Integration Testing (V)	Integration Testing (V)	Integration Testing (P)	Integration Testing (V)	Integration Testing (P)
	End to End Testing (V)	End to End Testing (V)	End to End Testing (P)	End to End Testing (V)	End to End Testing (P)
	Security Testing (V)	Security Testing (V)	Security Testing (P)	Security Testing (V)	Security Testing (P)
	Throughput Testing (P)		Throughput Testing (P)		Throughput Testing (P)
	CT Testing (V/P)		CT Testing (P)		CT Testing (P)
			DT Testing (P)		DT Testing (P)
					OT Testing (P)

applied to different pipeline requirements is shown in Figure 7.1. While standards exist and can be found easily online, best practice involves starting with known tests and expanding until they fit individual requirements.

Continuous processes support every DevOps level. The basics behind CT require checking everything and creating processes with known feedback at dedicated intervals. The known feedback then supports continuously looking to verify improvements throughout the software lifecycle. When we start with flow, testing decreases delivery lead times, establishes pipeline quality and prevents defects from reaching work centres. Removing defects improves metrics by eliminating operational bugs and drastically reducing the time to resolve.

Good flow supports good feedback. Establishing high-quality flow through CT ensures that those responsible for fixing applications, from the initial dev team to operational centres, have the data needed to implement rapid changes. Flow begins with frequent information about processes through consistent testing. Each testing element then supports ensuring fixes occur when they are smaller, cheaper and more manageable. The sooner a potential problem can be detected, the more likely the initial change affects fewer areas.

Feedback requires continuous monitoring, and monitoring applies testing even if the monitoring is no more than checking process occurrence and reporting. Any process creating an artifact can be considered testing. Testing looks for set barriers where results are validated. Telemetry functions to capture status at set points. Metrics, logs and traces may not be considered testing but the process ensuring the ability to capture metrics, logs and traces at defined points is a test. One should consider how tests report, whether by automated gating like GitLab runners reporting results, an operational dashboard like AWS's CloudWatch, or only during weekly staff meetings. An example of CT blueprint is shown in Figure 7.2.

FIGURE 7.2 Continuous testing blueprint

Continuous Testing Blueprint

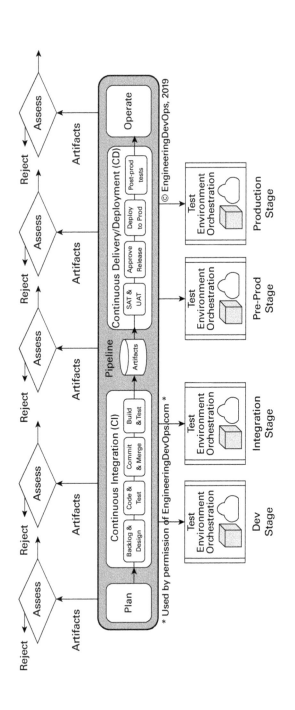

© EngineeringDevOps, 2019

* Used by permission of EngineeringDevOps.com *

Once flow and feedback are in the CT process, you can spend numerous cycles emphasizing continuous improvement. TDD creates a learning culture centred on operations. It is not enough to have testing in the development cycles; these practices should continue when code reaches the user. Constantly running operational tests verifies that tools continue to function effectively. These can occur behind the scenes through operational management, such as load balancing, auto-scaling, password remediation and other functions requiring regular change. One can also examine injecting stress and implementing other methods discussed in the testing for improvement section.

The CT step requires finding where production-like environments occur throughout the lifecycle. If the production environment mirrors the development environment, tests can be minimized. If development code deploys to multiple environments, more tests can be applied, the more similar a testing environment is to the actual environment, the more likely tests are effective. Early practices emphasize manual tests, which often means that tests are difficult to replicate and repeat. The desire is to invert the testing pyramid. Figure 7.3 shows the potential benefits of flipping that test pyramid, with each

FIGURE 7.3   Flipping the test pyramid

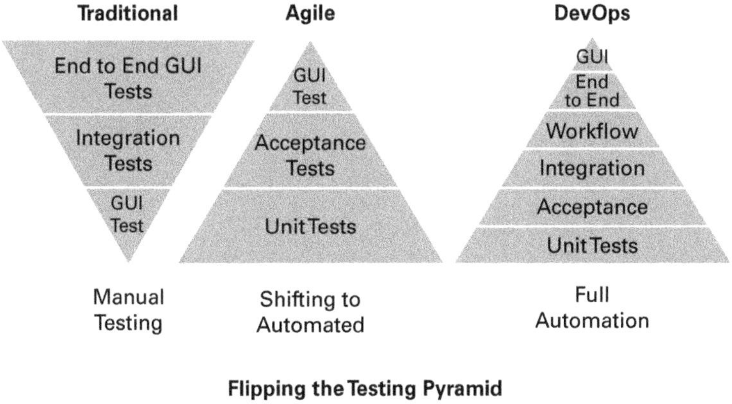

Traditional	Agile	DevOps
End to End GUI Tests	GUI Test	GUI End to End
Integration Tests	Acceptance Tests	Workflow Integration
GUI Test	Unit Tests	Acceptance Unit Tests
Manual Testing	Shifting to Automated	Full Automation

Flipping the Testing Pyramid

level's size showing the amount of work cycles spent on the individual processes.

The goal for the organization is to reduce manual tests that require more code and money. Frequently, manual tests may be in separate repositories, not verified across multiple levels, and manipulation may allow individual events to pass just to deliver successful results. An example of manipulating tests occurs when an item continually fails but rather than applying the red-green-refactor approach, the test only allows progression. Automated tests run constantly and can be used by multiple teams. The broad acceptance creates cultural learning with all participants understanding common progression. One cannot alter individual results in CT; all testing artifacts create acceptance, and only code meeting progression standards advances to the next stage.

The end goal is to be able to test, test and test again with only minimal intervention. Early testing allows for fixing problems early and ensuring those errors do not replicate. You must be careful to remember how Conway's Law impacts the testing cycle. Conway's Law states that organizational system design tends to mirror communication structures. Organizations reflecting highly hierarchical communications and manual decisions have difficulty implementing continuous testing.

Accurate testing requires implementing different tests at many levels. Development testing focuses on guaranteeing code quality by catching issues early through unit testing, code linting, static analysis and code reviews. Linting is automated testing evaluating source code for programmatic and stylistic errors. The term originates from people carding sheep wool who removed undesirable fluff and foreign matter from the wool delivered to production. Integration testing moves to the next step in validating service through data-driven testing with mocks and stubs, E2E practices, establishing regression and applying performance standards like speed, data usage and load balancing.

These practices then deliver results to delivery testing as the final gate before production. Delivery uses functional evaluations, dynamic security standards, and may introduce red/blue teaming to verify success at different levels. Remember, static security tests for existing bugs while dynamic processes use various, sometimes random, inputs to eliminate potential gaps. The final stage is deployment testing to evaluate how well the code or application performs in production. This stage is frequently not even referred to as testing but simply as an organization's operational processes. This stage introduces Runtime Application Self-Protection (RASP) to provide individualized security to verify that all calls between the application and the system meet security standards. This level also reviews all generated system metrics, traces and logs and applies reversion tests. Reversion tests ensure new builds can revert to previous versions without impacting user success.

Each application in CT supports continuous monitoring (CM). As we discussed in Chapter 5 on observability, monitoring means enabling those results to appear when collected. CT and monitoring exist within a tight coupling. When one implements monitoring, it supports the overall test process and vice versa. Without testing, monitoring does not exist. At the same time, one should establish tests that verify later applications support monitoring. For example, while logs may be accessible through the code, one must ensure those logs remain accessible when the code reaches larger systems. We evaluate improvement thought patterns in the next section.

Testing for improvement

The purpose of testing is to allow overall improvement. In addition to correcting errors early, systems with fewer bugs provide more quality and customer value. Our CT process should cover functional and non-functional applications to verify that relevant tests occur as early as possible in the pipeline. As an optimizing solution, parameters should automatically select tests, and the test results should be critical to the next stage promotion. As mentioned earlier, pipelines advance by successfully promoting artifacts and testing then ensuring the artifacts selected are correct.

Despite having automated pipelines, one should not expect that every test automatically succeeds. Creating for continuous success means the testing parameters are not specific enough to verify errors. A common metric can be evaluating test coverage. For example, a team may require that 80 per cent of code verifies through automated testing. This metric sounds useful but leaves 20 per cent of the code unprotected and untested. You can easily see where evaluating simpler coding bits would generate 80 per cent coverage while more complex functions are ignored.

Maturity is not preferred as a standard, but one can quickly see how testing occurs through maturity levels. At the chaos level, no structured process exists, and all testing is ad hoc. Defined processes have plans for most tests regarding functional software but skip non-functional tests and largely ignore training processes. These latter items occur at the repeatable level and also include peer reviews of the testing process. An organization with a managed test maturity not only conducts tests but measures how practical those tests are through E2E quality evaluations. They can suggest the test results should appear and whether those tests were effective. The end goal is to become optimized where tests provide defect prevention and long-term product quality control with no failed tests reaching production. Some preventative measures are possible before writing code, such as with chaos engineering.

Chaos engineering

Chaos engineering is a relatively new field that offers a unique approach to the testing process. The goal is to identify problems before they become problems, allowing iterative fixes and continuous development. The purpose is to use the process of testing a system across a distributed network to ensure that the various paths and policies can withstand unexpected disruptions.[4] This type of testing enables errors to be found early, potentially preventing malicious uses and solving problems a typical user may introduce. The basic principles and procedures run in a similar path to stress testing.

The common point at which to begin chaos engineering studies arises from theories compiled by Nassim Taleb in *The Black Swan*.[5] The Black Swan concept is that something that always happens today cannot be predicted to occur similarly in the future. An easy example is the turkey raised for a holiday; the turkey eats every day and has a wonderful life. From the turkey's viewpoint, the axe is not expected to come on that day before the holiday. In software, we want to prepare for those unexpected events. In a practical example, Japan's 2011 earthquake registered a 9.0 on the Richter scale, followed by a massive tsunami. Japan's nuclear facilities had prepared for one or the other event but not the combination.[6] Chaos engineering could have helped by looking at the effect of random events, a flood and an earthquake, on the distributed network of nuclear disaster recovery.

We then return to using chaos engineering in the software environment. Netflix receives credit for pioneering these applications when in 2010 they introduced a tool called Chaos Monkey to randomly terminate VMs and containers in the production environment. The goal was to ensure that the termination of the Amazon Elastic Compute Cloud (EC22) would not affect their users' service experience.[7] The tool expanded to an entire group of tools known as *Simian Army*, available through open source on GitHub. This developed two core principles for chaos engineers: develop systems that do not have single points of failure, and never be confident that a system does not contain a single point of failure.

Developing effective chaos engineering practices reads much like other experimentation techniques. You should first set a baseline using established metrics and observability as the normal baseline. From that baseline you generate a hypothesis to consider potential system weaknesses. The hypothesis looks for ways to stress points to identify those single failure areas. Next, one conducts experiments, considers effects and then evaluates effects. A quick checklist:

- Set the baseline
- Create the hypothesis
- Experiment to validate the hypothesis
- Evaluate results

These methods allow for finding the core areas in a distributed system. It would be best to look for things that are known and understood, things that are known but not understood, things that are known but lack observability, and things that lack observability and are not understood. Examples might be user logins from particular IPs, power services for edge devices or unexpected surges in system demands.

Building from the initial practice, one can look to computer scientist L. Peter Deutsch and his analysis of the eight fallacies of distributed computing.[8] These fallacies are:

- The network is reliable
- Latency is zero
- Bandwidth is infinite
- The network is secure
- Topology does not change
- There is only one administrator
- Transport cost is zero
- Networks are homogeneous

Each of these likely has a complete list of explorable topics. This section, like others, covers those wavetops in identifying areas for exploration. As a last step, some best practices can help avoid issues when launching a chaos test. The first practice returns to understanding usual system behaviour. Without knowing the basics, one may not know where to test. Next, you should simulate realistic scenarios. Expanding into future possibilities may yield benefits, but engineers should remain tied to reality to avoid unnecessary expenditures or fixing non-existent problems. Following those realistic scenarios, you should test using real-world conditions. Chaos engineering should occur primarily in production environments as it can be expensive to simulate large, distributed environments solely for testing. If you know a system has a hard break at a specific throughput, then testing above that throughput may not be effective.

Finally, when running chaos experiments, you should minimize the blast radius. Limit your experiments to a small area, with redundancy available, and not during peak times. While perhaps counter to the overall theory, you should remember that in injecting failures you want to minimize overlap with real errors as much as possible. Chaos engineering is not a panacea, but can help keep our DevOps confidence high as you gain additional feedback and improvements for the overall SDLC.

People, processes and technology for testing

Similar to other DevOps elements, some solutions rely on having the right people, processes and technology to support flow, feedback and improvement. These sections are critical, as every forward-looking flow depends on effective testing. People must be at the heart of an experimental culture. Then the company processes should support their testing process through effective means such as hackathons and well-regulated experimental techniques. These must then include tools allowing proper data analysis, and visualize results to make decisions from testing.

Testing people

It is possible to hire individuals solely as test engineers. These personnel require a deep knowledge of code, an infrastructure understanding and the ability to work through architectures. As with all other positions, all individuals need to root in a DevOps philosophy. Also important is the ability to provide context around testing solutions. Two central frameworks drive initial DevOps delivery: constructing a minimal viable product (MVP) and a walking skeleton. The MVP defines the absolute minimum necessary to meet user requirements, and the walking skeleton is one level below. The skeleton looks like the desired MVP but lacks detail. Testing personnel should incorporate solutions to ensure products demonstrate the right functions when fleshing in skeletons or advancing MVPs.

A tester needs to be inquisitive; they must always think not about only product function but about improving solutions. Most testers come from a self-taught background, which helps identify knowledge areas but can be challenging to integrate. In a test engineer, one looks for general programming knowledge, technical skills, testing expertise and some soft skills to integrate with the team. General programming should focus on development languages such as Java, Ruby and Go, but knowledge can rapidly transfer into different functions. Specific technical skills should address infrastructure, as communication protocols are a frequent testing problem. Some of these technical skills appear again in testing skills. Most testing skills address protocols and strategies for approaching tests. Like all DevOps, finding the right test engineers involves creating the flow, feedback about how the engineers work, and then experimenting to improve.

Testing process

The testing process should be an analytic one. Testers must have a framework so that tests exist to support other functions rather than derailing existing production. Sound tests are the framework for advancement. The basic process for a tester is:

- Define the story you want to tell
- Verify source credibility
- Automate everything
- Measure twice, cut once
- Present data in a meaningful manner, apples to apples

These steps should look very similar in process to constructing metrics. At heart, tests consider a different metric solution. One should be careful that testing processes only evaluate for the desired information, as too much data can be worse than insufficient. It would be best if you built tests analytically, as there must be a clear relation between test goals and the provided data. If those connections are not apparent, the test will likely fail to provide solutions. You should also ensure the test objectives are clear and any assumptions and subordinate factors are understood. Finally, the test should be structured based on desired output rather than instinct. Simply building a test to verify that something works is not sufficient.

Some process approach highlights appeared earlier in the continuous testing section, building good test cases and integrating chaos engineering. Effective processing removes blockers that prevent pipeline advancement and ensures only quality code reaches production. These blockers may be in the code, a quality assurance (QA) group that assumes responsibility for manually signing code, or simply a lack of test process understanding. Every DevOps practitioner assumes some responsibility that testing processes are in place, but establishing a testing expert, testing group or community enforcing testing practices helps supplement those initial approaches.

Again, some of the best practices appeared earlier. The best DevOps process seeks to automate as many tests as possible and then conduct paired programming or manual review if automation fails. These techniques support test-driven development (TDD). The TDD approach states that no story or task appears without first developing a verification test. Looking at the parking application, if the task integrates a user to an account, the test verifies an account exists, can be linked to payment, and then attaches to parking spaces. Each may have separate tests as tasks decompose into more minor elements, but understanding the need for tests accelerates development. Further support includes implementing the right testing technology.

Testing technology

Preferred testing tools should be designed to improve delivered code quality through managing testing processes. The best tools help automate and streamline the testing process to identify issues and, when identified, fix those issues early. As with every other DevOps aspect, specific tools change frequently and you should always pick the best option for your organization. One of my favourites, covered earlier, is Robot Framework. Other common options include Mocha, Parasoft and Selenium.

Mocha offers a feature-rich JavaScript test framework designed to run through Node.js or in the browser. As GitHub sponsors the system, it can be either open-source or a purchased upgrade. The tests run serially, so one at a time, which creates a flexible reporting structure. This structure catches exceptions to any designed test case. The system offers full online documentation to work through various testing issues.

Parasoft is a more complete tool but one you need to purchase. The tool offers different subsets for working with Selenium, testing APIs, or languages like C++ and Java. Testing programs such as C++ hold external certifications from security organizations to verify authentications. Each program for Parasoft can be purchased individually or as a larger set.

The last-referenced tool is Selenium, a well-known testing framework. This also supports the previous purchasable tool in Parasoft. Selenium, again, is an open-source, automated tool that can work with web applications across many browsers. However, this tool can only work through web applications so items like desktop and mobile applications are untestable. Selenium generally provides a combination of smaller tools such as a Selenium IDE, WebDriver, RC and Grid. Each of these focuses on a different aspect of testing.

With those three tools in mind, I would encourage you to research testing options for your DevOps environment. If you keep the general structures and guidelines throughout this chapter in place, finding the right tool can be easy. Knowing that each organization finds its own path makes me hesitant to recommend any tool, but the three above and the Robot Framework options can get you started.

Summary

This chapter covered the long road from testing basics to the specific applications that can drive success. Testing basics included how to design test cases for any problem that might be faced by a DevOps culture. One should remember that testing is not just for technical solutions but can assist with personal decisions. Some of these factors become more apparent as one implements continuous testing solutions for DevOps.

We then continued our exploration through testing processes for improvement. One interesting example in this area was using chaos engineering to build sound development and effective operational environments. Finally, we discussed finding the right people, processes and technologies to support solutions. The next chapter wraps up all the technical solutions we have discussed across various chapters and begins to explore the tools for the right DevOps mindsets within your organization.

Notes

1 Test, https://www.merriam-webster.com/dictionary/test (archived at https://perma.cc/2JDA-T648)

2 SQL Injection, https://www.imperva.com/learn/application-security/sql-injection-sqli/ (archived at https://perma.cc/MMW4-QECF)

3 Gillis, A (2023) Smoke Testing, https://www.techtarget.com/searchsoftwarequality/definition/smoke-testing (archived at https://perma.cc/26AU-B6C4)

4 Lutkevich, B and Gillis, A (2023) Chaos engineering, TechTarget, https://www.techtarget.com/searchitoperations/definition/chaos-engineering (archived at https://perma.cc/4L6Z-5HFT)

5 Taleb, N (2008) *The Black Swan*, Penguin Books

6 Acton, J and Hibbs, M (2021) Why Fukushima was preventable, Carnegie Endowment for International Peace, https://carnegieendowment.org/2012/03/06/why-fukushima-was-preventable-pub-47361 (archived at https://perma.cc/E6X2-98KR)

7 D'Antoni, J (2022) What is Chaos Engineering? A guide on its history, key principles, and benefits, Orangematter, https://orangematter.solarwinds.com/2022/08/18/what-is-chaos-engineering/ (archived at https://perma.cc/F8SG-H8J5)

8 Simple Oriented Architecture (2018) Understanding the 8 fallacies of distributed systems, https://www.simpleorientedarchitecture.com/8-fallacies-of-distributed-systems/ (archived at https://perma.cc/L7ET-NZC6)

PART THREE

The DevOps mindset

CHAPTER EIGHT

The DevOps mindset

Until now we have emphasized the importance of understanding DevOps and integrating technical tools into those solutions. But DevOps cannot be just a technical solution; it must incorporate cultural change. Integrating innovative technical solutions with cultural implementation takes a unique mindset. Understanding that mindset can help you make effective and confident decisions on where and when to implement. This understanding starts with being a broad-minded, philosophical manager. The decisions made by DevOps are not just technical engineering solutions but also require the consideration of human factors. Human decisions require human interaction, so understanding those drives and motivations helps us accelerate DevOps delivery. Some key chapter topics are:

- Understanding interaction with individuals and teams
- Overcoming bias
- Preparing the culture

After establishing the culture, building communication paths and planning the future, one of the next important steps is understanding bias. When I discuss bias, this means cognitive bias, those decisions people make based on factors unknown to their conscious mind. This chapter will examine those biases and provide steps to prevent them from infecting your decision-making processes. The last element will discuss evaluating and building cultural relevance. Feedback does not stop with the product delivery; one must prepare to constantly evaluate whether your team continues to be successful and relevant from numerous perspectives.

Understanding interaction with individuals and teams

One of my favoUrite pastimes is thinking about thinking. I enjoy evaluating workflow processes, understanding how you reach conclusions and helping others to reach confident conclusions. There are four main areas where I spend the majority of my thinking time: phenomenology, social exchange, socialist expressions and conversational topics. Phenomenology begins with a school of philosophical thought based on things themselves. Phenomenological methodology evaluates everyone's experience based on individual perception, but our DevOps integration requires a consensus view incorporating those elements into a team connection. Further, consensus requires understanding social exchange and how you exchange and prioritize work elements, especially when the work is a non-material product such as functional or compliant code or story points within a sprint.

Phenomenology in DevOps thinking

Despite being difficult to pronounce, phenomenology is a compelling philosophical approach. Phenomenology studies the structure of the conscious mind as experienced from the individual perspective. Every thought and every action drives your objective perception by understanding the content and meaning associated with the perceived object.[1] Many philosophical thinkers, including Husserl, Heidegger, Merleau-Ponty, van Manen, Sartre and others, explored phenomenology, but my preference for DevOps is the theories rooted in Heidegger. Heidegger bases his experiential understanding on the world; all experience must occur only by what already exists. He grounds those experiences within the time they must occur, an instrumental concept from the DevOps cultural standpoint. Equally important are the insights Heidegger provides into technological experiences.

Every conceptual action results in an effect and creates a target, a starting point and a path. This phenomenological look amplifies our ability to find blockers within a DevOps culture. When we take the initial idea as a coding platform for DevOps, we create the target to deliver production code that meets acceptance criteria, hence creating customer value. The analysis creates a starting point where we are today with our teams, and the path describes the sprint cycle and work needed to reach the target. The difference in this approach should be recognizing these points. Recognizing those points allows one to manage exchange between items to quickly deliver the most effective tools and creating those paths demonstrates the philosophy behind DevOps outcomes

Heidegger and van Manen studied the lived experience of human cultural activity with a cyclical method to interpret expressed meaning.[2] This qualitative method emerged from Edmund Husserl's transcendental studies in the early 1900s, with Heidegger expanding to a cyclical approach several decades later. In the early 2000s, van Manen applied thematic analysis to transform lived expression through textually articulating meaning, similar to how one converts DevOps use-cases into a call to action.[3] As we saw in the early XP guidelines, one of the keys to effective DevOps was creating the metaphor or analogy, allowing a common experience framework.

These phenomenological structures also apply to management theories. The German sociologist Max Weber favoured a hierarchical structure, the antithesis of what we seek for our DevOps workplace. William Shutz's seminal work took Weber's ideal workplace and examined the action-model relationship between researcher and subject. Schutz believed the key to effective management was not the static structure but the interpersonal relationships within the environment.[4] Linking productivity to interaction depends on strong, cultural understandings. Experiencing interaction supports the cyclical qualitative approach articulated by Heidegger and expands those thoughts into an organization. Thinking about progressive discovery during DevOps helps build a shared cultural understanding around valuation by how individuals experience the process.

In analysing your team cultures, you must understand the lived experience of those supporting the software development lifecycle. The experience qualitatively compares how inner-world perceptions affect outer-world applications, whether choosing a particular application aspect deters from others or was chosen based on the team's nature. Schutz referred to these interactions as the meaning relationships associated with the action model. He stated that the observer follows a three-step model to drive understanding: assess the general memories of the life-world actions, explore specific memories tied to an individual, and create the observer's inferred assessment. Studying these relationships occurs through the observer's approach based on the directness and intimacy of the interview.

While Schutz used interviews, this same model can be interpreted across DevOps cultural artifacts like pull requests, retrospectives and other feedback tools. DevOps as a culture favours personal interaction. Schutz provides a guideline between the direct technical standards associated with software and the intimate connection between the involved humans.

DevOps prefers technical solutions and automated interaction, but intermingling can happen as humans develop those solutions. One common practice in sensing tools is asking users for surveys and gathering developer inputs routinely. This step should match with regular, personal, individual interactions.

Process evaluation links understanding to individual perception. Perception changes cause social interaction changes based on accepting normalcy within cultural practices.[5] The DevOps method regularly assigns value throughout the development cycle but does not consider how these values are determined or chosen.[6] Van Manen found that qualitatively examining experience through a cyclical method guards against the cliché of conceptual and predetermined experiences by allowing the researcher to explore the lived experience's essence.[7] Guarding against the cliché ensures we are not taking actions simply because others have but are building a rationale through individualized experiences. This process shows where technology interprets by changing relationships from an experienced-through event to one experienced-with due to external influences. Some other philosophical approaches hold technology as a quasi-other affecting conversation, including online interaction. Still, the explored DevOps relationship builds a technology through human interactions as framed by Schutz. Heidegger helps us further characterize concepts associated with technology and interaction.

Heidegger used *enframing* to describe human-used technological processes that are not technological in origin.[8] Enframing describes gathering events within a human context to create an ordered structure. The simplest explanation appears as coding; coding provides a language interpretation, an abstraction, where humans can order technological action. Clarifying work associated with technology neither appears as a human activity nor does it create a single path. Combining the two means the path influences the internal experience at the start and delivery at the finish. Analysing these interpretations creates an opportunity to assess participants' lived experiences. Enframing then develops the metaphysical characterization of how technology appears as work and experience based on individual actions. The DevOps professionals in the value cycle create technology, use technology and have their succeeding actions ordered by their work experience.

Heidegger also clarified the ability to define work by the participants' experience with internal viewpoints and the external world. Heidegger identified work as unique characteristics: a bearer of traits, a unity of manifold sensations and formed matter.[9] From the DevOps perspective, cultures bear certain traits expressed ephemerally as code, becoming a formed product. Analysing those traits appears similar to the start, path and end for a broader phenomenological perspective. Each of these matters to the team and to the overall perspective. Framing the different elements allows for identifying blockers in code and in human interaction.

A qualitative understanding of cultural interaction drives building technology to support further feedback and improvement. We can model the exchange of different coding features as an element of community responsibility rather than strict use-cases to ensure the delivery creates economic gains. Understanding the cyclical cultural model leads to knowing what each individual or team experiences and provides an instructional process. These processes lead to continually emerging growth based on the feedback and improvement associated with each new event, whether human or technological. Isolating these elements leads to the next cultural consideration: social exchange.

Social exchange

The social exchange theory states that all exchanges between people realize some element of social interaction. The theory determines if an exchange will occur when profit, defined as reward minus cost, reaches a sufficient level for the involved groups to perceive a beneficial exchange. In essence it states that 'social behaviour is an exchange of goods, material goods but non-material goods'.[10] The theory originated from Homans' 1951 work *The Human Group*, exploring the behavioural decision theory with activities, interactions and means defining the group. Activities are those repeated actions taken, the DevOps culture elements including sprints, retrospectives and open exchange. Interactions are the defined elements between teams in large structures or between individuals on the team. The means are the communication media, often the git repository, the coding environments or the customer interaction.

Social exchange follows the constructivist worldview to address individual interactions and interpret the meaning others express about the world. Applying social exchange theory to your teams helps enframe the lived experience of DevOps practitioners by establishing exchange requirements within each experiential cycle. We will cover some of these required elements in the final section of this chapter.

Exchange mechanisms appeared in Homans' work as the initial conceptual understanding of social exchanges. Later research explained how exchanges between clear-cut economic functions and social responsibilities appear in corporations. This laid the foundation that culture has more impact than code, although all code has a social impact in changing those who interact with it. For example, developing and implementing sound security practices can be considered technical solutions or societal responsibility. Connecting social responsibility to coding builds a broader tie to the individuals on the team, increasing their satisfaction with software development. DevOps studies continue to stress that happy developers are effective developers. This interaction allows you to understand why value changes are made rather than simply stating baseline requirements. From analysing other SDLC methods, we understand that breaking requirements and planning from delivery can delay or disrupt effective practice.

Social capital is the critical exchange element through organizational structures.[11] Homans demonstrated mathematically that social capital could be measured to show exchanges between different areas. The concept supports this research when concluding that individuals can make quantified decisions based on qualified experiences. With the growth of software factories as a model for DevOps delivery, we can recognize the equivalence of software development and traditional labour. There is an association between DevOps through just-in-time delivery methods and capital accumulation within the company, delivering effective products quickly.[12]

While some may tie these conclusions to a broader corporate revenue stream, the decentralization of DevOps, with many teams working on items in parallel, means that a minor decision in one team can impact overall revenue. The DevOps change disseminates value decisions to a lower level and emphasizes tight ties to development teams. This dissemination, and the corresponding technology based on version and source control, makes it possible to identify social exchange mechanisms down to the individual developer or operator.

Connecting the GQI study through evaluated cyclical experience to social exchange allows for discovering how groups determine acceptable behaviour and the medium of exchange. Van Manen offered a qualitative perspective, stating that we must turn to experience as the lived-through events to guard against the cliché, conceptual and predetermined to study not the overall meaning but the moment the individual reaches their intuitive grasp.[13] Adopting this perspective means the focus for discovering value exchange processes will move from the terminology to the underlying experience as each individual proposes value to their delivery. Current work studying the human experience in DevOps is lacking, with no articles logged in ProQuest over the past five years.

In three case studies, research demonstrated social exchange, showing that values begin as economic comparisons and expand to social consideration.[14] These cases exhibited four themes: computer ethics, social information, cooperative work and participatory design. Estimating comparative value between coding elements like security and functions associates with the participatory design and cooperative work for those same elements. Simultaneously, these elements require social information to gain user agreement and demonstrate an ethical approach towards secure software. If we return to the parking structure, we must ethically sell items, gather social information within the application bounds, work cooperatively between multiple venues and encourage participatory design. A good parking application not only changes the parking environment, it can also contribute to the local corporate economy and yield long-term impacts. When code designs are poor, the negative outcomes then prove detrimental to the overall economy. Understanding how we exchange different priorities for which garages integrate when, and how you protect user information, becomes critical to our overall DevOps culture.

Social exchange rules in industrial organizations start with the core contract being centred around high trust, beginning as an economic exchange between parties.[15] We want DevOps to be more than simply buying an application, but a continuous culture embedded within the larger organization. Social exchange practices affect leader-member relationships, organizational support and organizational politics. Each of those elements exchanges with the others regularly but most organizations fail to recognize that an exchange is occurring. Especially relevant is the research finding that leader-member relationship exchanges are less stratified in modern companies than in traditional, hierarchical organizations. This lack of stratification, especially in technology industries, suggests the appropriate framework for open communication facilitated by DevOps cultures.

Quantitative knowledge-sharing assessments show how this process increased productivity.[16] Our DevOps feedback process of knowledge sharing was demonstrated from a social exchange perspective to survey established norms and workplace usage. Contrary to what was expected, the study found unexpected results demonstrating that the increased sharing of specialized knowledge improved productivity more than withholding information. This supports social exchange in the DevOps culture as the groups' activities, interactions and means accentuate sharing information. Value exchange between workplace units, whether individuals or teams, can improve product delivery. Understanding the culture and motivations is the first step; the next must be identifying those internal thought processes that can prevent success.

Overcoming bias

In examining bias, it helps to have a good explanation, as we often use the term to cover a wide variety of options. Merriam-Webster defines bias as 'an inclination of temperament or outlook, especially a personal and sometimes unreasoned judgment'.[17] This links to the previous phenomenological exploration, where experience drives perception and then affects results. When assembling teams, different individuals have different inherent biases; there is an organizational bias and there may even be local cultural bias. To produce the best products, it is key to identify bias and work through paths to resolve any issues. This section works through cognitive bias as a systematic thinking error occurring when you process information from the outside world. The following are the most common biases in DevOps.[18]

Confirmation bias

In DevOps, confirmation bias is a tendency to prefer a set codebase or tool. One often sees teams selecting a tool not based on external credentials but because of previous experience. I worked on a team that switched from Jenkins to Git based on a criteria model. As the teams hired more developers, the new individuals had experience with Jenkins and wanted to return to those solutions. The challenge in DevOps is to constantly use feedback to verify that beliefs are accurate rather than subjectively evaluating concerns.

Hindsight bias

Hindsight bias is very familiar to me from my intelligence background. After an event, it is always easy to align the causes looking back but not as easy when looking forward. This is a constant challenge for developers. One sees this in security where observing where an attack occurred afterwards is easy but the challenge is predicting future attacks. As mentioned with the Fukushima earthquake example, preparing for hindsight can restrict the ability to prepare for the future. Identifying hindsight bias benefits in avoiding taking unacceptable risks in planning and development.

Anchoring bias

Similar to hindsight, anchoring bias is when someone becomes overly influenced by the first piece of information received. When developing in a new cloud, environment, cluster or merely adopting a new tool, you want to be careful not to be overly influenced by the first experience of those situations. A version of anchoring was mentioned above where developers preferred Jenkins over Git based on their first experience with the tool rather than a structured evaluation. Anchoring is a critical mover in brand loyalty discussions from a marketing perspective and can be manipulated in DevOps by creating first-movement opportunities. The DevOps goal to deliver quickly aims to reaffirm anchoring by suggesting the first choice continues to be the best option.

Misinformation bias

DevOps teams use retrospectives to help combat the misinformation effect. Misinformation suggests that memory is malleable and later recollections may change the events associated with the initial experience. An example may be delivering a piece of code, proving initially difficult but with a later solution expediting the developed processes. You want the team to remember the difficulty and the time spent overall rather than the easy solution that appeared later. Accurately evaluating work on an iterative basis through retrospectives is one way DevOps resolves this bias.

Actor-observer bias

The actor-observer bias again ties in the phenomenological perspective and becomes extremely important to team functionality. This bias suggests that you often attribute personal actions to external influences and others' actions to internal influences. You might state that developing a new security model to comply with external standards was the standard for your team but that another developer's code resulted from faulty preparation. A common expression for this between teams appears in the 'Us vs. Them' model. One must be careful that adversarial relationships do not appear, and if they do, they are resolved by objective comparison rather than being biased towards their internal perspective. Another common DevOps bottleneck occurs when dev teams perceive security as trying to slow development rather than realizing security teams are also meeting external requirements.

False consensus bias

Most DevOps teams are inherently familiar with the false consensus effect as overstating how much agreement occurs. During regular meetings, teams resolve this common bias by looking for confidence votes and story-pointing. These interactions help ensure consensus actually appears rather than simply stating a consensus was reached. You do not want a technical lead to simply state the solution; instead, the solution should be discussed and evaluated from a team perspective. Building an accurate consensus avoids the false consensus bias.

Availability heuristic

The availability heuristic can be challenging for DevOps teams as it relates to the tendency to believe something will happen based on the examples already on hand. For example, if you release a security patch for software, that program may still have failing security benchmarks even if the patch was the first one released. Avoiding the availability heuristic involves using research time, sometimes known as a spike, to fully examine options. Another option creates criteria for all decisions to allow objective evaluation rather than simply the information on hand. Relying on only the information on hand can result in poor decisions and magnify risk since full evaluations have not happened. Risk evaluations use probability and impact to consider all items from multiple perspectives.

Optimism bias

This is the penchant for overestimating that good things will happen instead of negative ones. The optimism bias can be especially prevalent in DevOps as you always believe the code will work and run smoothly. While we want to be confident in our code, just as with the availability heuristic, realistic risk planning and management are required to mitigate bias. Understanding the risks that can happen when deploying software helps one understand where optimism is warranted and where more extensive mitigation should happen.

In every element of cognitive bias, the answer is to think objectively about the factors involved. Taking time for research, building up decision criteria and evaluating risks allow for sound decision making. Bias cannot be eliminated but effective planning can help mitigate those risks. DevOps' constant flow and feedback should provide steady information to make decisions. You should recognize where bias occurs and work consistently to identify and then minimize the impact of that bias on overall delivery. Not all bias is bad, and sometimes bias leads to better choices, but the overall emphasis should be on recognizing which biases appear and where.

Preparing the culture

Understanding team interactions and the bias represented in those interactions brings us to the next step in effectively preparing the culture. This section examines how to evaluate the culture within your teams. As with every other DevOps section, you must create steps to verify what teams are doing, and whether those decisions align with the overall cultural model.

Maturity levels

One area I have intentionally skipped until now is the maturity level concept. Personally, I am not in favour of maturity levels as too many organizations use them in the same way as poor metrics; they can become targets rather than progress measurements. Sorting maturity as targets separates good team goals from what the organization wants to advertise in the next conference or slick sheet. At the same time, there is a place for maturity and including these aspects within any effective self-assessment creates feedback for continuous improvement as a DevOps target.

When required to perform a maturity assessment, I typically use five levels to create an assessment: Chaos, Repeatable, Defined, Managed and Optimized. Each level incorporates multiple aspects and allows for customization and experimentation. You should assign levels to the process desired within the organization. Evaluation can be at a high level of DevOps maturity or you can approach smaller areas such as testing, observability or security. Understanding each level allows you to define the specific aspects. Items might include multiple sub-items to measure:

- Testing – automation, coverage, test design, inputs, pipeline inclusion.
- Observability – points of observability, access, sharing, automation, integration to alerting and improvements, data collection, dashboards.
- Security – security scanning, remediation, proactive alerting, pipeline integration, security policy.
- Architecture – enterprise or API options, defined governance, metrics established, stakeholder perception, change management.
- Infrastructure – compute limits and automation, storage virtualization, orchestration. Application delivery, load balancing.

Chaos describes where tasks are accomplished, but no one can describe a consistent process or application. At the repeatable level, the teams begin being able to do things in parallel but the emphasis becomes doing a thing again rather than understanding why a thing occurs. However, repeatability becomes the first step towards creating a mature culture. These first two steps begin to recognize the required actions but they appear as distinct sticky notes on the whiteboard rather than establishing any flow between different items.

Defined begins what one can first think of as maturity. In a defined stage, one establishes clear processes with metrics and explanations. Even though Agile prefers functional software over comprehensive planning, a framework for planning can drive flow and feedback. Establishing some known principles provides the platform to grow. In the visual model, defining areas allows for stability, securability, scalability and adaptability across phases for design, support, develop, deploy and operate. Defining processes and building the common understanding between teams and management allows you to realistically assess progress as reaching the managed level. Defined maturity organizations demonstrate automated builds, cross-functional teams and product-focused objectives while remaining open to cultural change.

Managed maturity means that processes exist and are established, observed and integrated in the sense that variations result in action. Examples of solid management include automated dashboards, retrospective practices and clear, observed flows. Organizations at the managed level tend to demonstrate happy individuals who use integrated toolchains to prevent failure. Test and deployment stages are automated and continuous delivery happens.

Once a process or an organization reaches the managed level, the only further step would be optimized. High-functioning cultures typically alternate between defined and optimized regularly. These changes are not bad but occur because, much like all other items of observability, assessments are made at a point in time. Optimized cultures appear as DevOps- Done during work tracking discussions. All necessary changes are in place, automation becomes a first step and employees get work done. Optimized delivery reflects continuous integration/continuous delivery. Suggestions and improvements become the basis for experimentation, and those results support any future process.

Organizations fluctuate between the defined, managed and optimized levels as newly incorporated processes and decisions can revert to early stages. When optimized observability demonstrates the need for changes, those changes must first be defined within the process, managed as you become familiar and then optimized. That optimization results in generating further data for experimentation. The variability between these levels is why I refrain from using maturity to measure success. That said, you should know how others use maturity levels to assess software development. Success should directly relate to delivering value quickly; stopping to consider maturity rather than operational success can lead you down the wrong path.

Team maturity

With the previous terms solidly in mind, it can be effective to give a synopsis of how those maturity levels occur within a team setting. First, you should consider how you obtain information. In Chapter 5 we discussed establishing various metrics; those metrics will be the core guidance for assessing team maturity. The DORA metrics often appear in measuring mature teams but deal primarily with production aspects. Instead, the emphasis should be on ensuring that cultural practices associated with teams support our strategic goals.

It would be best if no one ever worked on a chaotic team, but I am sure we have all been part of those environments. Chaotic teams lunge wildly from project to project, limited prioritizations exist and the general feeling is dissatisfaction. One of the simplest ways to judge this process level is to ask what a developer is doing and why they are doing it. An inability to answer those questions means there is no process guiding cultural decisions. One sees dissatisfied workers in these environments and may even see duplicated work. The lack of a common standard creates an inability to focus on clear goals. Teams at the chaotic level have not even begun to consider the basic DevOps principles of flow, feedback and improvement.

The first step to move out of the chaos level is to make work repeatable, which often happens through observability. Implementing work boards such as Scrum or Kanban, moving to sequenced pipelines and using automated tools such as GitLab, Jenkins, ArgoCD, Flux and others helps one visualize how work progresses and at what point efforts are currently. The biggest gap in a repeatable maturity environment appears in the lack of accurate feedback. Teams will repeat efforts because they know how to repeat them rather than choosing the best solution. Many operations teams can be stuck in the repeatable maturity level as they follow checklists and conduct routine activities but never generate feedback to reduce or automate repetitive work. One DevOps maxim is that anything that must be done twice should be automated; leaving these items in a manual approach removes one of the biggest strengths of the DevOps culture.

Moving from repeatability to a defined maturity involves knowing why processes occur. This movement relates to the longer nature of integrating features with individual coding samples and linking those features back to overall profitability. A defined element states what is happening, how it happens, where it fits in the process and when completion may occur. This emphasizes more than a repeatable step but the ability to lift and shift different processes into different places. Teams with defined characteristics can be exchanged with other teams and explain their processes to others. From the Agile perspective, defined teams deliver functional software and provide the documentation to allow others to benefit from their work. This repeatable and defined expression then allows for management to succeed.

The managed maturity level appears in teams that are integrated and successful. Managed teams have internalized the flow, feedback and improvement associated with DevOps. Those organizations understand their internal process and how they fit with other organizational pieces. Higher levels can assign functional tasks rather than having to establish specific requirements. These teams manage based on consistent, quality delivery rather than limiting to specialized items. The DevOps essence establishes continuous delivery of new products, changing versions and meeting adaptable demands. Managed companies constantly look for ways to benefit from feedback to improve flow and conduct experimentation cycles.

An optimized maturity level incorporates everything from the managed level and becomes more so. Optimization means not only are processes managed to create feedback but the feedback process is managed to produce the best, most actionable feedback regularly. These organizations are truly the opposite of chaos in simply allowing work to happen and managing all work through the continuous injection of order at every part of the production cycle. Contrary to chaos, not all optimized cycles are apparent to outsiders; often, optimization makes the work appear easy even when the constant struggle to maintain feedback can be challenging. The best-optimized cultures are the ducks on the water; all appears calm on the surface, but they are working hard underneath to remain afloat. Optimized cultures accept that maintaining those standards requires constant effort; the work of DevOps never stops but remains a continuous journey. At the same time, these cultures are confident in their ability to deliver work successfully.

Summary

This chapter took us from the high-level discussion of team interaction through phenomenology and social exchange to how those thoughts appear within the workplace. Phenomenology relates the social structure behind experience in terms of where and when individuals make decisions. Social exchange theory then built a framework for exchanging individual decisions with others to create a more valuable product. These interactive basics then allowed for a discussion about how bias affects decisions, where bias occurs in DevOps and how to mitigate those biases. Mitigation and risk management lead to characterizing cultural environments, aligning metrics and recognizing when a DevOps culture is mature. Each of these elements is critical in understanding a DevOps mindset, and the next chapter will examine some practical examples in establishing a DevOps workplace.

Notes

1   Smith, D W (2018) Phenomenology, *The Stanford Encyclopedia of Philosophy* (Summer 2018 Edition), Edward N Zalta (ed.), https://plato.stanford.edu/entries/phenomenology/ (archived at https://perma.cc/Z427-DY58)

2   Laverty, S M (2003) Hermeneutic phenomenology and phenomenology: A comparison of historical and methodological considerations, *International Journal of Qualitative Methods*, **2** (3), 21–35

3   Gill, M J (2014) The possibilities of phenomenology for organizational research, *Organizational Research Methods*, 118–137, doi: https://doi.org/10.1166/1094429113519348

4   Schutz, A (1980) *The Phenomenology of the Social World* (4th ed.) (G Walsh and F. Lehnert, trans.), Northwestern University Press

5   Zahavi, D (2019) *Phenomenology: The basics*, Routledge

6   Kim, G, Humble, J, Patrick, D and Willis, J (2016) *The DevOps Handbook*, IT Revolution

7   van Manen, M (2017) Phenomenology in its original sense, *Qualitative Health Research*, **27** (6), 810–25 doi: https://doi.org/10.1177/1049732317699381 (archived at https://perma.cc/ZA62-6ABP)

8   Heidegger, M (2013) *The Question Concerning Technology* (W Lovitt, trans.), Harper Perennial

9   Heidegger, M (1988) *The Basic Problems of Phenomenology* (A Hofstadter, trans.), Indiana University Press

10 Homans, G C (1951) *The Human Group*, Routledge

11 Durlauf, S N (2002) On the empirics of social capital, *Economic Journal*, 459–79 doi: https://doi.org/10.1111/1468-0297.00079 (archived at https://perma.cc/H8PP-CSQA)

12 Dyer-Witheford, N (2015) *Cyber-Proletariat: Global labour in the digital vortex*, Toronto, Pluto Press

13 van Manen, M (2017) Phenomenology in its original sense, *Qualitative Health Research*, **27** (6), 810–25, https://doi.org/10.1177/1049732317699381 (archived at https://perma.cc/ZA62-6ABP)

14 Friedman, B, Kahn, P H and Borning, A (2008) Value sensitive design and information systems in P Zhang and D Galetta, *Human-Computer Interaction in Management Information Systems Foundations*, M.E. Sharpte, pp. 348–72

15   Frieder, R E (2018) The rules of social exchange: Unchanged but more important than ever, *Industrial and Organizational Psychology*, **11** (3), 535–41, doi: 10.1017/iop.2018.108 (archived at https://perma.cc/4EPR-6CKQ)

16   Rudramuniyaiah, P, Joshi, K, Shah, V and Ramanujan, S (2020) Examining cognitive and emotive influences on knowledge sharing behavior among IT professionals: an empirical analysis, *E-Service Journal*, **11** (3), 1–35, 90–91, doi:10.2979/eservice.11.3.01

17   Bias, https://www.merriam-webster.com/dictionary/bias (archived at https://perma.cc/R38L-2PPX)

18   Cherry, K (2022) 13 types of common cognitive biases that might be impairing your judgment, Verywellmind.com (archived at https://perma.cc/58MF-3BCA), https://www.verywellmind.com/cognitive-biases-distort-thinking-2794763 (archived at https://perma.cc/FC8U-PQVX)

CHAPTER NINE

DevOps practices

We have made it here through the technical and theoretical, completing a significant step in your journey to become a confident DevOps practitioner. At this point, you should be thoroughly grounded in the basic DevOps philosophy, understand many technical terms and be able to compare DevOps benefits to other SDLCs or possible outcomes quickly. The next step moves from your theoretical understanding to the practical application of building a DevOps culture for a business or team. These areas include:

- Team working agreements
- Conversational practices
- Architectural patterns
- Picking the right technology
- Maximizing dashboard usage

Each area can help teams grow only if they adhere to good flow, feedback and improvement practices. The foundational step relies on selecting the right people and supplying a healthy cultural framework. People use processes to invest and develop technologies that amplify DevOps confidently. Finally, we remember that DevOps is a cultural solution to a technological problem and that each element shapes outcomes from a different perspective.

Finding, hiring and training people

The DevOps process at heart begins with people. High marketplace competition across the software industry means emphasizing hiring and retaining the right people. The most essential DevOps skills are emotional intelligence skills, while the Third Way builds technical prowess. The DevOps practitioners who should be hired are those who are eager, innovative and communicative while technically capable of coding, managing infrastructure, working within an architecture and dedicated to security. Companies need different codebases, so sometimes selecting a particular technology can be beneficial. However, selecting technology skills over communication or eagerness will likely prove culturally detrimental in the long term. Many companies search for DevOps or IT positions using examples like the compiled statements below:

- As a junior DevOps engineer, be responsible for assisting in all aspects of deploying, documenting, monitoring and maintaining the infrastructure and delivery pipeline critical to business success.
- As a senior DevOps engineer, you will be responsible for design, implementation, configuration, optimization, management and documentation.
- As a DevSecOps engineer, be passionate about building world-class security frameworks
- As an IT operations engineer, you will be responsible for working within a team framework.

- An IT ops tech will support the installation and maintenance of employee equipment and systems.

All these positions are important individually, but the team remains the most essential DevOps element. Building a DevOps culture means using the team as the smallest unit, the one susceptible to our unit tests, and the place where most measurement and observation occurs. Gathering the best people can be effective, but not as effective as maintaining highly performing teams.

Building teams

As with metrics, teams take time to form, and the longer the team survives, the more effective practices become. Change is necessary to improve, but centring teams around core ideals helps maintain focus. Amazon promoted the idea of a two-pizza team, where team sizes are kept small enough that they are never too large to be fed with two pizzas. In practice, most teams should have 5–10 members. This practice allows interaction but prevents individuals from disappearing into the background. Teams then align to a common purpose rather than a project. DevOps teams should not be project-aligned solely to build a specific application but functionally aligned to build applications within a common framework. Doing so prevents constantly juggling teams as projects end.

Another procedural guide helps drive successful team formations. This guide uses a scrum master or team leader to keep teams on track. Some organizations assign these roles as additional tasks, but good scrum masters accelerate team flow. The scrum master possesses comb-shaped knowledge, a broad base with multiple narrow skills. These individuals ensure use-cases are captured, acceptance criteria defined and work aligned with team working agreements. The product owner on the team possesses E-shaped knowledge, a broad depth and specific knowledge on two or three subjects. Coders should be T-shaped, with a breadth of coding knowledge but specific knowledge about one area or application. You can supplement teams with champions or representatives for security, platforms and architecture. A champion is a team member with specific responsibilities, while a representative is more narrowly focused and available on demand.

The best DevOps book I have read on team structures is *Team Topologies* by Matthew Skelton and Manuel Pais.[1] The authors break out the essence of working in DevOps teams and structure much better than I could within this chapter. Teams are broken into four essential types:

- Complicated sub-system teams – handle unique and specialized work.
- Stream-aligned team – completes any and all of the various DevOps business tasks.
- Enabling team – manages temporary special functions such as architecture or security.
- Platform team – manages the environment on which teams operate; development for developers.

Each team has strengths and weaknesses but they emphasize flow and communication to achieve effective outcomes. The underlying perspective is that even with all DevOps teams, not all teams are equal. At the same time, managers must prepare to handle DevOps flow rather than committing to static, Waterfall deliveries. One important note is that Skelton and Pais do not include distinct operational teams, as one expects teams to either run their own products or be a distinct stream-aligned team committed to the operational experience.

Culture has been a continuing theme, and a good DevOps culture possesses four pillars: trust, respect, failure-accepting and blame-free. Trust means we expect everyone to bring their best effort including sharing all plans and data when developing features. A good analogy is that we leave the keys to the kingdom out, trusting that anyone who grabs them uses them appropriately. Respect appears in trust. Respectful interactions mean one does not stereotype others for race, religion, coding background or other factors. When we disagree, we do not just say 'no'; we identify bias and present respectful arguments. Respect also means not hiding; we admit problems and errors and seek a group consensus. These factors lead to the last two pillars.

The last two elements are failure-accepting and blame-free. DevOps depends on iterating fast, failing quickly and learning from feedback to improve. Failures encourage growth by thinking about a response to failure. Cultures with zero-risk attitudes that need perfection are unlikely to accept failure. Failure now does not mean permanent failure; every failed test or failed build creates an opportunity to refactor and improve the code overall. One common standard to address failure should be practising until it hurts, especially in dealing with operational practices such as incident management. Sometimes repetition can be stressful but practising common approaches allows for better failure recognition early and ensures all team members bring the same standards to solutions.

The last cultural pillar is blame-free. No failure or error should be associated with an individual or team for punishment. We do not want teams to point fingers but to think about who wakes up if something fails inopportunely. Code criticism is never personal; correction should be core to feedback and improvement. One of the best pieces of leadership advice I ever received was that one should not take work criticism as a personal assault. Work, code and operations are all things we do but not who we are. Representing blame-free as a core cultural pillar helps embed these philosophies within teams.

One final team element to consider must be hiring effective managers. Teams generally work and manage themselves, but generating organizational value requires perspective. Managers address multiple teams and integrate several value streams, including platforms, specialized practices and regular features. The most challenging managerial task is often accepting the lack of control within DevOps. Typical programme managers use

Gantt Charts, control diagrams and status reports to inform on progress. In the DevOps culture, observability is built in and progress is always available to all. The challenge for the manager will be integrating progress from the team to the business level through connected features, epics and portfolios.

Conversational practices

Building a team depends on progressing cultures by embedding conversational practices to emphasize trust, respect and blame-free outcomes. Conversations appear simple but depend on two practices: teamwork agreements and communication training. The first element provides progress guidelines; the second is the ability to tie work to experience. Each contributes to overall success, emphasizing flow, feedback and improvement.

Team working agreements are individual to a team. Most important to agreements is physically writing them and posting in an observable location. These agreements should include high-level goals, intermediate objectives and standard practices, and typically restate the cultural pillars and their daily expressions. An example appears below:

- Goals – deliver effective, valuable features promptly. Demonstrate respect and trust in a blame-free culture. Exemplify observability in all practices.
- Intermediate objectives – characterize work to the smallest possible increment. Help others when needed. Implement automated tests whenever possible.
- Daily – be on time and present for all meetings. Report work hours daily. Link tickets between work tracking and merge requests. All code is commented. Pair programming and code reviews are the preferred standard of working.

You can see the derivation from the top level to the daily. Each team may represent these differently. Teams often include contact numbers, working times and scheduled meetings within agreements. Another good inclusion links onboarding tasks, knowledge hubs and shared environments for users. Placing all the information into a single area creates team observability, documenting required functions and establishing common standards. The next step allows teams to communicate effectively about these steps.

Like many DevOps practices, there are many excellent books about team communications. The best book I have found is *Agile Conversations* by Douglas Squirrel and Jeffrey Frederick.[2] These authors provide a detailed understanding of the flow and blockers within DevOps communications and suggest four Rs as the essential conversation elements: record, reflect, revise and roleplay.

Two additional Rs appear as subsets of the last two: repeat and role reversal. The first element, record, should be essential for all communication growth. Conversations should be recorded in writing or in a media format for replaying when learning. Recording presents a solid basis to move discussions forward. It prevents hearsay discussion such as 'I think someone said this', or 'I thought they said that'. The familiar track allows movement to the next conversational tool: reflect.

Reflection means going back over the recording and ensuring accurate communications. We all know items in an off-hand conversation are not always clear or as intended. A good conversation example would be telling a friend you put new tyres on his car because the old ones broke. The friend might assume you purchased brand-new tyres when in fact you put used tyres on, new to the car but not new from the manufacturer. Reflection helps clarify meaning, explain acronyms and ensure all parties have the same meaning. Once reflection occurs, the conversation can be revised.

Revising a conversation means returning to the original track and clarifying confusing issues. In the previous tyre example, one could see how stating that old tyres were replaced with functional, used tyres would help clarify issues. In coding examples, participants might lose or misunderstand detailed technical explanations. Detailing meanings during revising provides a better track of how the conversation might have gone. Detailing leads to roleplay, understanding the various terms and then retrying conversations. Roleplay leads to repeating conversations and sometimes role reversal. Role reversal means retrying the conversation from an another perspective to see if one reaches the same conclusions.

These methods are not for every conversation. Using them with initial sample conversations can help improve the overall communication flow. Later, methods can help with challenging conversations. Once a team understands the communication barriers, their communication will likely improve. A sound communication basis allows for effective processes to keep DevOps flow, feedback and improvement at value-producing levels.

Establishing effective processes

Beyond hiring and maintaining the right personnel, DevOps requires understanding some core processes to deliver quickly. The process depends on two interconnected pillars: technology and people. Previous chapters have highlighted the architecture, observability, pipelines and testing baselines, but those elements can expand into additional organizational patterns. Technology leads to specific paths informing goal accomplishment. This section explains some basic architecture for technology and the Scrum and Kanban methods often used for daily DevOps work.

Architectural patterns

Generally, most architectures deliver seven to ten core designs. These designs include some combination of physical style, processing style and information interaction to derive goals. My experience categorizes architecture into three rough groups. The first group is physical, including layered, microkernal, microservices and space-based architecture. The second is an action group exhibiting service-based, event-driven or orchestration architectures. The final group is relationships with peer-to-peer or master-client architectures. Each architecture appears briefly but I encourage you to conduct additional research into areas critical to your organization.

Architectural patterns solve functional problems. In some cases, more than one architecture can solve the same problem. Elements driving one architectural decision over another relate strongly to available resources, expertise and time. Understanding different architectural approaches drives informed decisions based on feedback. Just because an architecture was selected does not mean it will always be the best. You must remember the sunk cost fallacy, which states that just because a certain expenditure level has occurred, it does not mean continuing to throw good resources after bad for minimal results; feedback is crucial to success.

The first physical architecture example is layered design. A layered design states that every element within the architecture fills a unique task, and those tasks are open and closed within an independent layer. This design prevents a layer from advancing without completing a task. This inherent separation works well for teams that either lack experience or prefer a traditional approach. Connections between layers can create tight coupling and create problems in changing events. However, one can implement this model quickly.

Moving on from layered design, one sees space-based architecture. These architecture types use multiple processing elements with a virtualized middleware. Instead of using one set of layers, this design allows each process or subset to manage individual processes before reporting back to middleware solutions. These solutions typically handle larger loads with multiple concurrent requests featuring continuous requests. The biggest problem can be that multiple inputs can sometimes conflict in the data and

FIGURE 9.1   Layered design

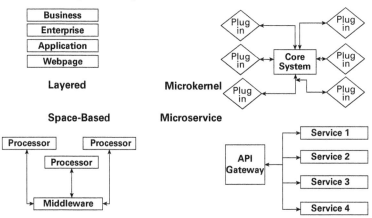

create collisions, multiple inputs with similar tags. The other challenge can be that with continuous inputs, it can be difficult to observe stable outputs without significant memory usage.

The last two physical designs are microkernel and microservices. Microkernals involve plug-ins to perform specific functions for a core system, while microservices decouple components from any core system to function as an interconnected mesh. Microkernal structures allow small changes to a centrally functioning system, such as adding new dictionary inputs or style guides to a word-processing system. Another example might be an employee management program that wants to add employee pictures to a legacy system. On the other hand, microservices create separate components for each function through remote access protocol connections.[3] Each microservice can be tested and deployed independently rather than requiring the microkernal's core system. Modern cloud-native approaches often use microservices approaches to develop quickly and distinguish tasks. The downside can be ensuring that a microservice has sufficient scope to perform the needed task but restricting that scope to only requirements without impacting the overall performance.

FIGURE 9.2   Action-based architectures

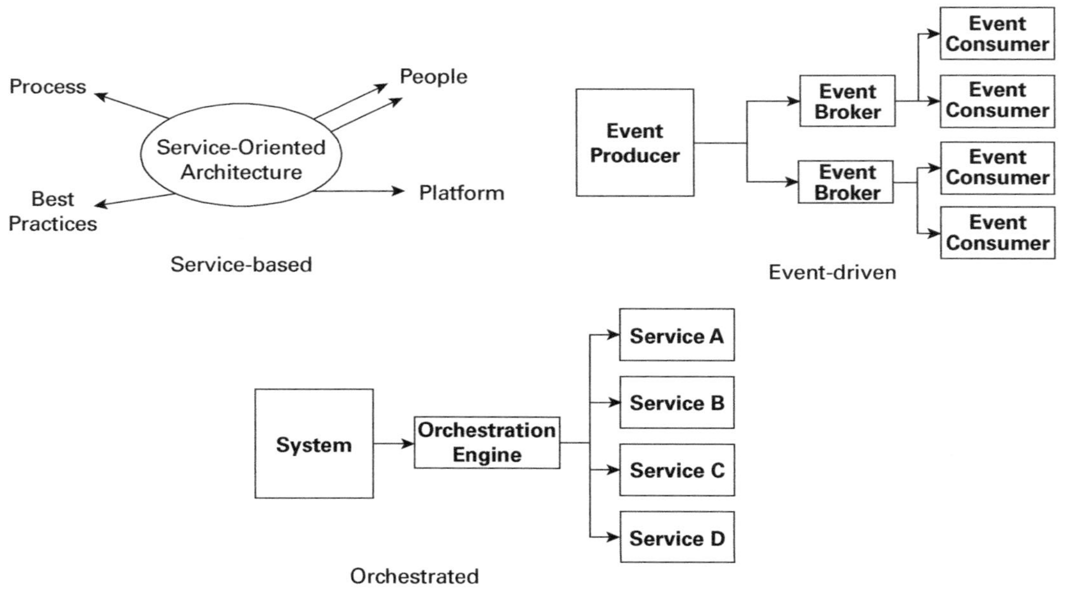

Event-driven

Event Producer → Event Broker → Event Consumer, Event Consumer
Event Producer → Event Broker → Event Consumer, Event Consumer

Service-based

People
Platform
Service-Oriented Architecture
Process
Best Practices

Orchestrated

System → Orchestration Engine → Service A, Service B, Service C, Service D

Action-based architectures can be service-based, event-driven or orchestrated. Service-based architectures are a hybrid of the microservices approach, using an API call or interface instead of distinct microservices. These features use shared databases at the domain level to allow access from multiple remote layers. Sometimes these architectures combine multiple functions across an entire architecture into common locations.[4] Extending this model leads to event-driven architectures. Each element functions from decoupled, single-purpose event-processing components that receive and process events asynchronously. Two shapes appear: broker-driven, where events are chained together independently, and the mediator that drives steps without central control. Event-driven fits well for the earlier parking example where multiple requests occur continuously with common responses.

The last action-based architecture is the orchestrated pattern. Orchestration combines the layered model with the service-driven model. An orchestrated pattern uses multiple event services, each communicating across multiple areas. These models typically start with a business pattern, move through an enterprise bus, and allocate resources, a service level and the specific services required. This design's complexity means it frequently appears within legacy systems as part of a monolithic structure. The more orchestration required, the more complex the connections and the more difficult it is to fix errors. The advantage is that layers can be reused multiple times, limiting initial cost but likely creating user errors and data collision.

Finally, architecture can feature relationship patterns such as peer-to-peer and master-client. A peer-driven architecture often occurs in file-sharing platforms like Skype, BitTorrent or Napster. In this case, each element can act as either a client or server and change its role over time by requesting service from peers or providing service to peers. These networks increase in power as more individuals join the network but lack centralized control. The shared service allows the easy transfer of large files but

FIGURE 9.3   Peer-to-peer and master-client

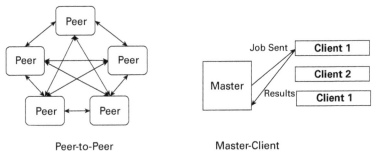

Sources: https://devblogs.microsoft.com/cppblog/vscode-embedded-development/;
https://stackoverflow.com/questions/74459113/spyder-ide-with-python-3-10-seems-freezing-when-click-run-button-but-it-works-f

makes security or any type of predictive performance virtually impossible. The master-client takes the opposite approach in that a single master controls all nodes. No task will report completed until all clients report to the master. Master-client allows for decomposing tasks but can create issues with client dependencies, failure of the master or isolated client actions. One advantage is processing data in edge locations that cannot send raw data due to size. An excellent master-client relationship could be weather services, where data compiles at the edge location and only the results return to the master.

Each of these architecture patterns demonstrates only the wavetops of the possible in designing systems. Software architects spend their whole careers designing and implementing different solutions. The advantage of quickly summarizing is observability of what method one intends to reach. An e-service site might be better suited to a microservice, a security scanning tool to a microkernal, a messaging service to an event-driven architecture and a crypto-mining concern to a peer-to-peer relationship. At the same time, a security service could use micro-services for individual tests, microkernals within components, an event-driven architecture for alerts and a master-client relationship to identify bug bounties. The most important part is realizing significant information exists on all these types and making architecture requires continuous flow. At the same time, one should also build processes supporting individuals making decisions daily.

Scrum and Kanban

The key to confident DevOps is observability. Observability features technological improvements and a clear understanding of the work to reach goals. Scrum and Kanban workboards are the two best processes for delivering effectively on work and maintaining observability. Each works slightly differently, but problems often arise when individuals adopt the visual method without understanding the underlying concepts. Scrum focuses on driving work in time-determined intervals, while the Kanban approach uses a continuous flow. Knowing the difference can help in making confident decisions and ensure valuable work is completed quickly.

Regardless of the method, the effort begins with laying out work on small tickets. Different teams use different approaches but I prefer initiatives, epics, stories, tasks and sub-tasks as my categories. All of these terms are collectively called issues. These definitions are:

- Initiative – large projects taking six or more months to complete. Managed at the business level.
- Epic – scaled to a quarterly approach, typically can take from 6–12 weeks. Managed at the team or group of teams.
- Story – issues completed within a sprint and managed by team or individual.
- Task – smaller than a story but required to move forward. Handled by individual.
- Sub-task – smaller than a task. Typically captured so vital steps are not lost.

One of the most essential aspects in categorizing work is recognizing that these are not firm boundaries. These are soft outlines intended to guide flow, not become blockers so that an event must be a story at a certain point or an epic at a certain point. Deciding which level to use comes from individual consensus within the team or team groups. Some functions may be more straightforward for one individual and be a task, while others consider the same work as a story or an epic. All items in the list should include, at a bare minimum, a use-case, acceptance criteria and a narrative description. The use-case should clearly state that if I was this person, such as a customer, I want to be able to use this app to do this thing. The acceptance criteria should establish some metric standards for validation, i.e. the app has to have a button for the thing, the thing has to work and it has to update a database. The narrative then includes further details: the database must be SQL, the app must be in Android, existing repo locations and other factors. All of these factors allow one to prioritize the issues. Items should also be related in that initiatives hold several epics, epics hold several stories and so on.

The next step aligns the work by priority. You must decide on items to work on first and whether priority appears from business needs, technological steps or other factors. Both methods align work in backlogs. A backlog is the prioritized list of items ready for work, including use-cases and criteria but not yet started. Some teams like to accomplish the shortest and easiest tasks first, while others may start with larger tasks and then build smaller pieces. Columns are used across Kanban and Scrum boards to identify the work stages as, at a minimum, to do, in progress and done. Some teams use more columns with additional categories for items like review, testing and preparation. I prefer to leave comments reflecting these states attached to the work item as visualizing work across multiple teams using different workflows can be difficult. Imagine if one team uses pair review, peer review and testing as states while another team uses testing 1, deploy 1, test 2 and team review. It can be challenging to ascertain exactly which team is making progress. Software that can simplify this process appears in versions like Trello, Jira, Asana and others.

The core for both methods is completing work by pulling items from the left side of the board (To Do) to the right (Done). The difference is that a Kanban board continuously pulls from the backlog into a To Do state, while a Scrum board defines a sprint's worth of work. A sprint normally runs from one to four weeks. A work-in-progress (WIP) limit will identify each Kanban column. The WIP identifies the maximum work present in any column. The maximum column number should not be exceeded if work slows as individuals complete assigned work as they then help the team to clear columns. The goal is to keep a continuous flow of work. Kanban methods work well for non-development teams as policy items move, or are held in review status. Team members pull work from the prioritized backlog into the To Do column as WIP room appears.

In Scrum, each item has story points highlighting the required work potential. Story points vary from team to team but my typical standard is that one story point is about four to eight hours of work, two equals one to two days, three is more than two days, five is a week and eight or higher is more than a week. Scrum teams should try to divide any story eight points or larger into smaller working increments. Teams begin the sprint by planning and pointing work before moving items into the To Do column. In a mature team, work is assigned when items reach In Progress as team members pull work from the To Do column.

Either solution provides an effective process to build confidence in accomplishment. Both methods should employ planning for the backlog and regular retrospectives to review the work accomplished. Reaching Done means functional software was created, and Done column items can be demonstrated. Nothing says confidence like displaying the proposed intellectual task as a functional accomplishment. Additionally, demonstrations provide a clear point to move on to the next task, with acceptance of value from the customer. I recommend experimenting with these methods in teams to find the best approach. Remember, just as in measuring other metrics, you should allow three to six months for teams to get comfortable with the process and build expertise before measuring pace. All these processes help but one must also understand how technology supports DevOps operations different from the tools used in software development.

Learning technological solutions

Throughout the book, we have discussed many different technological solutions for achieving results beneficial to DevOps. While tools at the root level are practical, understanding the broader tools necessary, such as IDE options, platforms and dashboards, helps make not just one team or instance better but the entire organization. DevOps tools should increase flow, feedback and improvement daily. Not all teams require the same tools, but learning the interactions between those tools can help with making good decisions about pursuing the most valuable path forward.

IDE and test

It would be awesome if we could write code in a typical Word document: 'write Hello 100 times' or 'search the database for every item that includes an "A" followed by a "B"'. Unfortunately, we format those items as abstractions since code contains computer instructions. Every type of code uses different abstraction variants. Remember, machines always talk in machine code, a binary variant of ones and zeros telling the computer, at the base level, which electronic switches to trigger for which effect. Abstraction means that writing code to see effects requires an integrated development environment (IDE) that interprets or compiles the code into effective commands.

Any text editor can write code, but only an IDE can perform the functional tests beyond initial text editing. IDEs are software applications combining software editing with build, test and package functions. One common resource is Visual Studio Code, an open-source option that supports several languages. Another example would be Anaconda, again open-source and frequently used for data analytics approaches, offering specific Python and R language applications. A combination version would be Jupyter Notebook, a server-client application that allows editing and running code by combining code commands with descriptive comments.

Three types of IDES appear frequently: local, cloud and standardized. Local IDEs are those individually built on local machines. These highly customized approaches often run into problems as software scales. Cloud offers more options and more integration. One cloud benefit can also be a large user base capable of providing community support. Standardized options expand from the local to build options for a specific enterprise or approach.

IDEs always perform some generic functions. Some do more, and some do less, so choosing the right tool depends on team skill and individual preferences. All IDEs should automate code editing and correct syntax. Some expand from that basis to offer intelligent code completion, like Copilot with Gitlab and IntelliSense with VS Code. The tools should allow refactoring support by highlighting certain functions as different visual elements. One example from Anaconda is colour-coding different commands and different functions. Other benefits include local build automation, some testing and debugging. Keys for picking the right IDE are the right programming language, cooperating with the operating system, DevX customized options and any automation available to improve speed. One final element for IDE should be integrated testing.

The previous section covered continuous testing and processes in great detail. The advantage of IDEs is that the closer testing occurs to coding, the easier it is to resolve difficulties. An effective IDE should include unit tests, syntax correction and some functional tests. VS Code offers a wide range of test extensions, as does Anaconda. Sometimes the tests run integral with code, and at other times may use kickstart options to run parallel tests with code development. The Jupyter Notebook functions can run tests for an entire notebook or within individual cells. Combining tests between IDE-embedded and distinct plug-ins allows comprehensive coverage.

Once the preferred IDE with requisite functions is selected, the next step is incorporating those aspects into standardized delivery. In an artistic example, these items show the first step, helping select whether one paints an oil canvas, sketches in pencil or ink, or builds statues. Moving on from these aspects means ensuring you have the best workshop or platform to support confident DevOps delivery.

Dev and ops platforms

From the DevOps perspective, a platform contains the environment where software can be executed. This platform may be the hardware, virtual operating system, web browsers or a wide range of programming interfaces. When designing systems, one works through the four Cs: cloud, cluster, container and code. Platforms provide a means to integrate these developments and expand success. A platform finds tasks that could be done independently, requiring integration to reach effective goals. An example would be bundling GitLab as development, Argo or Flux to assist in building Helm charts, a Docker environment, orchestration systems and standard protocols with an overall abstraction level. Most tasks can individually integrate, but bundling those tasks together reduces friction early in the process. At the same time, these platforms should create operations observability to maximize product success.

The goal behind a development platform should be to make life easier for the developer through improving the developer experience (DevX). A platform would provide the tools and clusters within a virtual environment, allowing developers to focus on building applications rather than infrastructure. Platforms allow teams to focus on building software rather than creating the subordinate infrastructure. When deciding to build software, teams should focus on creating the best ROI through a new app, seizing competitive advantage or simply being a first mover rather than infrastructure.

The best platform analogy is building a new shelf. First you go to the store, buy tools and materials, and then return home to build. On your return, you may be missing sandpaper, the right wood type or a particular screw. A platform gives you the full toolbox and basic blueprints. At that point, you can decide if you want multiple shelves, a birdhouse or any other project as all the pieces and tools are available. Effective platforms solve security early, smooth versioning issues and provide virtual spaces to build and deploy, build and test and then package software for other environments.

Operational platforms expand from the development platform to allow managed use. An effective platform can be run from someone else's server (cloud) or within one's spaces. Platform management allows for separating data and ensuring other woodworkers do not copy your designs. On the operational side, a platform allows for structuring teams, parsing data access and ensuring all tools function effectively. Platform lifecycles are distinct from application lifecycles, and an application may spin up and down multiple times, change users, change protocols or make other variations. The platform ensures tools are present, the workshop is clean and there is a common, community knowledge base for success. Operations means managing users, curating knowledge and keeping clusters running. Within those clusters, developers lead in bringing in unique software, managing users and expanding forward.

Platforms change the DevOps mindset from build and run from tip to tail to just building and running the efficient pieces. The DevOps goal is always to automate anything done at least twice; platforms support that mindset. Platforms provide the initial automation to gain observability, implement pipelines and concentrate on valuable software. These tools can also provide a common spot to share and integrate data to improve feedback through dashboards.

Dashboards

One last technological DevOps decision deals with dashboards. Dashboards are the pretty cover to the complicated processes within the DevOps engine. At the highest level, dashboards should demonstrate any metric your team tracks. Grafana, Prometheus, Jaeger, Open Census and OTel are all options to gather data and present metrics usefully. The most important aspect should be that dashboards are not the end point of discussion. Dashboards gather all information in a shared place, visible between all business workers, and allow outcome modelling. It is one thing to see an error published when committing code and another to see a red dot on the pipeline execution graphic. Visualization allows abstraction, and just like with code and platforms, every abstraction level produces additional benefits.

Dashboards are highly customized applications. Each dashboard supports specialized viewers. Individuals who prefer one dashboard over another might see similar data, just in a different format. When building a dashboard there are two questions: how do you learn from the dashboard, and how does it create action? These mimic the first steps we took in creating metrics: how do you know, and what do you see next? Integrating the thought process into visualization allows sharing between teams, isolating problems and leaning into experimental solutions.

Project managing dashboards appear best as workflow boards like Kanban or Scrum, burndown charts showing work completed and GitHub project boards. Application monitoring dashboards use tools like Jaeger and Open Census. Jaeger performs open-source, end-to-end trace requests to evaluate response time, including service mesh. Open Census allows one to view the host application's data but can be exported to other aggregation dashboards. Prometheus scrapes metrics from nodes, Grafana uses event-driven metrics with panels correlating multiple inputs and OTel establishes a single, open-source standard to capture and deliver metrics, traces and logs from cloud-native applications. Each tool can be used in various proportions to build an effective dashboard.

Kubernetes implementations can challenge our dashboard structure due to the numerous containers and service mesh integration. The problem is that each cluster of containers can be interpreted separately with no centralized application data and rapidly changing clusters. Data must be aggregated to a stable environment to observe through providing context, history and the overall environment state. There are a couple of keys to succeeding with Kubernetes: first, do not just aggregate logs. Logs must be contextual and bringing them to a single point does not create the needed success. You cannot just rely on picking the right application or using a managed Kubernetes service. Kubernetes requires active monitoring because of the distributed and ephemeral nature of each cluster

Overall, dashboards are a key to bringing together information. It would be great if there were one customized solution to provide the best outcome, but much like other DevOps approaches, you will have to start from the beginning and experiment towards success. Finding the right dashboard will be largely trial and error for processes like observability, pipelines and testing. I would start with the options available through some services, then adjust to show flow.

Summary

Building from technology to find the overall process governing DevOps decisions can be difficult. Expediting this process requires hiring the right people, creating efficient team practices and emphasizing conversation. None of these things happen or will continue to happen if not supported by top-down direction and bottom-up participation. This participation requires solid connection in building architectural patterns supporting delivery. Solid Scrum and Kanban techniques that emphasize flow further support those software architectural patterns. Picking the right IDE, using platforms and clearly displaying flow through dashboards can help distinguish between indifferent DevOps and confident delivery. Our next step explores how to emphasize stable practices with security and stability to ensure external factors do not crush your success.

Notes

1   Skelton, M, and Pais, M (2019) *Team Topologies: Organizing business and technology for teams with fast flow*, IT Revolutions

2   Squirrel, D and Frederick, J (2020) *Agile Conversations*, IT Revolutions

3   Harris, C (2023) Microservices vs. monolithic architecture, Atlassian, www.atlassian.com/microservices/microservices-architecture/microservices-vs-monolith (archived at https://perma.cc/JHZ2-W7C9)

4   AWS (nd) What is service-oriented archiecture? AWS, https://aws.amazon.com/what-is/service-oriented-architecture/ (archived at https://perma.cc/ZAZ2-HYAX)

CHAPTER TEN

Stability and security

Stability and security appear as opposite sides of the coin, but both are central to DevOps. The initial thought diagram shows that DevOps constructs must be adaptive and scalable, but the structure falls without stability and security. Stability persists through always offering working options; security, on the other hand, serves two purposes: to guard value or signal a threat. This chapter combines operational and security features to examine various aspects essential to DevOps but often left behind.

- Forming security teams
- Operationalizing enterprise concerns
- Establishing continuous monitoring techniques
- Setting a secure culture
- Leveraging site reliability engineers
- Picking secure technology

Each area offers a part of the overall goal. Security and stability must contribute to the overall flow, feedback and improvement to create valuable products. You can be confident in your DevOps teams and product delivery when you resolve security and stability issues.

Security and stability professionals

As with other DevOps elements, success in stability and security requires finding the best people. If we return to the original DevOps basecamp graphic, we see how secure and stable features hold up our ability to develop, deploy and operate features.

These individuals must be embedded in the DevOps culture but have a slightly different approach. They must be dedicated to keeping functions working despite constant development. There is a slight change in their security outlook from typical DevOps, as we want folks who understand the need to do things correctly and operate expeditiously. This can be challenging but is not insurmountable. Looking for some of the characteristics in the following paragraphs will help you pick the best folks and establish top-notch teams.

Over the past several years, many now refer to DevOps as DevSecOps, emphasizing security as the middle element. The

FIGURE 10.1   DevOps basecamp

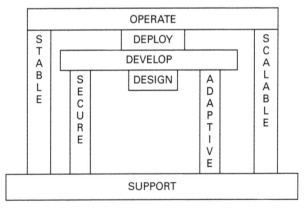

term DevSecOps is attributed to Shannon Lietz in 2013, although she traces the history back to early software developments in 1976.[1] The central concept involves shifting security left, accomplishing security tasks earlier and ensuring stable and secure software, but my view is that all delivery should include security. Some organizations still working on security basics may need verbal influence to stress what should be standard delivery.

The importance of security in DevOps is early inclusion. Many developers use DevSecOps guidance to help advance new or maturing teams. Returning to the *DevOps Handbook*, only two of the over 20 chapters briefly mention security. Some groups support DevSecOps models to assist moving forward. A group of prominent individuals authored the DevSecOps Manifesto and suggested some guidelines, similar to the Agile Manifesto, to include security early and often. The Manifesto guidelines are:[2]

- Leaning in over always saying 'No'.
- Data and security science over fear, uncertainty and doubt.
- Open contribution and collaboration over security-only requirements.
- Consumable security services with APIs over mandated security controls and paperwork.
- Business-driven security scores over rubber stamp security.
- Red and blue team exploit testing over relying on scans and theoretical vulnerabilities.
- 24×7 proactive security monitoring overreacting after being informed of an incident.
- Shared threat intelligence over keeping info to ourselves.
- Compliance operations over clipboards and checklists.

These guidelines should be seen exactly as Agile, with the preferred on the right and options on the left. In some instances you can see the stricter alignment, such as the leaning in over always saying no or the 24×7 monitoring over incident reactions. In both cases, these would be absolute on the left with little room on the right. We adjust to adopting these instances by choosing the right security experts.

Security experts

One of the challenges with security experts is growing from past models to today's standards. In the old days (pre-2010), security experts gained their positions as experts on development or operations, and then someone asked if they wanted to change. The individual moved from their team to building and running compliance teams. The older security standards were about scan timing, whether compliance occurred and satisfying audits. This practice means security experts spent the last 10 years thinking about paperwork results rather than active integration. DevOps means bringing those experts back together and integrating into daily delivery experiences.

When you think of security experts, they should know three areas: standards, risk management and business solutions. Each area shapes security thoughts and guides future discussion. The first item is standards. Whatever industry area in which you deliver products, there are required security standards. In the United States, medical care is governed by the Health Insurance Portability and Accountability Act (HIPAA) or, if working in government, you have the National Institute for Standards and Technology (NIST). From a generic perspective, there are the ISO 27001 and 27002 guides. Further, legal restrictions such as the General Data Protection Regulation (GDPR) in Europe or the North American Electric Reliability Corporation Critical Infrastructure Protection (NERC CIP) for US utilities often apply. Any expert needs to be intimately familiar with the challenges associated with those elements.

Commercial organizations supplement, enhance and explain these standards to others to gain revenue from solving security assistance issues. The proliferation of third-party groups emphasizes why your experts must live and breathe relevant standards.

Many approaches contain hundreds of pages, contradictory guidance and one-time exceptions. Only through regular use and application can one truly understand security standards. The difficulty is more than recognizing breaches or incorporating firewalls, but delves into daily practices for users, screen-saver times, backup power and other items customarily ignored. Once your expert learns the basics, establishing sound risk management fundamentals is the next step.

As with the initial security standard, many standards offer different approaches to risk. For example, the NIST standard uses the Risk Management Framework, with these steps:

· Prepare
· Categorize
· Select
· Implement
· Assess
· Authorize
· Monitor

These will undoubtedly help define individual risks, but the most crucial aspect revolves around two areas: first, categorizing the risk through assigning a probability, timeline and impact. Probability defines the event likelihood, the timeline addresses when events happen and impact shows the product effects. For example, on our parking application, a DDOS attack might be unlikely, can occur any time from today onwards and create a significant impact if customers cannot reach our service. The second step is mitigation by accepting the risk, avoiding it, controlling it, transferring it to others or monitoring it. In this case we accept that a DDOS happens (accept), only allow registered users access (avoid and control), use a third-party service (transfer) or use solid operational practices (monitor). Understanding standards and risk moves to the final requirement for an expert, understanding business solutions.

The last area for the experts to show their skills should be generating business solutions. There are a multitude of different tools that advertise security guarantees. An expert should distinguish between the different variants and find where we can rent or buy a solution rather than building our own. The sheer number of tools available can be overwhelming, and experts should be able to rapidly narrow those by efficiency and price. One common area appears in AI/ML security solutions. The expert should differentiate between generic ML solutions and learning that mitigates the overall risk. Another solution for experts is creating teams to increase the shared benefit.

Security teams

A security team brings multiple experts together to share ideas and improve flow, feedback and improvement. These experts work together to identify crown jewels within the organization, areas requiring protection. The teams have two goals: aligning operations to compliance standards and filling security framework holes. Each happens best by working with other DevOps teams. When I support security, I assign team roles with active participation in the DevOps teams, learning the language, understanding the flow and communicating security benefits. From the earlier team discussion, good security teams enable functions that improve everyone.

In compliance alignment, we previously mentioned that security experts should live and breathe compliance standards. The next step is applying those standards to regular actions. One can move forward only by knowing the security standard and the operational guidance. As mentioned earlier, security can either guard or signal. This practice requires knowing all organizational gaps. These gaps appear in three areas: compliance, vulnerability and organizational. Distinguishing categories helps find the best ways to eliminate problems at notification rather than after damage occurs. Compliance gaps are when one knows a standard must be met and is not. Vulnerability gaps assess current defects and use proactive measures to stop defects from reaching production. Organizational gaps are issues in the corporate process with training, cultural acceptance and team interaction.

Addressing the compliance gap addresses known standards to create market value through advertising security fixes. If a product falls within HIPAA, NIST or PCI DSS, meeting the standard is the primary way to be competitive. Companies advertise compliance through maturity levels, evaluations like SOC2 or ISO 27001, or achieving a certification like the US Government's FedRAMP or Authority to Operate (ATO). These gaps must meet internal evaluation standards combined with external approval. An organization runs tests to demonstrate standards and then produces artifacts for external review. Sometimes, compliance can involve third-party assessments, penetration testing or even red/blue team exercises.

Vulnerability gaps deal with technical challenges posed by producing new code. The broad security community routinely evaluates new products for fun and profit. One sees these evaluations by known security tools, practices like Hack the Box competitions or bug-bounty items. Hack the Box competitions offer a target for prizes by breaking more areas faster than competitors. Conferences like Black Hat and DEFCON routinely bring groups together to discuss vulnerabilities. Bug bounties are when companies offer rewards for anyone finding software vulnerabilities.

Typical vulnerability identification emerges from the published Common Vulnerabilities and Exposures (cve.mitre.org) on a public website. Some are associated with known fixes and others still need solutions. Solutions apply mainly to published software or when development includes open-source and third-party inclusions. Most software depends on other tools, libraries and code as dependencies to work effectively. Scanning tools like ACAS, ZAP, Anchore, Fortify and others can identify these gaps in production and prevent publication. Vulnerabilities tie into the risk equation of risk (R) equals threat (T) times vulnerability (V) (R=TxV). Without a vulnerability, risks are minimal but similarly, without a threat, risks are also minimized. Removing known and suspected vulnerabilities zeroes out half of the equation.

Threats emerge internally from the organizational gap. External threats, those seeking to harm your organization, can never be fully addressed, but one can remediate internal threats. Having good people creates value. Similarly, people can create errors. The most secure system is the one with no users; a locked system in a locked room with no external connections generates complete security but produces no value. Introducing users creates organizational gaps, but one can mitigate these with sound management practices. Training and culture are the two biggest wins for organizations. These elements must adjust for constant change in people, tools and processes to ensure familiarity and secure practices. One of the best ways to deal with all gaps is to link security teams with development elements and connect security teams to operational and enterprise tasks.

Emphasizing operations

The basic DevOps philosophy suggests a 'you build it, you run it' approach. This philosophy means that every dev team should be capable of running their production environment. Self-operations work excellently for small instances, but an independent ops team becomes necessary when the goal is to expand value to millions of customers. Ops teams categorize issues and bugs whose resolution might distract developers and reduce organizational flow value flow. These flows work best with a help desk and hot fix resolutions, although one key element remains interaction to update baselines continually.

Interacting with a designated ops team can be challenging. One must first recognize that ops teams are no less critical than other developers; after all, ops works with the customers, the direct value source, so revenue flow ceases without ops. The first step realizes that interactions with a code base occur as three levels: simple, complicated and complex:

- Simple: Adding two apples to two apples equals four apples. Changing any number changes only the total number of apples. Making one change in code creates a direct result.
- Complicated: Buying two apples requires managing the store inventory, personal inventory and available funds. Code changes create defined results in multiple areas requiring mapping.
- Complex: Every issue ties to a random number of other issues, the Gordian knot. Buying an apple relates to store space, business income, personal outcomes, recipe management etc. Complex issues occur in code with tightly coupled, extensive interactions where it's difficult or impossible to identify all outcomes from a code change.

The software development goal produces a baseline with primarily simple issues, and the operational goal solves customer issues from complex and complicated to simple resolutions without excessive development. Development constantly resolves complex and complicated issues to build simple, loosely coupled coding integrations. Architectural patterns and solutions in the previous chapters helped model building within these frameworks.

Once identifying an issue, one must also assess how change affects other elements. An ops team solving all customer issues would be spectacular, but sometimes bug fixes, CVE elements or improved user interfaces must be reflected within the standard code base. Interactions between DevOps teams are defined as dependent, independent and interdependent:

- Dependent: Changing one item changes the other; heating water raises the temperature in the pot. Adding columns to a shared user database interaction affects all other users.
- Independent: Items do not interact; heating water does not change the refrigerator temperature. Creating a user login does not affect the overall codebase.
- Interdependent: All items interact with all other items. DevOps interactions are interdependent as teams rely on each other. Any significant change by Ops should be reflected in the overall baseline code.

Ops do not operate independently. Their success depends on establishing dev team connections, understanding new code flow and managing release cycles. Software development never ceases so ops teams will constantly add new upgrades and features to already-delivered software. In the cloud-native environment, these changes occur as a continuous flow. Upgrades that impede flow are detrimental to the overall DevOps outcomes.

Ops teams emphasize keeping developers working on new code and the next feature as long as possible. Sometimes users have issues requiring resolution that are inherently uncomplicated from an experienced operator's perspective. If each customer reaches out to the original developer, it can impact flow. For example, if your car starts leaking, you do not contact the engineering team but instead visit a local mechanic. Sometimes the manufacturer contacts teams about a recall notification or a problem with preemptive fixes. The same distinction applies to ops. One way for teams to manage user inputs is through a tiered value flow like this:

- Tier 1 – Consult: the issue can be solved with current documentation as written, i.e. I need a new user account.
- Tier 2 – Configuration: the issue can be solved with an application of current standards, accesses and permissions, i.e. my system cannot reach a tool I need.

• Tier 3 – Code: the issue cannot be solved without changing existing code, i.e. I need new database fields or I want the button on the other side of the screen.

Ops teams should be familiar with all published documentation to resolve Tier 1 issues quickly, and remind users where they can locate instructions. Tier 2 issues require the most expertise from the help desk, merging current standards with their system understanding. These problems happen when users import new tools and then security standards prevent integration without additional privileges. Ops teams function as the administrators for deployed instances or enterprise-level solutions. Tier 3 issues require new code to resolve them. If the code change is short, one to three sprints, the ops team writes the code and resolves issues. New issues can be added to the overall dev backlog if more time is required.

Resolving issues relies on an effective ticketing system. Ticketing characterizes the issue within a tier, passes it to the right individual and ensures resolution. Writing strong service-level agreements (SLAs) supported by objectives and indicators supports executing the ticketing system. Ticketing also provides a historical backlog to identify common issues, update needed documentation and experiment with group solutions such as manufacturing recall. Operationally focused elements of the DevOps teams are not merely an administrative function but a vital integration into maintaining flow throughout the process.

Processing for security and stability

Defining stable and secure processes can be challenging. We do not merely affect static guidelines but a continuous model changing daily. The goal becomes keeping the car between the lines and keeping a constantly changing shape within dynamic lines with moving traffic on the road. Good stability and security processes are akin to teaching someone to juggle, ride a unicycle and move through a crowded market. Each contains difficulty but learning the three together requires an interdependent approach.

Providing security compliance for delivered components, often through established controls, can be critical to effective software. Establishing delivery model controls depends on several factors, including what standards exist, volatility, agency theory and transaction costs.[3] Volatility controls how much standards change. Subscribing to an external policy addresses compliance but sometimes one loses control over how often elements change. Agency theory entails how much control your company has over changing more extensive standards and how you affect those changes. For example, changes in user passwords are relatively easy but massive protocol changes, such as when Google went from HTTP to HTTPS, take more work. Transaction costs are company costs to make those adjustments.

Security control frameworks sometimes address integrating software but often focus on policy, while mitigation attempts begin with artifact creation to assess controls.[4] Those all provide implementable solutions but no factor addresses initially bracketing preconceived security experiences to understand how those affect the social basis of exchange between project teams. Stability and security processes require observability by all teams having pipeline artifact access, system processes from dashboards and voluminous standard documentation.

Security creates key DevOp functionality when needed functions become part of the overall culture. Seventeen per cent of articles from 2016 to 2019 discussed the importance of a security culture.[5] Some organizations can manage technical solutions to cultural security with automated models providing continuous security.[6] The selected cultural strategy matters as sound strategies are statistically significant in reducing organizational security breaches. In addition to reducing breaches, processes maintain value by creating customer stability. Sound cultures include extra-role functions as processes employees follow even when required by policy. Defining initial standards allows the integration of operational monitoring practices, incorporating SRE personnel and building security emphasis within the organizational culture.

Continuous monitoring for operations and security

In Chapter 7 we discussed continuous monitoring from a testing perspective; the emphasis here establishes monitoring for end-user satisfaction through product usability. Continuous monitoring builds past the development functions to create current knowledge and build a database supporting potential audits. Running a market can be the same as a juggler on a unicycle moving through a crowded marketplace. There is a planned route but all the other shoppers constantly present new obstacles and must be monitored. The previous understanding focused on the infrastructure monitoring associated with pipelines and internal interactions, while operational monitoring switches to application and network monitoring. Application monitoring, as stated, examines released software to measure user effectiveness. Network monitoring tracks the various systems essential to cloud-native to ensure components interact effectively.[7]

Monitoring provides several ops teams benefits. The first is improved network observability by obtaining expansive clarity. One collects metrics at set times and monitoring tools enhance awareness. Next, enhanced awareness allows for rapid response by connecting the right people to the correct issues. Our ops team evaluates submitted tickets as tiers but constantly uses monitoring to review performance and submit needed improvement tickets. From personal experience, our team saw numerous customer issues and made timely fixes to resolve future concerns. At the same time, the team identified a subsequent change preventing similar issues and used a Tier 3 ticket to add solutions to planned releases.

The third benefit of operational CM is decreasing the overall system downtime. In Chapter 4 we discussed Sigma standards and uptime importance. Tracking issues at the minor level allows for resolution before severe issues occur. If our juggler sees a turn upcoming, they can make preventative adjustments early, and our ops teams can do the same. Finally, CM improves overall business performance. One key in complicated software delivery remains knowing what your system does better than anyone else. The conversation with the customer should always begin with showing our performance. If the customer has an issue, we should rapidly identify where that issue exists and suggest fixes. Monitoring tracks upcoming software updates and ensures user experience remains positive for all individuals.

Monitoring should focus on four key issues: server status and health, application logs, resolving or identifying system vulnerabilities, and user activity. Server status remains the first option in cloud-native implementations; without network connectivity, cloud-native options disappear. As mentioned with chaos engineering, the cloud is an inherently complex problem; constantly monitoring small changes allows for predictively addressing more significant issues. Application logs track how well the system performs. Routine log review and metric comparison allow ops to verify that applications run per specifications. Developers sometimes stop monitoring performance when delivered, so ops teams resolve those gaps.

System vulnerabilities lie at the heart of the security picture. Pipeline monitoring identifies known vulnerabilities but those expand once delivered. Third-party dependencies often develop vulnerabilities after delivery, as was the example with Log4J. Continuous tracking for new items helps resolve issues quickly, mainly when many companies immediately publish fixes. This monitoring element allows ops to verify the right version is running and implement patches.

The final issue deals with monitoring user activity. As mentioned, devs often stop when code enters production, but ops teams continue assessing product use. Sometimes, usage changes can result in market advantage. In any case, understanding usage accelerates flow. A good example is knowing that users purchased a product but use an intermediate stage to convert formats. In early cases, Microsoft Excel could not interpret some spreadsheets produced through data gathering. Teams would gather data, convert it into a new table and then upload it into Excel. Understanding user behaviour allowed Microsoft to incorporate those integration tools directly, improving user experience and ensuring customers spent more time within their tool.

The last element to emphasize with continuous monitoring is that it must be automated and observable. As with development, the necessary information should be automatically collected and compiled. These compiled sites should be available across multiple teams. We use the ops team to filter users from development while allowing devs to see and understand how functionality can drive success. Devs can use shared data to test new features without impacting customers. For example, database changes can test in shared platforms for performance metrics without downgrading user performance. Code dependencies are evaluated here without risking the entire system. A specific example would address Kubernetes version upgrades and integration tools such as Crossplane, Amazon EKS and Pluto that keep applications running throughout changes. Equally significant, good operational CM functions help create the environment to employ successful SREs to balance development with operational responses.

Site reliability engineering (SRE)

One recent DevOps integration was the site reliability engineer (SRE). These folks, including those without DevOps, occupy an organizational position of linking multiple teams together as high-level problem solvers. SRE improves context across an organization by working horizontally and vertically, operating within a service-level agreement framework and monitoring metrics related to resolving issues. In many organizations, SREs lead the incident response team when items cross a certain threshold to ensure work continues to flow, preserving incident feedback and preparing teams for future incidents. Google was one of the first to implement SRE, and they define the role as treating operations as a software problem.[8] If you remember the discussion of the Andon cord in Lean manufacturing – the cord Toyota used to stop the line when problems emerged – SREs are the folks who receive the call when one pulls the Andon cord. One of the best collections of SRE stories and experiences appears in *Seeking SRE* (2018), edited by David Blank-Edelman.[9] If you intend to implement SREs, I strongly advise some targeted research. SRE work is more than can be addressed here but this section frames some initial thoughts.

If we look at the SRE from the moment you pull the cord, the first job provides context for the event: why was the cord pulled, what are the impacts and where should solutions begin? In software development, the SRE requires basic infrastructure knowledge and an understanding current corporate practices and user practices. The cord-puller knows something is wrong, but the SRE builds across higher levels, for example if a developer recognizes an issue when continuously failing a pipeline or an automated test. When working with the code, if the individual recognizes the problem is beyond individual code and may be a system-wide vulnerability, they pull the cord and the SRE appears. The SRE can then evaluate the issue, determine how it applies to other production code and recommend solutions. Sometimes solutions can change faulty dependency, make a policy change or implement company training. The variety in solutions explains why context is essential, and the SRE must be comfortable working with individuals from developers to the C-suite.

SREs identify where potential cord pulls happen even when individuals do not yet see SLA framework errors. The framework begins with an agreement, then assigns objectives and determines indicators showing progress before you need to pull the cord. An SLA defines the level of service between a customer and the supplying organizations, and SLAs may exist between external or internal groups.[10] An example of an SLA might be 99 per cent system availability. The important SLA element occurs in defining a commitment to another party.

SLOs (service-level objectives) move on to define internal goals necessary to keep the SLA within compliance. An SLO provides the metrics suggesting what needs to happen and allows tracking of the error budget.[11] If the SLA was for 99 per cent availability, the SLO should reflect the same goals. If the external agreement was for 99 per cent availability but our SLO only looked for 80 per cent, that's a significant difference between when the customer was upset and when internal managers began to panic. The error budget defines the amount of deviation space within the system over a time interval or one minus the SLO number. In the 99 per cent availability example, that number would be 1 per cent; with 99.99 per cent availability, the error budget would be .01 per cent. Error budgets include time length for the SLA, as a 1 per cent error over a year requires different tracking than assessing for 1 per cent daily.

The last element is the SLI (service-level indicator). The SLI provides the organizational metrics defining availability. As with all good metrics, tracking availability shows the control chart with one line set for 99 per cent, and then the wavering line depicting actual availability. When that line dips repeatedly below 99 per cent or makes regular dips towards the line, the SRE could act to assess root causes, generating changes. Since these issues solve operational problems with software solutions, the SRE becomes responsible for tracking, resolving and reporting metrics.

Good metrics also suggest actions to affect those metrics. The SRE then becomes the organizational individual or team that acts based on metrics. Often we think of metrics as a red line to generate immediate action. SREs track those events before reaching the red line to identify early trends and keep items within defined goals. SREs often use a set of metrics that Blank-Edelman depicted as the virtuous cycle, listed below:

- Time to Detect (TTD) – the amount of time to initially detect a problem. If availability is measured every six hours, it could take up to five hours and 59 minutes before a problem is identified.
- Time to Engage (TTE) – how long to activate the individuals that can solve the problem. If availability runs through a cloud provider that only updates your request daily, this could be 24 hours.
- Time to Fix (TTF) – the time to fix a problem. If availability only requires a textual change, say from having three pods available to four pods with an additional 100 GB of RAM, it might be only 10 minutes.
- Time to Mitigate (TTM) – the total time for the above three metrics. If we add the above, the mitigation time might be 30 hours and 10 minutes

SRE teams strive to resolve these metrics most efficiently. In the above example, the longest metric was the TTE. The number could be significantly reduced if one could engage a different framework with the cloud provider to establish more direct environment control. In tracking metrics related to identified SLIs, the SRE provides contextual awareness for ensuring system reliability.

The final SRE area is incident management. In this case, an incident is an unexpected internal or external event that seriously disrupts SLA. The first detection of an incident should occur through the SLI changes. On the other hand, public notice through a CVE of a new vulnerability, like Log4J, could also launch an SRE into action. The SRE would assemble their team and resolve issues. Typical incident management processes require identification, categorization, prioritization, response and closure. In this case, the SRE locates the problem, determines organizational effects and potential importance, makes fixes and then provides documentation and training to prevent those problems from reoccurring. Incident management is a complicated task requiring significant practice before an incident occurs to ensure smooth processes occur. Many incident teams have been initially without common operations areas, such as a conference room or VTC accesses, or cannot communicate to the broader company. Practising effectively for SRE, or stability and security in general, benefits from strong cultures whose values emphasize those areas.

Stability and security cultures

DevOps depends on humans, and humans rely on culture. Ensuring the developed culture shares values depends on the associated cultural language, norms and artifacts. Language means the organization incorporates terminology to communicate about a process or event. Norms are how we express ourselves to others; for example, a norm might be knowing not to cook fish in the company microwave because the smell affects all others. Stability and security norms are the behaviours we expect from ourselves and others regarding developed software. Finally, artifacts are those items produced that help one recognize the culture. Compliance artifacts such as SOC 2 or maturity levels communicate practical cultural standards.

The first element for cultural integration remains language. Participants should discuss security and stability issues within a common framework. We introduced many security and development terms here but the essence requires a common understanding. When metrics and dashboards appear, individuals should understand the discussed terms. If the dashboard shows released

CVEs, and their company product connection, common terms would relate to high, medium and low impacts. One way to emphasize language is to maximize company communications and inter-team reporting. These items do not require formalization but provide an opportunity to explore language items. In past teams, one example was that no acronyms were allowed in any writing; any time an acronym appeared, the explanation had to also appear.

Using languages can be strengthened by introducing norms. Norms are the informal rules governing society when individuals practise a behaviour because they believe others in the community will practise the same behaviour. Much of our DevOps discussion has focused on establishing norms regarding how you practise technological solutions to derive value. This norm defines value as an ROI versus a new idea. A value associated with a norm might be integrity in communications, and the norm might be that all testing tools run to the maximum extent possible before committing code. Each organization may establish different norms and values related to the desired culture. Common norm differences in organizations may be how one communicates with senior members, whether those discussions are open and collaborative or hierarchical and formalized. Formalizing norms occurs through cultural artifacts.

DevOps teams produce a lot of different artifacts. These compare to the modern culture with about 328.77 million terabytes of data created daily.[12] Pipelines, boards and team communications are significant items in producing large numbers of artifacts. Artifacts are categorized within three levels, listed below:[13]

• Primary artifacts – used in production (hammer, fork, camera, computers, Kubernetes, pipelines, Scrum boards).
• Secondary artifacts – relating to primary artifacts (documentation for how to use pipelines or Kubernetes).
• Tertiary artifacts – representations of secondary artifacts (system architecture, team working agreements).

An entirely different topic suited for a different text would be how one manages artifacts within a culture. Many modern management practices are devoted to creating and managing artifacts within the culture to the most significant effect. If you remember the documents produced at each stage of the waterfall process, each becomes a primary artifact, with secondary items describing how and when to use them, and then as a tertiary Gantt chart showing the representation of all those items. The important cultural element should be identifying the artifacts describing the culture and ensuring they fall within values and norms. Establishing monitoring, SRE practices and a sound culture helps select stable and secure technologies to ensure confident DevOps.

Stable and secure technologies

One poor assumption often made by business professionals about technology is that an item that is stable and secure today will remain so into the future. Predictability and adaptability are valuable business attributes and DevOps enhances those ideas by encouraging constant adaptation. Two common examples of not adapting to new technology were the IBM CEO declaring that personal computers would never be valuable and the Kodak CEO stating there was no reason to move from wet film to digital practices. We can see how those failed to meet the test of time. A more recent example would be how Blackberry failed to adjust to the smartphone market.

If we assume that software and computer systems constantly change, then no secure and stable technology picked today will remain so. As a DevOps professional, there are ways to remain ahead of these trends. One philosophy I advocate is that if you constantly develop and deploy new software, any malware or CVE must keep up with that trend. If it takes hackers 30 to 60 days to exploit a new vulnerability, and you release software on a 30-day cycle, that makes it difficult to obtain any purchase on a deployed system. These options can make it expensive and challenging to maintain a high performance rate but two ways to remain ahead are introducing platform engineering and implementing effective scanning and operational testing within development.

Platform engineering

We briefly touched on platforms as the integrated technology set to build applications. Many teams start with software development by attempting to construct basic platforms. Platform construction can often take one to two years before it sufficiently matures to support development. When markets change every 30 days, the desired software application can be well behind by the time the platform is ready. Purchasing or renting pre-designed platforms allows companies to focus on the needed development aspects to increase ROI rather than building a unique platform.

A common analogy for employing effective platforms compares the process to building a woodshop. If you need to build a shelf for the house (the ROI-producing software) and you have not built one in the past, you likely lack the tools. You head to the hardware store and purchase wood, a hammer, nails, a saw and other items. When you return to the house, you realize you are missing items and make another trip to the tool store. This cycle repeats, and what was supposed to be a small project turns into a multi-day expedition and practice. Good platforms provide you with all the necessary tools and some basic blueprints for shelves, birdhouses or racecars. One can then modify the blueprint for multiple shelves, birdhouses with multiple holes, or different models of toy racecars. The best platforms might include a community to provide help, support systems and collaboration so friends can visit the woodshop and help. With that definition in mind, we can return to platform engineering in terms of a DevOps platform.

The most essential element of the platform for modern business is the collaborative environment. This collaborative area includes work management functions, IDE to write code, communication tools and source/version control options for the deployed code. This area also includes knowledge repos, the blueprints, suggesting known good options for pipeline approaches, previous code and possible integrations to third-party code. The next element requires a platform to provide the woodshop as deployment and production targets as clusters. In software, this means a place exists to test and deploy new code. As the developer, you own and manage target specifications. However, the purchased platform stays current with modern technology to keep clusters stable and secure. At the same time, the platform provides observability to manage items from users to operational code.

Many companies currently offer some portion of this integration. Examples like GitLab, Jenkins, Harness and Azure DevOps manage different elements. One challenge I see with many platforms is that rather than end-to-end options, they focus on a particular spot, such as operational deployment or development to production. This practice significantly improves an area but still causes difficulty in creating full observability or leaves significant training hurdles. The platform goal should allow developers to focus on development while automating other functions.

How do I pick stable and secure technologies?

Picking stable and secure technologies effectively constantly challenges DevOps professionals. As with many other aspects, one needs to manage these selections through careful metrics and understanding requirements. As mentioned before, not acting increases chaos while acting reduces chaos, but these areas must obtain constant feedback. If I were to merely list the best technologies from a company like Gartner, or recommend the top companies yearly from a State of DevOps report, that inclusion could take several hundred pages. Unfortunately, as in many other areas, the answer is found by asking: what does your company require for stability and security?

How does one define stability? At its root, stability means a minimum change but with pursuing DevOps we know that constant change exists as a desired goal. In this case, stability must relate to the produced product and developer happiness. We want to incorporate technologies that minimize disruption to production rates while continuing to keep user alignment. When Netflix moved from mailing DVDs to a primarily streaming service, the change in focus caused some disruption but resulted in a more stable footprint in the long term.

Managing internal stability tools aligns with the same concepts. Stable tools should support the internal culture and maintain user alignment. Changing versions can show a lack of stability. One wants to incorporate technology that minimizes external disruption while maintaining security. Automated upgrades and version updates are one way to minimize these options. One could look to iOS as a stable technology sending regular updates to users but remaining a user option as to when to implement changes. Then, once changes occur, the system highlights new changes affecting users and quickly introduces new features.

On the other hand, secure technology should never be a user option. We like to think that all users will inherently choose secure options but we know that when schedules matter, sometimes areas get missed. Securing these options occurs through choosing a good mix of scanning and dependency technologies, with an active security team to manage the constantly changing options. These options range from the primary unit tests incorporated with the IDE, to functional tests and pair programming, and finally to an active penetration test and red/blue program to manage deployed technology. Any scanning technology is better than nothing but one should find the best options to deliver quickly, provide useful tips and allow one to move on.

An example of less than useful is requirements in some compliance standards to have items that can only be verified manually. Examples include backup power sources, fire alarms or a policy document establishing user training standards. At the same time, some items security scans can flag for might not be appropriate for your organization. One item I found here was a government standard that required a Federal Information Processing Standard (FIPS) at a certain level but the software the team used could not incorporate that standard. A mitigation was in place but the scanning tools never recognized the mitigation and constantly flagged the software as non-compliant. Unfortunately, many of these manual resolutions only appear through using the system and working closely with customers.

One final element for scanning should be considering operational scanners. These move from internal development to scanning networks for unusual events. These scans start by identifying active devices on the network and move into tracking observability through logs and traces involved in the connection. The best of these identify patterns of connection, show behaviour, illustrate usage patterns and deliver through visual dashboards. A simple model might be something like Amazon CloudWatch, while items that involve Runtime Application Self-Protection could include companies like Contrast Security and Dynatrace. Again, just as with the security tools and good DevOps philosophies, you must deploy and iterate versions to find your best options.

Summary

Effective development cannot happen unless applications are stable and secure. Some of the other chapters discuss how to build adaptive software and scaling solutions but this chapter laid the foundation for the other half of the DevOps table. The first step was finding and shaping personnel to follow slightly different guidelines than those focused on development. We examined the difference between the DevSecOps Manifesto and traditional Agile, and how to pick security professionals and then integrate those folks into the teams necessary to your organization.

Moving from people, we developed the processes to show continuous monitoring with security and stability. The chapter expanded into how to use site reliability engineers to buttress your operational processes, which appear in the overall cultural outlook. These processes then link to finding the right techno-logical tools to monitor and observe, whether by implementing a platform or using unique scanning tools. These chapters have prepared you for a confident DevOps implementation now, but the next chapter will look at what you can expect for DevOps as we move into the future.

Notes

1   History of DevSecOps, https://www.devopsinstitute.com/the-history-of-devsecops/ (archived at https://perma.cc/HM5D-BUNL)

2   Devsecops Manifesto, Devsecops.org (archived at https://perma.cc/YC88-L9BP)

3   Wiener, M, Mahring, M, Remus, U and Saunders, C (2016) Control configuration and control enactment in information systems projects: Review and expanded theoretical format, *MIS Quarterly*, 40 (3), 741–D14

4   Cram, W, Proudfoot, J G and D'Arcy, J (2017) Organizational Information security policies: A review and research framework, *European Journal of Information Systems*, 26 (6), 605–41, doi:10.1057/s41303-017-0059-9; Mayer, N, Aubert, J, Grandry, E, Feltus, C, Goettelmann, E and Wieringa, R (nd) An integrated conceptual model for information system security risk management supported by enterprise architecture management, *Software & Systems Modeling*, 18 (3), 2285–312, doi:10.1007/s10270-018-0661-x (archived at https://perma.cc/7QD3-QRA7)

5 Sanchez-Gordon, M and Colomo-Palacios, R (2020) Security as Culture, *IEEE//ACM 42nd International Conference on Software Engineering Workshops*, pp. 266–69

6 Kumar, R and Goyal, R (2020) Modeling continuous security: A conceptual model for automated DevSecOps using open-source software over cloud (ADOC), *Computers & Security*, **97**, 1–28, https://doi.org/10.1016/j.cose.2020.101967 (archived at https://perma.cc/Q7BF-2XK6)

7 Bose, S (2023) What is continous monitoring in DevOps? BrowserStack, https://www.browserstack.com/guide/continuous-monitoring-in-devops (archived at https://perma.cc/8DW9-XR29)

8 Google (2023) What is Site Reliability Engineering? https://sre.google/ (archived at https://perma.cc/7FJH-TAVT)

9 Blank-Edelman, D (2018) *Seeking SRE*, O'Reilly Media

10 Overby, S, Greiner, L Paul, LG (2017) What is an SLA? Best practices for service-level agreements CIO, https://www.cio.com/article/274740/outsourcing-sla-definitions-and-solutions.html (archived at https://perma.cc/U9U5-T6TH)

11 Cruz, P (2022) SRE Fundamentals: Differences between SLI vs. SLO vs. SLA, The New Stack, https://thenewstack.io/sre-fundamentals-differences-between-sli-vs-slo-vs-sla/ (archived at https://perma.cc/D6VG-HWMM)

12 Duarte, F (2023) Amount of data created daily, https://explodingtopics.com/blog/data-generated-per-day (archived at https://perma.cc/D5TD-JG87)

13 Wartofsky, M W (1979) *Models: Representation and the scientific understanding*, Springer Science & Business Media

PART FOUR

The future of DevOps

CHAPTER ELEVEN

The future of DevOps

Our review of the concepts and philosophies of DevOps cannot be complete without looking at what will come next. More than other areas, DevOps encapsulates a constant push to constantly develop new and better, accelerating us into the future. To effectively accelerate, we must visualize the future and any upcoming expectations. This chapter will point you in a direction to keep all your current endeavours running well into the future. Some of the topics include:

- Training consistently
- Machine learning and artificial intelligence ops
- Advancing technology

Dealing with people involves incorporating global communities, finding simple tools to drive processes and maintaining consistent tempos. Some tempo decisions may be adjusted as many companies transfer to artificial intelligence (AI) and machine learning (ML) solutions to reach new heights. While those technologies may seem like bleeding-edge advancements, more innovations, such as quantum models and bioengineering, are still approaching. Solving these problems will require a strong and confident DevOps culture.

Advancing people

As we advance our DevOps people, we must consider the global DevOps community. We are global in interpreting Agile, and remote workplace centres can often feature global workers. Scaling Agile poses some unique challenges to our remote environment. These challenges include:

- lack of face-to-face communications
- improper task allocation
- cultural differences
- temporal differences
- linguistic challenges
- lack of coaching

Addressing these topics deals primarily with three issues: coordination, temporality and communication. Coordination advances through implementing computer-assisted design (CAD) processes and maintaining skills. Temporality resolutions occur by maintaining a clear tempo within the organization. Finally, communication always appears as a DevOps issue but has some unique hurdles within the global environment.

Implementing CAD for coordination can be quickly done. Throughout the book, we have mentioned various tools and technologies to assist in sharing architecture, coordinating code and implementing design structures. Driving down from CAD, computer-assisted software engineering (CASE) has existed for a while and appears in most IDE functions and is a primary benefit of tools like GitHub. As development environments become more complex, simpler design tools are imperative. These tools appear in recent pushes towards low-code and no-code implementations for designers. Using CASE tools improves design and code quality and accelerates delivery. On the other hand, these tools can cost significantly and require additional training, but smooth integration with other tools.

You can handle these hurdles by implementing better training standards through feedback and continuous improvement cycles within DevOps. Managing training should deal with having an employee knowledge, skills and abilities (KSA) assessment. Knowledge incorporates the academic tools for success, skills are the areas practised to improve and abilities are the current capacity to apply different knowledge and skill areas to generate results. Keeping workers sharp requires recognizing new skills and certifications, presenting tool training and managing corporate communication channels dedicated to training. High-level tools addressing issues include maintaining an employee learning budget, having programmes such as lunch and learn events and rewarding those who expand their skills. Also challenging to training can be integrating into development temporality.

Development temporality expresses the timeframe where development and administrative corporate functions occur. As technology advances, needs increase to deliver sooner to maintain market advantage. DevOps cultures strive for the no-heroes approach with visible work, clear goals, maximizing the work not done and eliminating items not creating value. Accelerating pipelines works, but one must remember that additional speed can stress those who are managing pipelines. Remote work supports teams anywhere and 24×7 development cycles but increases challenges in working together, source control and security. All of these resolve through communicating clear team roles and timelines.

Communication advances mean work can be faster and more efficient. Only 100 years ago, it could take days to coordinate a global message; today, those same communications occur in minutes. Visual, face-to-face meetings over video are a significant advantage in managing employees but only work when using video. Humans need visual interaction and visual communication should be a staple for remote environments.

Set out on Gemba walks, when you regularly walk around the workplace to learn about your colleagues' activities and to recognize small issues early. Remote workplaces remove this opportunity, so you should remember to schedule regular meetings with all employees. While these are valuable, they do lack the spontaneous chat that happens on the fringes around work meetings in a physical office. Future trends can improve some of these aspects but not all. I had the chance to test a tool where you moved an icon around a virtual workspace, and whenever encountering another icon, a video chat would start; that could bring the Gemba walk construction into the virtual age. More importantly, you must manage communication. Whether using asynchronous messaging channels or virtual meetings, you must invest time and effort to manage communications. Implementing expanded processes using ML and AI can bring people into the future.

Advancing process

Advancing process requires one to stay in line with innovation within the industry. You want to avoid being either a first adopter or a late adopter. First movers gain some advantage but can suffer some delays as they fix issues later adopters will use to their advantage. Good company processes utilize the three horizons model shown in Figure 11.1 to spend 70 per cent of their time on sustaining current features, 20 per cent on adjacent technology and then 10 per cent on new markets.

Sustainment includes development within the current scope, including new market technologies and versioning. Adjacent services typically include next-generation technology, such as major version releases and improving core technology services. The third horizon looks for visionary and transformative categories. In common parlance, this would be moonshots, large projects with distant deliveries relying on unknown unknowns to succeed, things that might happen but are currently unavailable. Navigating the horizons requires setting an innovation

FIGURE 11.1   Three horizons model

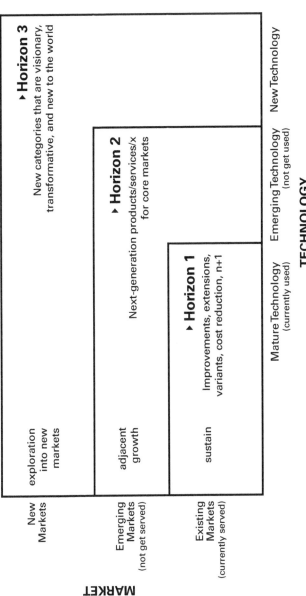

frontier that defines how far you will chase an unknown, the existence of interdisciplinary teams and identifying important industry problems.

New developments can be either cutting-edge or bleeding-edge technology. The primary difference is accepted risk, since one cannot build an effective bleeding-edge business. Cutting-edge development uses the most current and high-level IT with proven implementations. Examples include augmented reality solutions, 3D gaming experiences, socially moderated television such as having X feeds with a live show, and home 3D printing solutions. Bleeding-edge technology is highly risky, usually unreliable and expensive for early adopters. Some bleeding-edge technology examples include augmented reality devices supported by AI, retail-based 3D printing, holographic monitor displays and brain-to-screen technology.

Keeping ahead of the latest technology can be challenging. Fortunately, many media outlets help stay abreast of change. The Edison Awards (https://edisonawards.com/index.php) are an excellent choice that pick the best technologies each year in various areas. They focus on fielded technologies and should not be confused with the Darwin Awards for removing oneself from the gene pool. The Edison Awards highlight not only significant changes but small yearly improvements. In the past year, they offered architecture improvements, digital world mirroring options and bring-your-own environment options. These help with the small changes, but significant changes such as AI and ML solutions can require additional study.

Artificial intelligence

AI, or artificial intelligence, has monopolized many conversations over the past several years. Two broad categories of AI exist: task-oriented and general. A task-oriented AI focuses on completing specific tasks such as winning chess games. The first AI engine for chess was Deep Blue, which in 1997 became the first AI to defeat a human grandmaster. General AI is machines accomplishing multiple tasks such as winning a chess game, completing a coding program and holding a conversation simultaneously. Most AI implementations are narrowly focused, accomplishing a specific task faster and more efficiently than humans. The fear associated with AI solutions assumes that general AI machines could eventually replace human workers. Many AI tasks and tools like GitHub's Copilot work today to assist human workers in tasks while leaving the final decisions to humans.

Another option for AI looks at generative adversarial AI models. These tools set multiple AIs against each other to accomplish tasks and then learn by comparing outputs. An example occurred in the Defense Advanced Research Project Agency (DARPA) AlphaDogfight trials. The AlphaDogfight taught an AI model to conduct dogfights in an F-16 flight simulator, first against AI models and then with the winner combatting a human. The Heron Systems AI model beat the human in five straight fights, none lasting more than 30 seconds.[1] The advantage was that the AI had run four billion simulations before the trials, garnering experience unmatched by any human pilot and not suffering missions potentially resulting in a human's death or capture. These future AI models benefit significantly from integrated machine learning practices.

Machine learning

Machine learning (ML) practices are highly integrated with AI solutions. These models create complicated computer algorithms designed to learn decision trees and execute them quickly across large data volumes. In either case, ML systems are a subset of most AIs. Integrated data from ML systems predicts what comes next, a faithful metrics implementation through flow, feedback and improvement. One subset within ML involves deep learning systems designed to mimic human brain activities through multi-layered neural networks. Rather than offer a single algorithm, each neural network element processes data similar to what we know of human brain functions.

ML systems appear in many DevOps processes. As discussed, most software development produces significant data in many areas as gathered by observability processes through metrics. These systems use either unsupervised or supervised models to reach predictions. Unsupervised models draw inferences and find patterns through clustering group data points and dimensionality reduction. Reducing dimensions eliminates variables through elimination or extraction, moving those things that do not relate to the desired solutions. An ML solving our coffee problem from Chapter 5 might start with all location data and then rapidly remove elements unrelated to coffee within the kitchen or multiple kitchens.

Unsupervised models use regression or classification to address problems. Regression depends on inputting continuous output through linear regression as a best-fit line; decision trees offer two options at every decision point or the aforementioned neural networks. Classification seeks discrete outputs through logistic regression, support vector machines, hyperplanes and naïve Bayes. Logistic regression applies logarithmic scales to model events where exponential scales are more common than linear ones. Support vector machines (SVM) help find hyperplanes with multiple decision points. SVMs find a best-fit line in multiple dimensions, becoming the plane or shape to reach the next step. Naïve Bayes looks for the best fit through an initial assessment of the probability of Y occurring given an X. The advantage is that these machines operate much faster than humans and can be programmed to ignore the cognitive bias elements discussed earlier.

Every ML system only operates as effectively as the data entered. Data that already contains cognitive bias demonstrates the same bias in their predictions. If you work with an ML, preparing data takes four steps. First, one gathers metrics, logs and traces before aggregating that data into appropriate formats. Next, pre-process the data through cleaning, verifying and formatting into usable sets. Pre-processing matches formats between sets, ensures reliable data and de-duplicates some records. Once data is available, divide the elements into three sets: one to train the ML to process, one to validate accuracy and a third for model performance. At that point, one can train and refine the model to develop the needed predictions. AI/ML models pose significant advantages, but as they expand, the available technology can only limit the data needed for practical conclusions.

Advancing technology

Throughout our DevOps discussion, one common factor appears as humans select technology, shape it to their needs and then the technology shapes the humans. Then the cycle repeats as you select additional tools to maximize value. Only human imagination limits tools but at some point the technical capabilities shape the direction in which our imagination grows. I offer two suggestions for where expanded imagination may dramatically alter the ability to produce accelerated value: quantum computation and bio-design. Each of these offers not only a different thought path but new hardware-shaping input.

Today, we are all wedded to our basic laptops, hardware systems, servers, GPUs, cloud computing and other technology. Bio-design and quantum computing currently require moving from that model to different approaches. One common element is that neither requires binary restrictions that have formed the root of computing processes since Claude Shannon's 1948 paper, 'A Mathematical Theory of Communication'.[2] This article was the first to suggest that any analogue input could appear as digital components, the binary standard where all objects must be either a 1 or a 0. Quantum computation and bio-design turn this theory on its head.

Quantum computation

Quantum theories deal with the smallest discrete units of any physical theory; these particles behave differently than larger particles. One of the greatest human minds, Albert Einstein, called quantum mechanics 'spooky action at a distance'.[3] Quantum does not use simple switches since no quantum action finalizes until observed. Every quantum particle occupies four states rather than the two associated with binary. These states are spin-up, spin-down, positive and negative. At its heart, quantum computation harnesses the collection properties of quantum states to incorporate properties of superposition, interference and entanglement to perform calculations. This section presents an overview, but one could spend a career exploring the ramifications involved with quantum computing.

Superposition states that you can add any two quantum states, resulting in another valid quantum state. This theory allows for mathematical computations with quantum particles, critical for quantum positioning. Interference states that each particle interferes with itself in a wave state. On measurement, the initial superposition collapses into a single state. Basic interference states the process is random, but the third property, entanglement, prevents those options. Entanglement means any entangled pair, like generating a photon and splitting it, are related in a way that is indefinite until measured. Once measured, the act of measurement defines the state of the other entangled particle in a predictive way.

Those principles are all complicated and evaluate with matrix mathematics. One application of this uses Grover's algorithm to conduct unstructured searches in a disordered list to find solutions more quickly. This algorithm is known as the travelling salesperson problem: if a salesperson must visit X cities and carry Y items, what is the best combination to generate the most profit and the lowest cost?[4] A typical algorithm that requires finding a solution with 1,000 (N) possible elements must try, on average, least 500 (N/2) or at worst (N-1) possible solutions to verify accuracy. When quantum computation is applied, this same solution only takes 31.6 tries ($\sqrt{N}$). One can easily see the advantages in time and computation power required.

The lack of computation power needed is a significant advantage as most quantum particles require sophisticated environments operating at temperatures near 0 degrees Kelvin. For a quick reference, the conversion between a Celsius temperature and Kelvin is to add 273 degrees. Zero Kelvin is absolute zero in scientific terms, the temperature at which all molecular motion ceases. Quantum computation occurs in qubits, similar to bits on a classical computer, with each qubit holding one quantum state. The largest current quantum computer just surpassed 1,000 qubits.[5] One other limitation is that classical computation dedicates significant processing to error detection and correction. In common error detection without correction, it can be as simple as adding one bit to every byte (8 bits sent). Quantum requires nine error detection qubits for every message qubit sent. One can see where this rapidly becomes difficult with smaller machines.

Quantum offers significant opportunities to solve more complicated problems in less time. Most of the current advantages are in offering predictions for mathematically complex models. This benefit means quantum excels at problems like materials science, pharmaceutical research, sub-atomic physics and logistics. If your DevOps model supports these areas, experimentation in this area can help. Several quantum coding languages like Qiskit, SILQ, Q and others exist. These allow the use of classical computers to model quantum problems. One can use a service like AWS Braket to rent time and run code on actual quantum computers without physically purchasing the computer.

I again suggest evaluating quantum computing beyond this short reference if these areas are intriguing.

Bio-design

Moving away from any classic material study would be the field of bio-design. This field is still largely experimental, moving from using binary switches powered by electricity to using protein molecules to provide calculations. These models use protein or DNA particles to perform computations but are still largely experimental. All bio-design computers would be constructed from living things rather than silicon circuit boards. That prospect raises the possibility for power changes, rapidly expanding capability through growing new hardware solutions and integrating neural networks based on brain tissue rather than extensive algorithms. The hardest part of bio-designed systems will likely be translating biological results into mechanical answers.

Considering biology, the problem becomes whether one could generate a protein to show a certain answer. These answers might be accessible through DNA sequencing, environment changes like PH acidity or alkalinity, or even just the production of a simple protein. Since bio-design computers do not exist, even the basic algorithms and tools for evaluating those models are lacking. DNA uses four bases in two pairs: adenine with thymine and guanine with cytosine. These pairs are then extended across DNA strands to create proteins. At the core level, one could modify pairs to carry data, since they already carry some data. The challenge becomes converting those pair models into the data we need as DevOps professionals rather than the data supporting a living being. I am eagerly following this area to explore the new potential. Of course, all those technological potentials should be shaped by how we implement cultural processes for flow, feedback and improvement.

Final thoughts

First, thank you for joining me on this DevOps exploration. I hope it has garnered some thoughts and suggested some practices to improve your initial DevOps transformation or your continuing journey into these areas. Our journey started with a look at DevOps from a historical basis, compared it to other solutions in practice and then formed an initial foundation. From there, we moved into technical processes associated with architecture, observability, constructing pipelines and testing. In that sense, we took our initial human perspective and examined how it shaped the technology we use.

In the following part, we examined how technology shaped our practices. Understanding those tools associated with technology allowed the return to future DevOps practices, examining the practitioner mindset and how we maintain an effective culture through practices. This exploration evaluated cognitive bias and how individual experience works through social exchange to shape organizational interactions or the worker's phenomenological experience. Equally important, we took time to evaluate maintaining secure and stable practices in developing software. Finally, the focus changed to future technologies and how those may affect continuing to deliver confident DevOps solutions.

In parting, I would offer some thoughts to remember across your DevOps journey. First and foremost, DevOps is a cultural solution, not a technological one, and should always centre on people. People are the most important part; keeping people happy, effectively trained and managing flow is the primary step. Flow then generates the necessary feedback for continuous improvement. Second, I would recommend that one never sublimates learning for delivery schedules. Value is necessary, the customer is essential, but too often DevOps organizations start weeding out learning, hackathons and time to experiment in favour of delivery schedules. This generates short-term gains but moves the culture away from DevOps to more Waterfall practices in the long run. Solving this requires constant communication from leadership to developers and operators and regularly listening to those at the tactical level.

Third, and most important, DevOps is constantly changing. How one organization implements DevOps solutions will not transfer directly to another organization. Your confident DevOps interpretation may radically differ from the DevOps team around the corner or down the street. Do not let someone else's success detract from your current culture and model. Every DevOps solution is individual, so I have offered basic frameworks and models to guide your journey. Confidence emerges from knowing your solutions drive from the flow you want, feedback that creates action, and improving to generate additional value.

Thanks again for joining me on this journey. Please feel free to reach out directly and ask any further questions you have about this book. Whether you like the book or have issues, feel free to post reviews and comment to others. I remain adamant that DevOps cultures offer the best value-driven software development options and that the cultural model has wide-ranging benefits beyond just software. Some of these models appeared early as we saw how DevOps grew from physical manufacturing solutions and I think future organizations will incorporate more and more DevOps concepts. Lastly, this book would not have been possible without the dedicated support of my family and the folks at Kogan Page. I hope your DevOps journey is confident and successful.

Notes

1   Tucker, P (2020) An AI just beat a human F-16 pilot in a dogfight — again, Defense One, https://www.defenseone.com/technology/2020/08/ai-just-beat-human-f-16-pilot-dogfight-again/167872/ (archived at https://perma.cc/W2V2-PZ6B)

2   Shannon, C (1948) A mathematical theory of communication, *The Bell System Technical Journal*, 27, 379–423, 623–56, https://people.math.harvard.edu/~ctm/home/text/others/shannon/entropy/entropy.pdf (archived at https://perma.cc/3SG2-BS5L)

3   Turner, B (2022) Quantum 'spooky action at a distance' lands scientists Nobel prize in physics, Live Science, https://www.livescience.com/clauser-aspect-zeilinger-win-2022-nobel-physics-prize (archived at https://perma.cc/8N3X-YBC4)

4   Matuschak, A and Nielsen, M (2019) How does the quantum search engine work? Quantum Country, https://quantum.country/search (archived at https://perma.cc/2FN6-8KUH)

5   Wilkins, A (2023) Record-breaking quantum computer has more than 1,000 qubits, *New Scientist*, https://www.newscientist.com/article/2399246-record-breaking-quantum-computer-has-more-than-1000-qubits/ (archived at https://perma.cc/ZY89-9VX4)

Index

Page numbers in *italic* denote a figure or table.

abstraction 95, 98, 99, 226, 230
ACAS 239–40
acceptance criteria 79, 224
acronyms 216, 252
action-based architectures 218, *220*, 221
  see also event-driven architectures; orchestration architectures; service-based architectures
active applications 106
activities 72, 103, 195
  see also branches; code (coding); retrospectives (retros); sprints
actor-observer bias 200
adaptability 253
agency theory 244
Agile Infrastructure 21–22
agile methodology 16, 18, 20, 23, 52–61, *175*, 206
agile release teams 60
AI *see* artificial intelligence (AI)
AlphaDogfight trials 269
Amazon 33, 179, 212, 247
Amazon Machine Images 152
Amazon Web Services (AWS) 16, 26, 95, 122, 152–53, 173, 257, 273
Anaconda 227, 228
analysis 37
Anchore 156, 239–40
anchoring bias 199
andon cords 18, 86, 248
Apollo project 15
Apple 83
application monitoring dashboards 231
application programming interfaces (APIs) 110–11, 112, 139, 152, 162, 184
ArchiMate 114–15
architects 60, 112–13, 222

architectural decision records 147
architectural development model 104–08
architectural tradeoff analysis method 113–14, 115
architecture 93–118, 203, 217–23
Argo CD 162–63, 205
arithmetic logic units 95, 96
ARPANET 15
artifacts 144–47, 151, 152, 162, *174*, 244, 251, 252–53
artificial intelligence (AI) 238, 263, 266, 268–69
  see also machine learning (ML)
Asana 225
assumptions identification 131
attack surfaces 149
augmented reality 268
Authority to Operate 239
automation 18, 76–78, 81, 86, 230, 247, 256
  pipelines 43, 152–54, 157–58, 160, 162–63
  tests 175–76, 183–84
availability heuristic 201
Avocado 170
AWS (Amazon Web Services) 16, 26, 95, 122, 152–53, 173, 257, 273
Azure 95, 153, 255

backlogs 79, 224, 225, 242
baselines 82, 180
Beck, Kent 20, 52
behaviour 72–73, 101, 103, 106, 195
Benetton 69
bias 190, 198–202, 270
bio-design 271–72, 274
Bitbucket 152
BitTorrent 221
black box testing 169

Black Hat conferences 239
black swans 179
Blackberry 253
blame-free culture 13, 80, 213, 214, 215
Blanc, François 122–23
Blanc, Joseph 122–23
blockers 48, 76, 183, 191, 194
blue tests 166, 169, 256
Booch, Grady 100
Boolean 116, 144, 155
boundary testing 167
Braket 273
branches 62, 126, 148–49, 150, 155, 172
broker-driven architecture 220, 221
brown-field approaches 44
bug bounties 223, 239
bureaucracies 135
Business Source Licence 40

cached memory 97–98
Calgary Olympic Winter Games 16
CALMS concept 53, 69–70
    see also automation; culture; lean
        manufacturing; metrics; sharing
causation vs correlation 133
CD (continuous delivery) 62, 139, 149, 150, 157–58
central processing units 96
certification 16, 104, 184, 239, 265
Challenger 16
champions 213
change failure rate 78, 126
chaos 203, 205, 255
chaos engineering 86, 178–81, 183
Chaos Monkey 179
chip manufacturing 33
Chrysler Corporation 52
CI (continuous integration) 56, 62, 139, 149, 150, 157–58
CI engineers 157–58
class 99–100, 101, 102
CLI (command line interface) 62, 125, 160
cloud computing 24, 51, 95, 109, 122, 227
cloud-native approach 40, 95, 109–10, 219, 231, 242, 245, 246

Cloud Native Computing
    Foundation 138
CloudWatch 173, 257
clusters 95, 228, 229, 231, 255, 270
code (coding) 95, 143–45, 212–13, 228, 243
    code coverage scanning 154–56
    ownership of 55, 57
    single code base 110–11
    standards 55, 57, 112
code quality tests 158–59, 166–67
code review tests 165, 166–67
cognitive bias 190, 198–202, 270
collaboration 20, 235, 252, 254–55
command line interface (CLI) 62, 125, 160
commercial projects 14, 15, 236
commits 126, 128, 160–62
Common Vulnerabilities and
    Exposures 140, 239
communication 53–54, 71–72, 100, 103, 135–36, 264–66
    see also conversations; feedback;
        language; social exchange theory
comparative metrics 132–33
complex interactions 241
compliance 244, 251, 257
compliance gaps 238–39
complicated interactions 241
complicated sub-system teams 213
components 101, 102
composites 101
computer-assisted design 264
computer-assisted software
    engineering 264
configuration 242, 243
confirmation bias 198–99
conflict management 15, 22
consensus 71, 78, 190, 200–01, 214, 224
constructivism 195
consult tier (DevOps teams) 242, 243
consulting companies 1–2
contact lists 94–95
containers 40, 95, 99, 111, 139, 145, 152, 228, 231
    scanning tools 156
continuous delivery (CD) 62, 139, 149, 150, 157–58

continuous delivery engineers 157–58
continuous flow 13, 17, 60–61, 71,
    75–79, 173, 213, 223, 225,
    242–43
continuous improvement 13–14, 22,
    56, 84–88, 151, 175, 177–81
continuous integration (CI) 56, 62,
    139, 149, 150, 157–58
continuous integration engineers
    157–58
continuous monitoring 159, 172–77,
    245–47
continuous testing 172–77
Contrast Security 257
control charts 128, 138, 249
conversations 215–17, 246
Conway's Law 81, 134–35, 176
Copilot 227, 269
correlation vs causation 133
cost models 73–74
Covid-19 pandemic 33, 44, 110
C++ 184
created metrics 130
critical chain project management 16
Crossplane 247
Cucumber 170
culture 13, 26, 57–58, 69–72, 80–81,
    86, 189–209, 213–15
    security (stability) 244–45, 251–53
    see also maturity levels; mindset;
    social exchange theory
curly braces 116
cyclical methods 49, 73, 191–92, 193,
    194, 196

daily goals 215
Darwin Awards 268
dashboards 81, 151, 173, 204, 230–31,
    251–52
data 252
data sources 130–31
data tests 165, 167
databases 149–50, 167, 168, 224, 247
Debois, Patrick 21–22
decision trees 269, 270
decomposition 47, 74, 128, 133, 222
Deep Blue 268–69
deep learning systems 269–70

DEFCON 239
Defense Advanced Research Project
    Agency 269
defined maturity 203–04, 206
delivery testing 177
demos 83
dependency inversion principle 99–100
dependency scans 156, 162
dependent interactions 242
deployment 101, 102, 126, 130–33,
    137–38, 149, 177
deployment frequency 126, 130,
    131–33, 137–38
deployment testing 177
design 37–38, 40, 47, 56
detailing 217
dev, test and prod pipelines 143
    see also code (coding); production;
    testing
developer experience (DevX) 43, 227,
    229–30
development temporality 265
development testing 165, 176
    see also code quality tests; code
    review tests; unit tests
DevOps 12–14, 21–23, 67
    basecamp framework 3–5
    market value 1, 23–24
    SDLC model 41–45
DevOps Handbook, The 23
DevOps Institute 3, 23
DevOps Institute Ambassadors
    programme 3
DevOps Research and Assessment
    (DORA) metrics 23, 78, 126,
    133, 205
DevOpsDays 22
DevSecOps 211, 234–36
DevX 43, 227, 229–30
direct franchising 25
distributed computing fallacies 180
DNA sequencing 274
Docker 111, 152, 162, 228
Docker Bench 156
documentation 47, 54, 147, 243, 244,
    252–53
    see also records
dynamic tests 159, 166, 169

Dynatrace 257

E-shaped knowledge 212
Edison Awards, The 268
EKS 247
Elastic Compute Cloud (EC22) 179
ElasticStack 130
electronic discrete variable automating
    computer 95
emotional intelligence 53–54
    see also respect
enabling teams 213
encapsulation 98, 136
end to end (E2E) tests 166, 167–68,
    178
enframing 74, 193–94, 195
England-France tunnel project 16
entanglement 272
epics 223, 224
erroneous (error) testing 167, 171
ethics 197
event-driven architectures *218*, 221,
    222
evidence, absence of 133
experiments 85
    see also testing
extreme programming 52–58

failure-acceptance 214
false consensus bias 200–01
feature demonstrations (demos) 83
federal holidays 70
FedRAMP 239
feedback 13, 22, 53–54, 61, 80–84,
    132, 173
    see also continuous monitoring;
    continuous testing
Fibonacci sequences *35*, 36
flickering tests 171–72
flow 13, 17, 60–61, 71, 75–79, 173,
    213, 223, 225, 242–43
Flux 205, 228
Ford, Henry 14, 17
Fortify 167, 239–40
Fowler, Martin 20, 170
France-England tunnel 16
Fukushima (Japan) earthquake
    179, 199

functional pipelines 148
functional tests 166, 168
functions 154

Gantt charts 15, 20, 72, 215, 253
general AI 269
General Data Protection
    Regulation 236
generative AI 269
generative organizations 135
Git 72
GitHub 51, 62, 138, 147, 152, 179,
    184, 231
    see also Copilot
GitKraken 149
GitLab 62, 131, 149, 152–53, 156,
    173, 205, 227, 228, 255
GitOps 59, 61–63
Gliffy 114
global fixes 136
Go 182
goal setting 215
Google 32, 33, 86, 87, 244, 248
Google Cloud 33
Google Play 33
government sector 39, 44–45, 47, 70,
    123, 236, 239, 257
Grafana 130, 138, 139, 140, 230, 231
graphical user interface (GUI) 115,
    125, 160
green-field approaches 44
green tests 168
Grid 185
grocery sector 76–77
Grover's algorithm 272–73

Hack the Box competitions 239
hackathons 86, 87, 181, 276
hacking 122–23, 149, 152, 167,
    253–54
Harness 255
Harvard architecture 96, 97
HashiCorp 40
Health Insurance Portability
    and Accountability Act
    (HIPAA) 236, 239
Heidegger, Martin 191, 192, 193, 194
Heron Systems 269

hindsight bias 199
histograms 128, 138
holiday entitlement 70
home thermostats 97
Hoover Dam 15
Human Group, The (Homans) 72, 195
Husserl, Edmund 191
hybrid architecture 97–98
hypotheses 85, 180

IBM 32–33, 253
IDEs 166, 171, 226–28
implementation 38, 40, 47–48, 59–63, 72–75
improvement 13–14, 22, *56*, 84–88, 151, 175, 177–81
incident management 21, 214, 250–51
independent interactions 242
industrial age 14, 15
infrastructure 203
infrastructure as code (IaC) 25, 42, 62, 86
inheritance 98, 101
initiatives 223, 224
innovation 39, 266–68
inquiries 136
instruction set architecture 95
integrated development environments (IDEs) 166, 171, 226–28
integration stubs *161*, 162, 168
integration testing 165, *172*, *175*, 176
IntelliSense 227
interactions 101, 103, 195, 241–42
interdependent interactions 242
interface segregation 99–100
interference 272
intermediate objectives 215
internal controllers 49
International Organization for Standardization (ISO) 100–01
ISO 27001 236, 239
ISO 27002 236
ISO 42010 105
IT operations engineers 211
IT ops technicians 212

Jacobson, Ivar 100
Jaeger 230, 231

Japan (Fukushima) earthquake 179, 199
Java 44, 182, 184
Jeffries, Ron 20
Jenkins 152–53, 199, 205, 255
jidoka 18
Jira 225
JSON 114, 115–16, 139, 160
junior DevOps engineers 211
JUnit 154, 170
Jupyter Notebook 227, 228
just-in-time manufacturing 12, 17–18, 196

Kaiser Permanente 26
kaizen 17, 18
kanban 79, 146, 205, 223–26, 230
Karate Kid 67–68
key fobs 38
knowledge sharing 70, 78, 82, 87, 197–98, 255
knowledge, skills, abilities assessments 265
Kodak 253
Kubernetes 111, 152, 162, 231, 247, 252

language 100–08, 251–52
  see also standard query language (SQL); unified modelling language (UML)
'latest' command 150
layered design 218, *219*
lead time to change metric 23, 78, 122, 126
lean manufacturing 12, 15, 17–18, 77, 81, 86–87
legacy systems 44, 45, 109, 221
lifecycle model 30–64
lightweight methodologies 16, 20, 23
line testing 155
linear regression 270
linting 176
Linux 93, 125, 155
Liskov substitution 98, 99
LMO ('let's move on') 77
local fixes 136
local IDEs 227

Log4J 52, 246, 250
logical designs 37
login information 37
logistic regression 270
logs 120–22, 124–25, 144–45, 162, 231, 246
Lucidchart 114

Mac 125
machine learning (ML) 166, 238, 263, 266, 269–71
maintenance 34, 38–39, 45, 46, 48, 50
managed maturity 204, 206
managers 60, 72–75, 214–15
Manen, Max van 191, 193, 196
Manhattan Project 15
manual processes 21, 122, 125, 158, 159, 163, 257
manual tests 166, 175–76
master-client architecture 218, 221–23
Mattermost 77
maturity levels 178–81, 202–07, 239, 251
mean time to restore 126
meaning relationships 192
means 195
    see also communication
measurements 121, 122, 124, 126–29
mediator-driven architecture 221
merge requests 62, 215
metaphor 4–5, 55–56, 57, 192
metrics 87, 120–22, 124–40, 154, 159, 173, 247–50
    DevOps Research Association 23
    lead time to change 23, 78
    test coverage 178
micro-controllers 97
microkernals 219, 222
microservices 109, 110, 111–12, 219, 221, 222
Microsoft Excel 247
Microsoft 365 25
Microsoft Visio Pro 114
Microsoft Windows 25, 125
mindset 40, 189–209
    see also culture
minimal viable products 182
misinformation bias 200

mixed method experiments 86
Mocha 184
mocks 168, 176
monitoring 159, 172–77, 245–47
monolith structures 109, 110, 111, 221
Mozilla Public Licence v2.0 40
multiple metrics 126, 132, 134
multiple pipelines 45, 145, 146, 157, 158
multiple testing environments 171

Naive Bayes 270
Napster 221
National Institute for Standards and Technology (NIST) 236, 237, 239
Nessus 155
Nest 33
Netflix 110, 179, 256
network monitoring 245
Nmap 155
non-functional pipelines 148
norms 69, 198, 251, 252
North American Electric Reliability Corporation Critical Infrastructure Protection 236
NumPy 166

Object Management Group 100
object-oriented programming 98–99
objectives and key results 136–37
objects 99, 101, 103, 271–72
observability 119–41, 151, 203, 223, 244, 247
observable actions 121
observation points 122, 135
observing actions 121–22
Open Census 230, 231
open-closed principle 99
Open Group Architecture Framework 100, 104–08, 115
open policy agent (OPA) 138, 139, 140
open source testing 171, 179
open worldwide application security practices (OWASP) 138, 139, 140, 156
OpenTelemetry (OTel) 121, 130, 138, 139, 140, 230, 231

OpenVAS 155
operating systems (OS) 125, 137, 143, 155
operational monitoring 245
operational scanners 257
operational tests 166, 169
operators 43, 121, 196, 276
opportunities (SWOT) 61, 63, 79, 87–88
   agile methodology 58
   DevOps SDLC 44, 45
   SDLC 32–33, 40, 41
   TOGAF 108
   UML 103–04
   waterfall planning 51–52
ops teams 240–43
optical telegraphs 123
optimism bias 201–02
optimized maturity 204, 206–07
orchestration architectures *174*, 218, *220*, 221
organic metrics 129–30, 139
organizational gaps 238, 239, 240
organizational structure 134–36, 176, 192, 196, 197
   see also culture; monolith structures; silos
OS (operating systems) 125, 137, 143, 155
OTel 121, 130, 138, 139, 140, 230, 231
OWASP 138, 139, 140, 156

Pacific Railroad 15
packages 101, *102*
pair programming 16, *56*, 215, 256
Pandas 166
pandemic (Covid-19) 33, 44, 110
Parasoft 184, 185
Pareto measurements 128–29
'parking lots' 78
passive elements 106
patches 35, 36, 37, 38, 48, 51, 52, 61, 168, 201
pathological organizations 135
PayPal 26
peer-driven architecture 221–22
people observation 134–36

PeopleCert 23
perception 75, 193
phenomenology 190–94, 198, 200
Phoenix Project, The 23
physical architecture 218–19
   see also microservices
physical design requirements 38
pipeline gates 144
pipeline visualization 160–62
pipelines 38, 45, 77, 142–63, 205, 246
   automation 43
   testing plans 172–73, 178
Planet Fitness 25
planning 34–37, 39–40, 46–47, 51–52, 54–55, 56
platform teams 42, 213
platforms 228–30, 254–55
   see also cloud computing; clusters; code (coding); containers
Pluto 247
Polaris 15
polymorphism 98
pre-processing 271
pre-prod 144, *174*
primary artifacts 252, 253
primary pipelines 148
probability 16, 148, 201, 237, 270
procedure testing 170
process management 77, 158–59, 182–84, 204, 217–26, 243–47
   manual 21, 122, 125, 163, 257
process observation 136–38
production 143, 175, 177
profile 101
programme increment design 60–61
programme management 14–16, 20, 214–15
Programme Management Professional certification 16
project management 16, 230–31
Prometheus 121, 130, 138–39, 140, 230, 231
public relations 136
pull approach 17–18, 150
PurpleTeam 138, 140
push approach 79

Q 273
Qiskit 273
qualitative experiments 85
quality assurance (QA) teams 169, 183
quality control 128, 151, 165, 166, 178
quantitative experiments 85
quantum computing 271–74
qubits 273

RACI matrixes 137–38
RC 185
records 216
    see also documentation
red tests 166, 168, 169, 256
redundancies 37, 181
refactors 44, 168, 214
reflection 216
regression tests 166, 168, 270
remote working 110, 264, 265–66
repeatability 48, 178, 203, 205–06
repositories (repos) 148–50, 152, 255
representatives 213
requirements/solutions alignment 38
research 86, 87, 201–02
research time 201
respect 54, 213–14
retrospectives (retros) 78, 82–83, 135,
    200, 225
reversion tests 177
revising conversations 216–17
risk 240
risk analysis 49–50, 201
risk management (mitigation) 16, 148,
    237
Robot Framework 170, 171
role reversal 217
roleplay 217
Rollerblade 69
Ruby 170, 182
Rumbaugh, James 100
runtime application self-
    protection 177, 257
Rust 114

sandboxes 42
SCALA 114
scalability 43, 109, 111
scaled agile framework (SAFe
    model) 59–61

scanning technology 156, 162, 256–57
Schutz, William 192, 193
Schwaber, Ken 20
Scikit-Learn 166
scrum 26, 72, 79, 146, 205,
    223–26, 230
scrum masters 212
SDLC see software development
    lifecycle (SDLC)
secondary artifacts 252, 253
security 42–43, 154, 200, 203, 233–59
security experts 236–38
security patching 37, 38, 52, 61
security standards 236–37
security teams 238–40
Selenium 170, 184, 185
senior DevOps engineers 211
sequencing 103
server status 246
serverless structures 109, 110
servers 109
service-based architectures 220, 221
service level agreements 243, 249
service level indicators 114, 249
service level objectives 249
service mesh 112, 152, 156, 231
Shafer, Andrew 21–22
sharing 70, 78, 82, 87, 197–98, 255
'shiny topics' 78
sigma deviations 128
silos 23, 24, 26, 31, 45, 82
SILQ 273
Simian Army 179
simple interactions 241
simulation 109–10, 181
single code bases 110–11
site reliability engineering 247–51
Skelton 213
Skype 221
Slack 77
SLAs 243, 249
SLIs 114, 249
SLOs 249
small releases 48, 56
smart home thermostats 97
smoke tests 166, 168–69
social behaviour 72–73, 101, 103,
    106, 195
social capital 196

social exchange theory 72–75, 190, 194–98
social responsibility 73–74, 195
socialization 148
SOC2 239, 251
software architects 60, 112–13, 222
software asset control 148
software composition analysis 156
software development lifecycle (SDLC) 30–64
  traditional 85, *175*
SOLID architecture 98–100
solutions/requirements alignment 38
SonarQube 154, 156, 167
source control 147–48
space-based architecture 218–19
Space Shuttle Challenger 16
spikes 201
spiral approach 49–50
Splunk 130
sprints 76, 79, 82–83, 191, 195, 225, 243
square brackets 116
stability 233–59
standard query language (SQL) 167, 224
standard testing 167
standardized IDEs 227
standards 238–39, 244, 245, 257
  codes 55, 57, 112
  see also National Institute for Standards and Technology (NIST)
Starbucks 26
'State of DevOps' (Brown) 23, 257
state machines 103
statement coverage tools 155
static analysis 165, 167, 176, 177
static application security testing 165
stories 223
story points 225
stream-aligned teams 213
strengths 31–32, 61, 63, 79, 83, 87
  agile 57, 58
  DevOps 42, 43–44, 45
  SDLC 39, 41
  TOGAF 108
  UML 103, 104

waterfall 51, 52
stubs *161, 162*, 168
sub-tasks 223
subcontractors 70
subscription models 25
sunk cost fallacy 218
superposition 272
supervisory control and data administration systems 109–10
support vector machines 270
suppression 136
surveys 167, 193, 198
sustainable pacing 57
Sutherland, Jeff 20
SWOT model 30, 31–33, 39–41, 43–45, 51–52, 57–58, 79, 103–04, 108
syslogs 125
system design 95–98
system reliability engineers 136

T-shaped knowledge 212–13
takt time 17
task-oriented AI 268–69
tasks 223
team maturity 205–07
team working agreements 73, 215
teams 73, 205–07, 212–16, 226
  agile release 60
  ops 240–43
  platform 228–30, 254–55
  quality assurance (QA) 169, 183
  security 238–40
  whole team 55, 56
telemetry 121, 130, 138, 139, 154, 173
templates at scale 151–52
temporality 264, 265
Tenable 155, 156
'10+ Deploys a Day' (Hammond & Allspaw) 22
Tensorflow 166
Terraform 40, 160
tertiary artifacts 252, 253
test cases 169–72
test coverage 178
test-driven development (TDD) 56, 168, 169, 171, 172, 175, 184
test engineers 182

testing 164–86, 203, 227–28
    code quality 158–59
    dynamic 159
    line 155
    unit tests 154, *161*, 162
    see also experiments; quality control
thematic analysis 191
threats 33, 61, 63, 79, 84, 87–88, 240
    agile 58
    DevOps 44, 45
    SDLC 40, 41
    TOGAF 108
    UML 104
    waterfall 52
three horizons model 266–68
360-degree assessments 32
'Three Ways, The' 67–90
    see also feedback; flow; improvement
'thumbs' 78
ticketing 215, 223, 243, 245–46
time stamps 124, 125
time to detect metric 250
time to engage metric 250
time to fix metric 250
time to mitigate metric 250
timeboxing 77
timing 103
TOGAF 100, 104–08
Toyota 17–18, *19*, 248
traces 120, 121, 122, 125–26, 173, 231, 257, 271
traditional SDLC 33–41, 85, *175*
training 48, 54, 59, 73, 104, 108, 240, 257, 265
transaction costs 244
Trello 225
trunks 148–49
trust 22, 149, 197, 213, 215
Twistlock 156
two-pizza team concept 212

unified modelling language (UML) 71, 100–04, 113, 114
unit tests 154, *161*, 162, 165, 166, 170, *172*, *175*
unsupervised machine learning 270

upgrades 25, 48, 149, 157, 168, 184, 242, 247, 256
'Upskilling IT' 23
US Air Force (USAF) 2–3, 48, 61, 68
use-cases 37, 79, 103, 105, 224
user activity 247
user IDs 124, 125
user tests 166, 169

Veracode 167
verification 48, 184
version control 148–50
virtual machines (VM) 95, 109, 171, 179
virtual private clouds 95
Visual Studio Code 154, 227
volatility 244
Von Neuman system design 95–97
VS Code 227, 228
vulnerability 239–40, 246

waterfall methodology 45–52
weaknesses 32, 61, 63, 83–84
    agile 57–58
    DevOps 44, 45
    SDLC 39–40, 41
    TOGAF 108
    UML 103, 104
    waterfall 51, 52
WebDriver 185
Weber, Max 192
'weeds' 77
weighting 35, 36, 49–50
Westrum patterns 135–36
white box testing 169
whole team approach 55, 56
Windows 25, 125
work 194
Work Breakdown Structure 15
work-in-progress 79, 146–47, 225

XML 114
XP 52–58

YAML 114, 153, 160

zero attack proxy (ZAP) 138, 139–40, 142–43

Looking for another book?

Explore our award-winning books from global business experts in Digital and Technology

Scan the code to browse

www.koganpage.com/digital-technology

Also in the Confident series

ISBN: 9781398615724

ISBN: 9781398615670

ISBN: 9781398611924

ISBN: 9781398611887

www.koganpage.com

Printed in the USA
CPSIA information can be obtained
at www.ICGtesting.com
JSHW072046280624
65595JS00009B/14